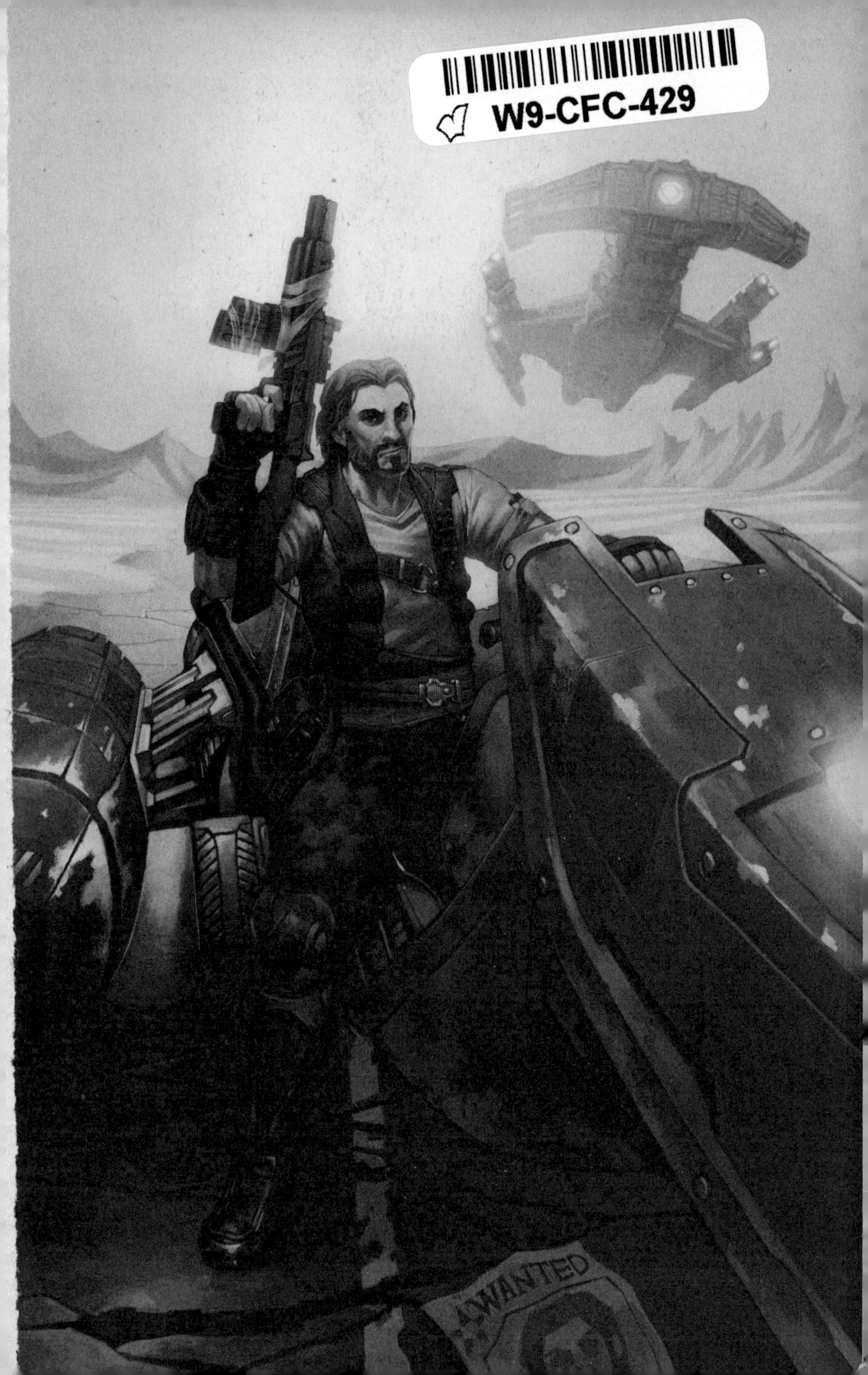
WANTED

## StarCraft: Frontline Vol. 4

Contributing Editor - Troy Lewter
Layout, Lettering and Retouch Artist - Michael Paolilli
Creative Consultant - Michael Paolilli
Graphic Designer - Louis Csontos
Cover Artist - UDON with Saejin Oh

Editor - Hope Donovan
Print Production Manager - Lucas Rivera
Managing Editor - Vy Nguyen
Senior Designer - Louis Csontos
Director of Sales and Manufacturing - Allyson De Simone
Associate Publisher - Marco F. Pavia
President and C.O.O. - John Parker
C.E.O. and Chief Creative Officer - Stu Levy

BLIZZARD ENTERTAINMENT
Senior Vice President, Creative Development - Chris Metzen
Director, Creative Development - Jeff Donais
Lead Developer, Licensed Products - Mike Hummel
Publishing Lead, Creative Development - Rob Tokar
Senior Story Developer - Micky Neilson
Story Developer - James Waugh
Art Director - Glenn Rane
Director, Global Business
Development and Licensing - Cory Jones
Associate Licensing Manager - Jason Bischoff
Historian - Evelyn Fredericksen
Additional Development - Samwise Didier and Tommy Newcomer

A **TOKYOPOP** Manga

TOKYOPOP and are trademarks or registered trademarks of TOKYOPOP Inc.

TOKYOPOP Inc.
5900 Wilshire Blvd. Suite 2000
Los Angeles, CA 90036

E-mail: info@TOKYOPOP.com
Come visit us online at www.TOKYOPOP.com

ISBN: 978-1-4278-1698-6
First TOKYOPOP printing: October 2009
10 9 8 7 6 5 4 3 2 1
Printed in the USA

# StarCraft®

## FRONTLINE™

### Volume 4

HAMBURG // LONDON // LOS ANGELES // TOKYO

# STARCRAFT

## FRONTLINE
### VOLUME 4

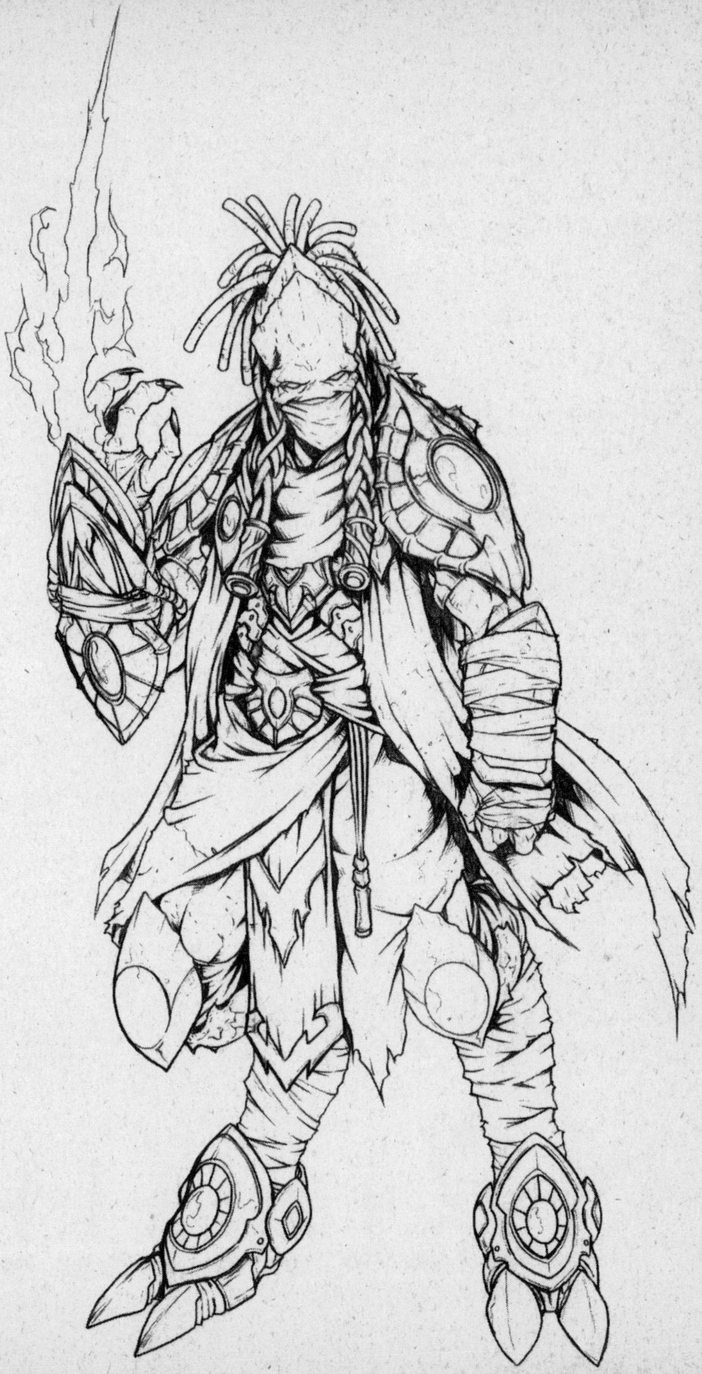

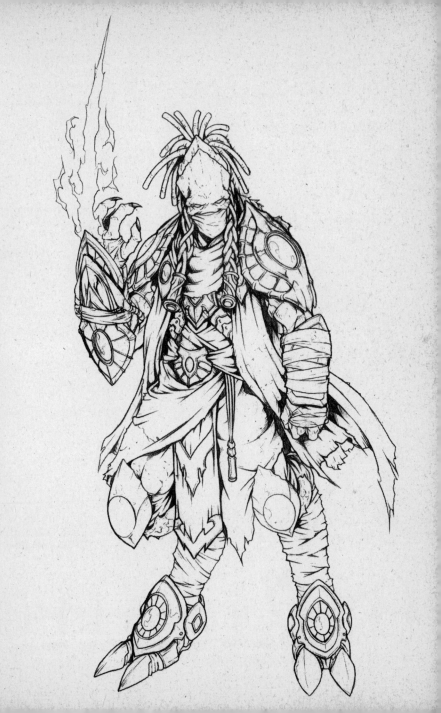

# STARCRAFT

## FRONTLINE
### VOLUME 4

## HOMECOMING

Written by Chris Metzen

Art by Hector Sevilla

Letterer: Michael Paolilli

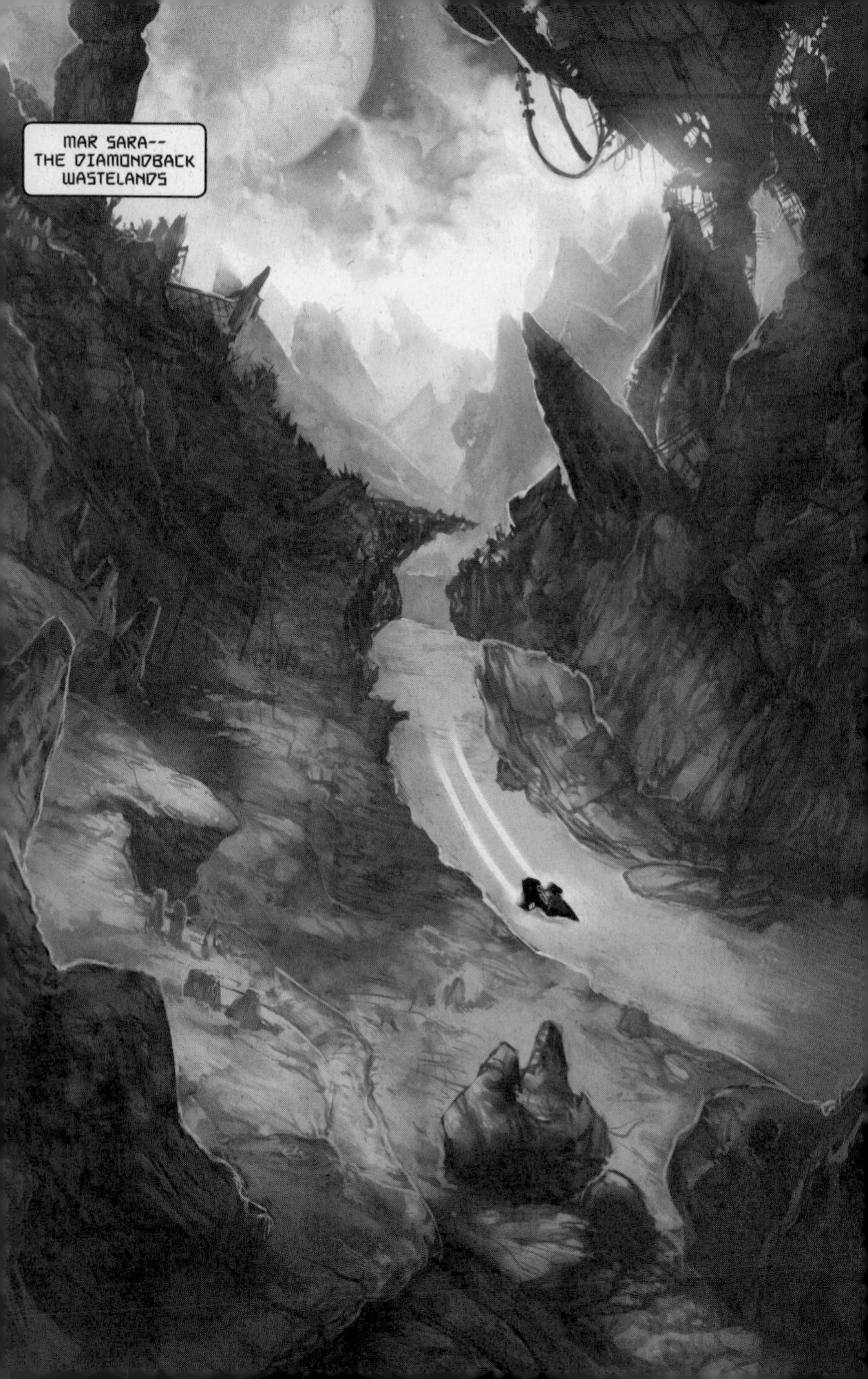
MAR SARA--
THE DIAMONDBACK
WASTELANDS

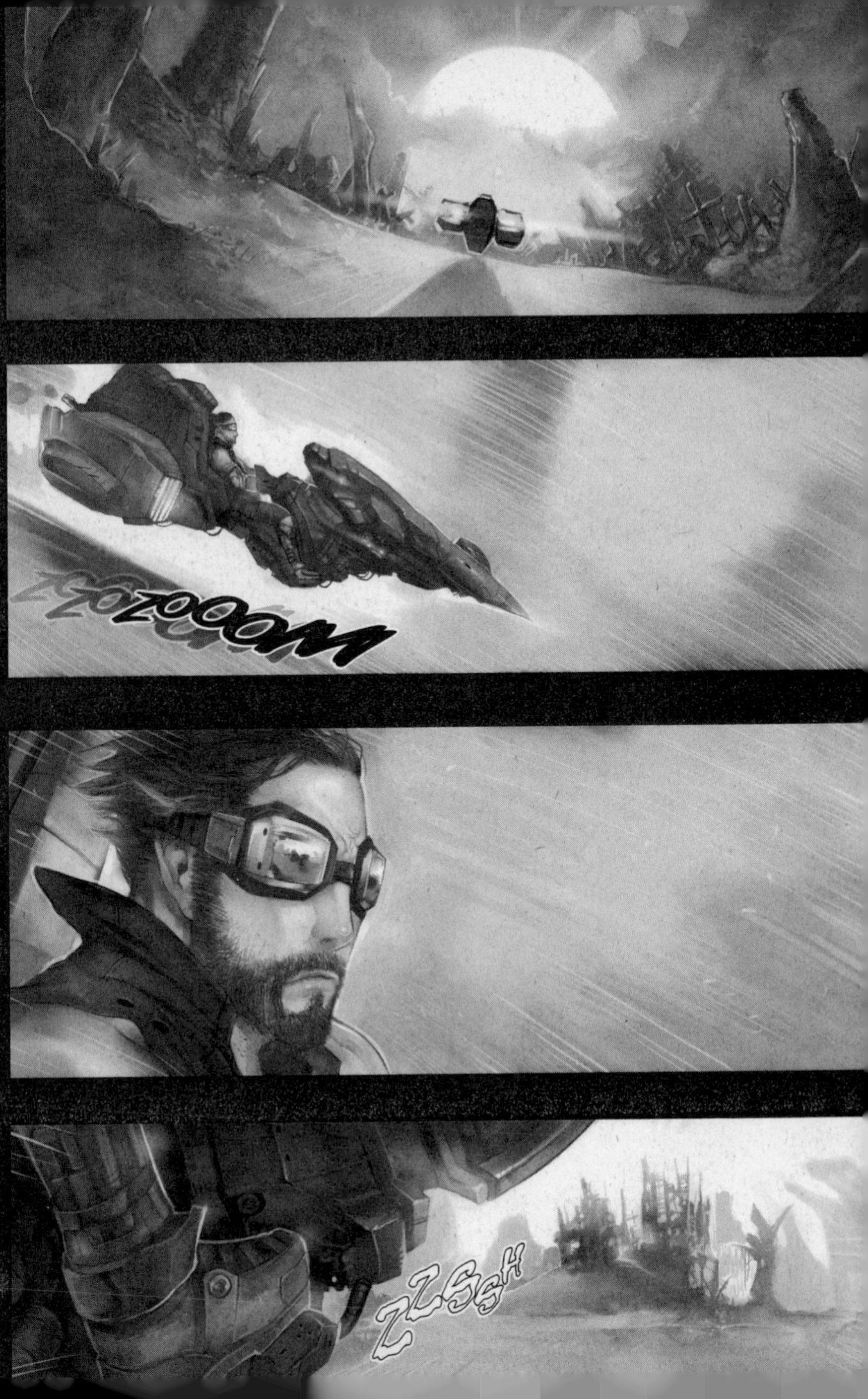
ZOOOOM
ZZSSH

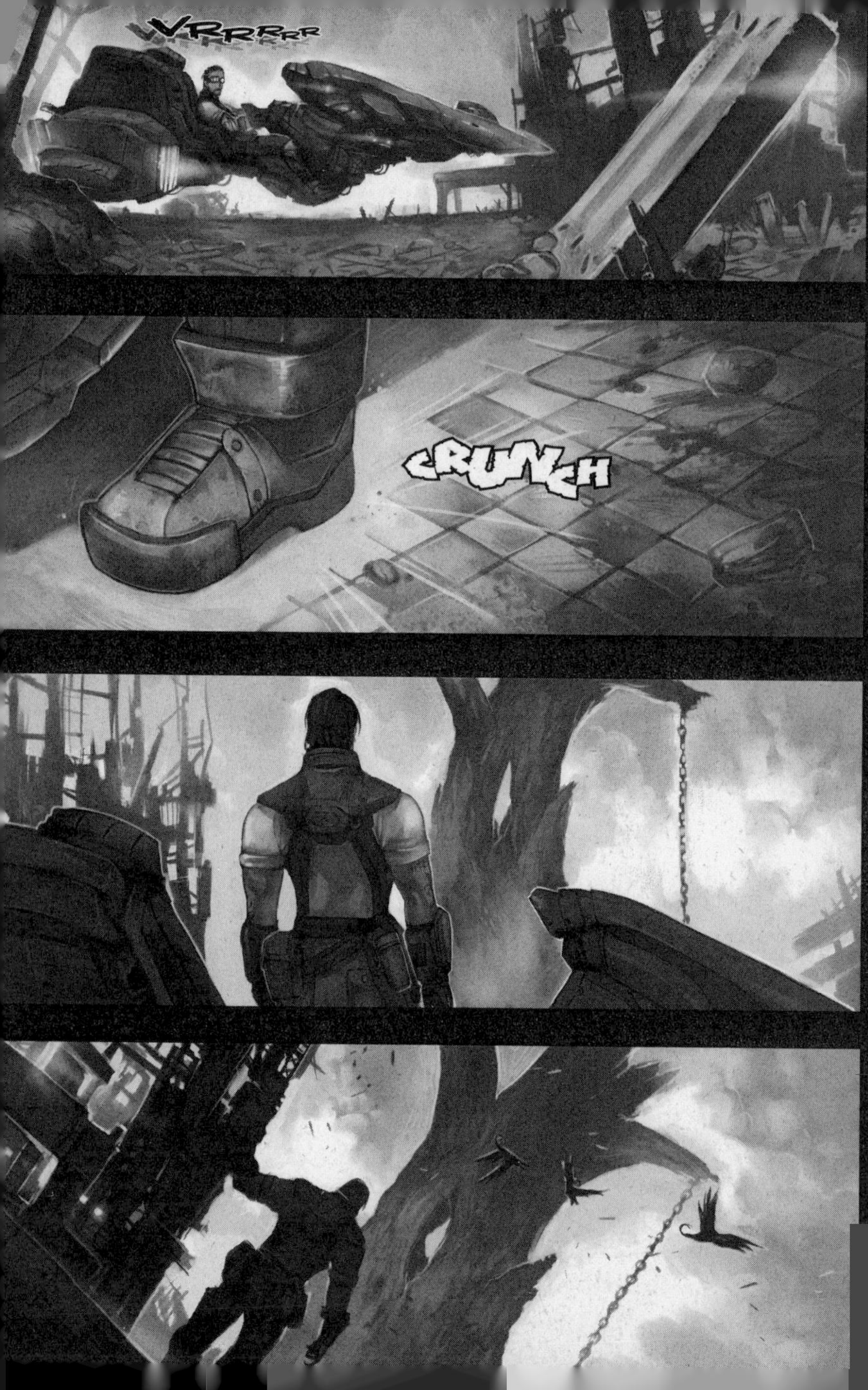
VRRRRRR
CRUNCH

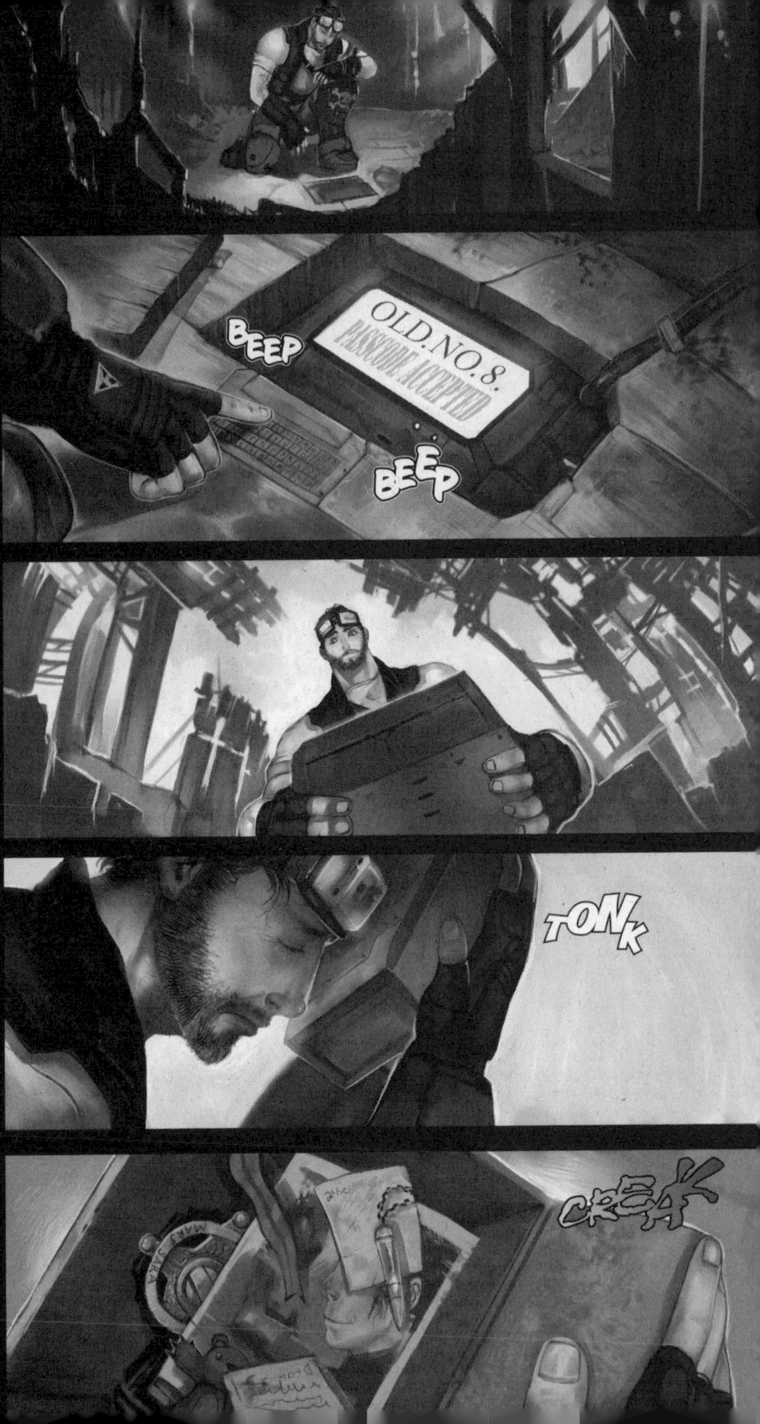
BEEP
OLD.NO.8.
PASSCODE ACCEPTED
BEEP
TONK
CREAK

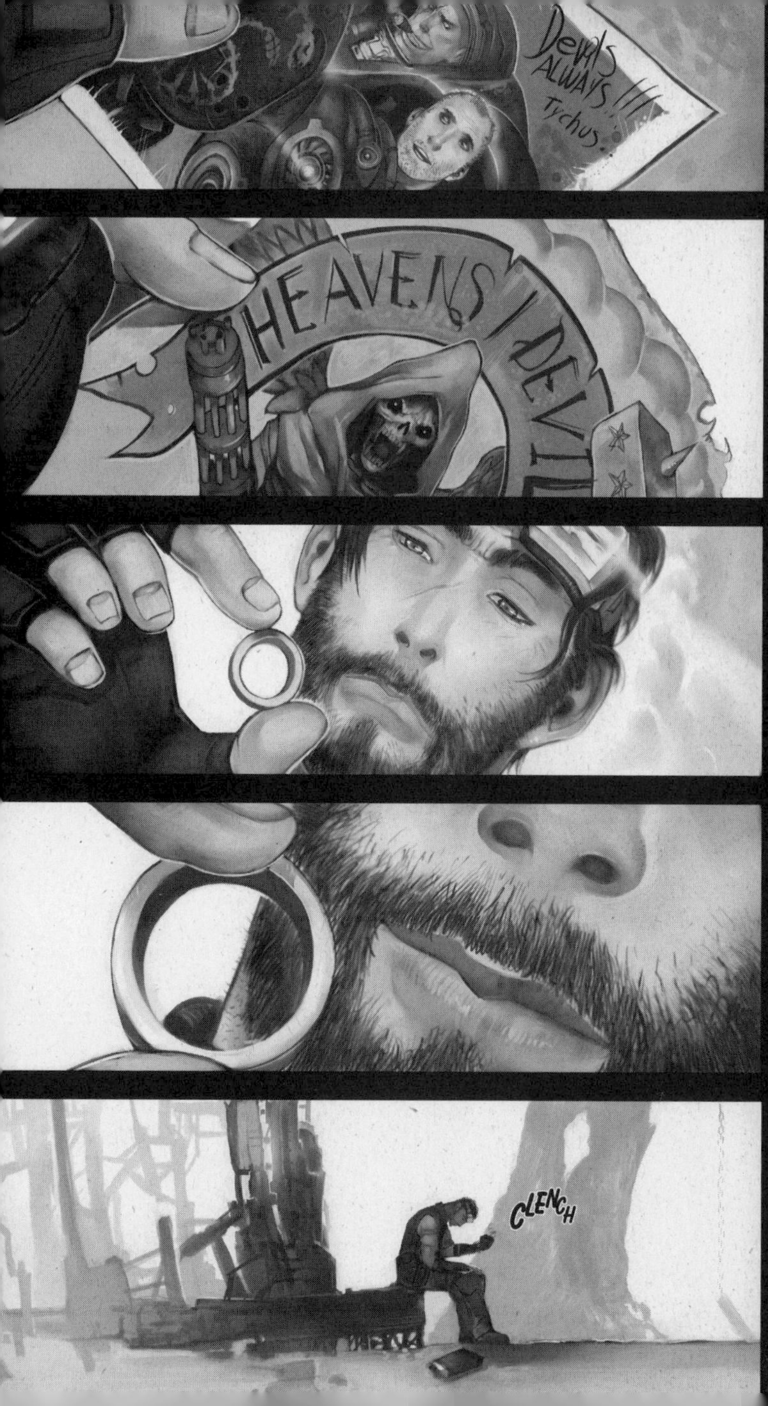
Devils ALWAYS!!!
Tychus.
HEAVENS DEVIL
CLENCH

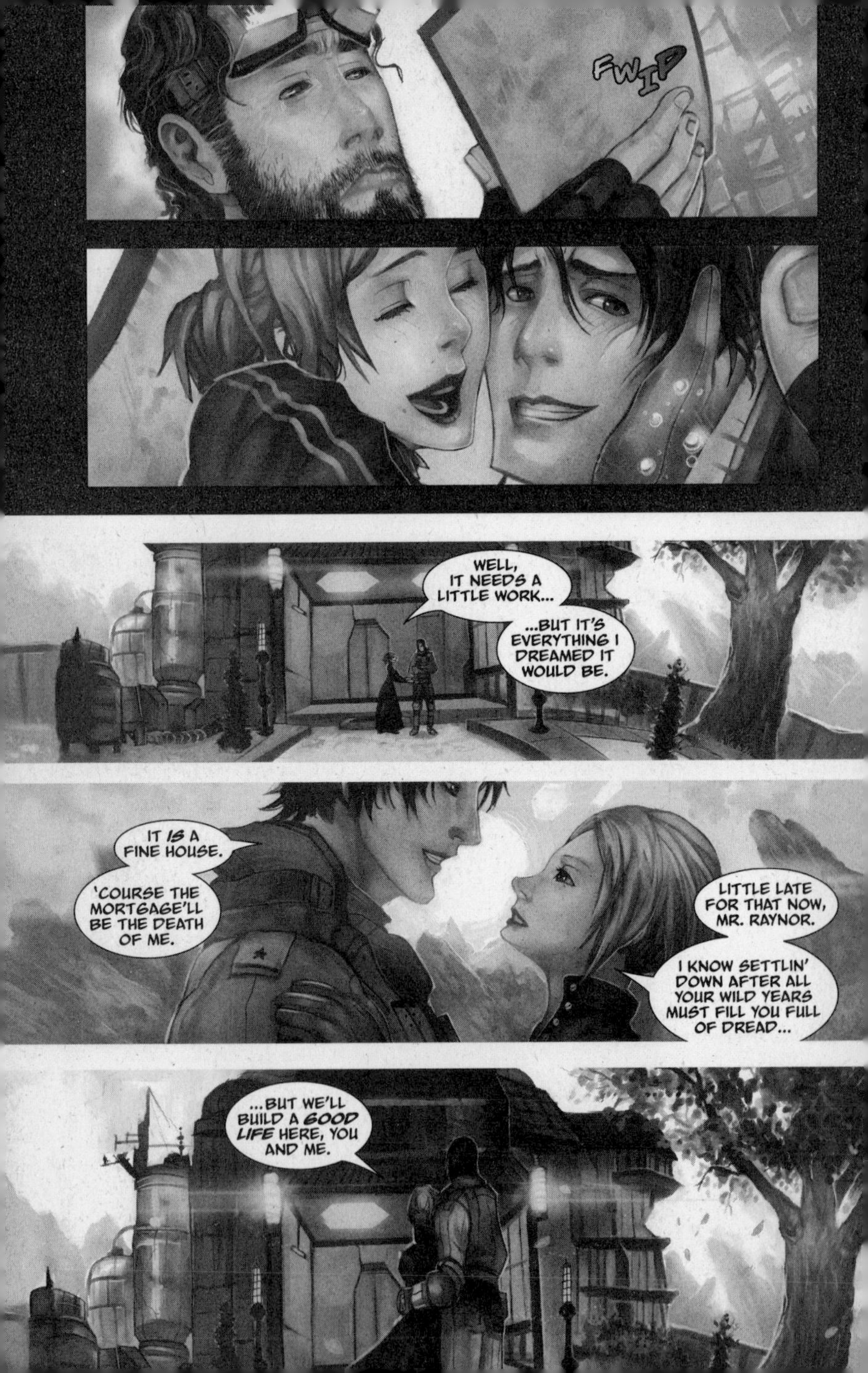
FWIP
WELL, IT NEEDS A LITTLE WORK...
...BUT IT'S EVERYTHING I DREAMED IT WOULD BE.
IT *IS* A FINE HOUSE.
'COURSE THE MORTGAGE'LL BE THE DEATH OF ME.
LITTLE LATE FOR THAT NOW, MR. RAYNOR.
I KNOW SETTLIN' DOWN AFTER ALL YOUR WILD YEARS MUST FILL YOU FULL OF DREAD...
...BUT WE'LL BUILD A *GOOD LIFE* HERE, YOU AND ME.

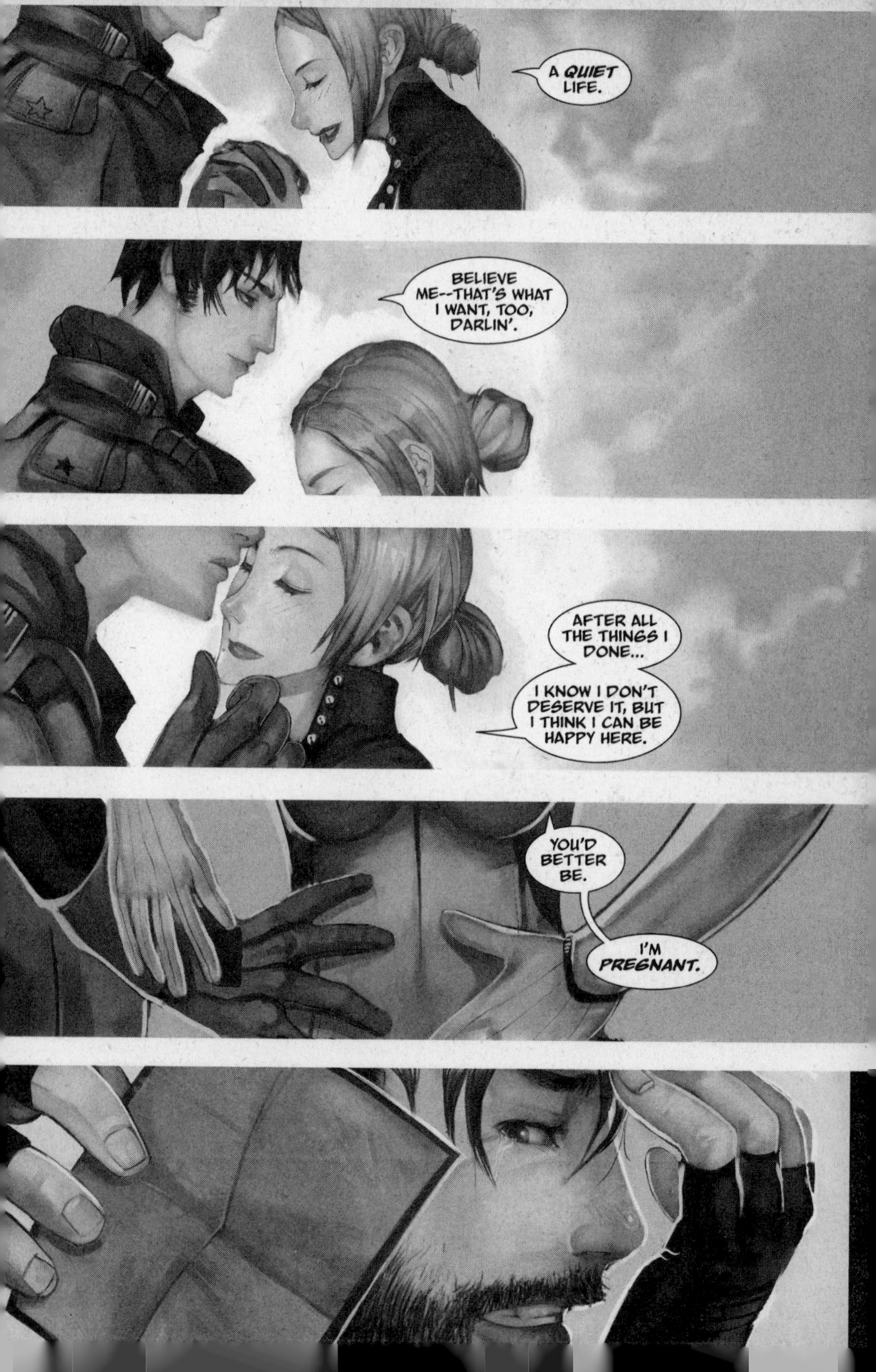
A QUIET LIFE.
BELIEVE ME--THAT'S WHAT I WANT, TOO, DARLIN'.
AFTER ALL THE THINGS I DONE...
I KNOW I DON'T DESERVE IT, BUT I THINK I CAN BE HAPPY HERE.
YOU'D BETTER BE.
I'M PREGNANT.

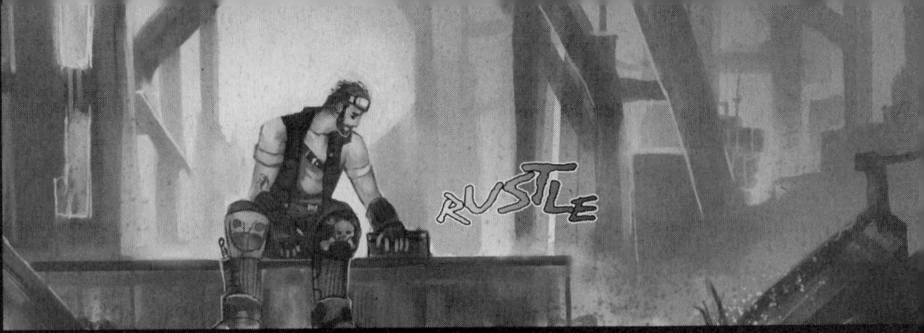
RUSTLE
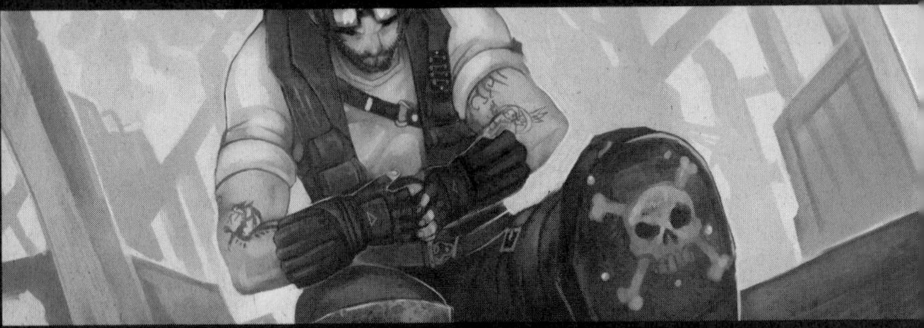
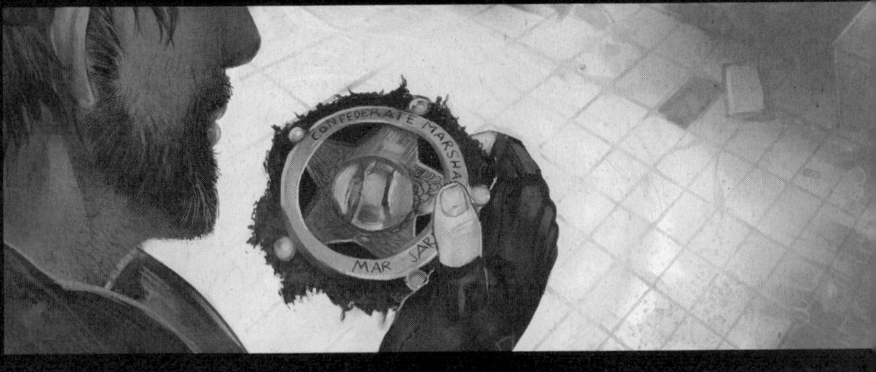
CONFEDERATE MARSHA
MAR SAR
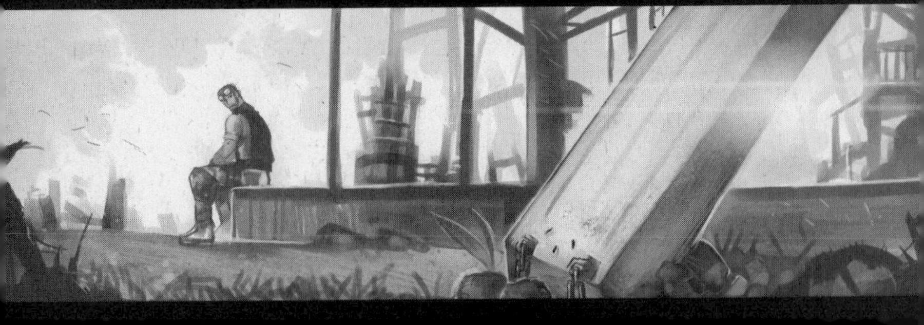

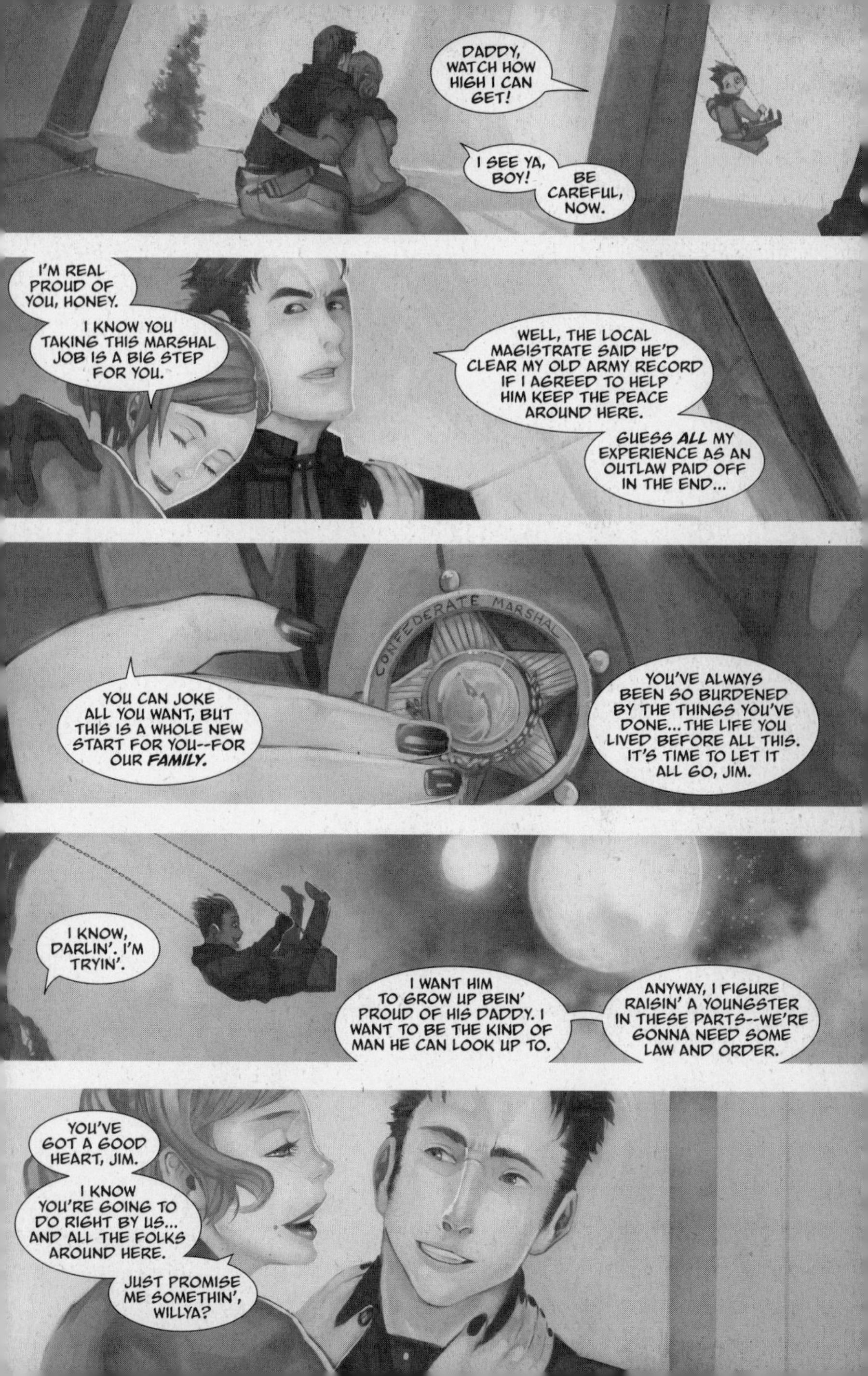
DADDY, WATCH HOW HIGH I CAN GET!
I SEE YA, BOY!
BE CAREFUL, NOW.
I'M REAL PROUD OF YOU, HONEY.
I KNOW YOU TAKING THIS MARSHAL JOB IS A BIG STEP FOR YOU.
WELL, THE LOCAL MAGISTRATE SAID HE'D CLEAR MY OLD ARMY RECORD IF I AGREED TO HELP HIM KEEP THE PEACE AROUND HERE.
GUESS **ALL** MY EXPERIENCE AS AN OUTLAW PAID OFF IN THE END...
CONFEDERATE MARSHAL
YOU CAN JOKE ALL YOU WANT, BUT THIS IS A WHOLE NEW START FOR YOU--FOR OUR ***FAMILY.***
YOU'VE ALWAYS BEEN SO BURDENED BY THE THINGS YOU'VE DONE... THE LIFE YOU LIVED BEFORE ALL THIS. IT'S TIME TO LET IT ALL GO, JIM.
I KNOW, DARLIN'. I'M TRYIN'.
I WANT HIM TO GROW UP BEIN' PROUD OF HIS DADDY. I WANT TO BE THE KIND OF MAN HE CAN LOOK UP TO.
ANYWAY, I FIGURE RAISIN' A YOUNGSTER IN THESE PARTS--WE'RE GONNA NEED SOME LAW AND ORDER.
YOU'VE GOT A GOOD HEART, JIM.
I KNOW YOU'RE GOING TO DO RIGHT BY US... AND ALL THE FOLKS AROUND HERE.
JUST PROMISE ME SOMETHIN', WILLYA?

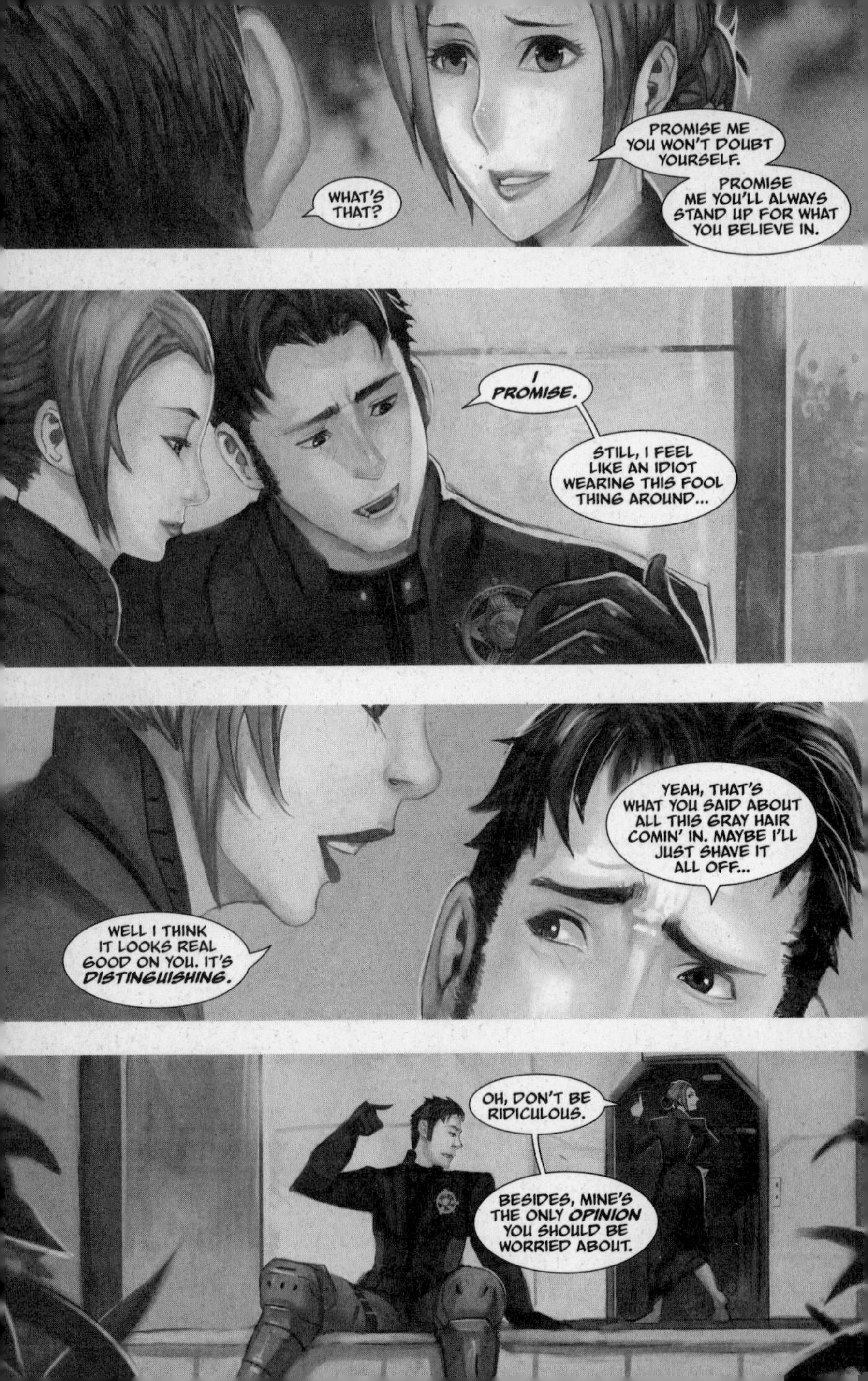

WHAT'S THAT?
PROMISE ME YOU WON'T DOUBT YOURSELF.
PROMISE ME YOU'LL ALWAYS STAND UP FOR WHAT YOU BELIEVE IN.
I *PROMISE.*
STILL, I FEEL LIKE AN IDIOT WEARING THIS FOOL THING AROUND...
YEAH, THAT'S WHAT YOU SAID ABOUT ALL THIS GRAY HAIR COMIN' IN. MAYBE I'LL JUST SHAVE IT ALL OFF...
WELL I THINK IT LOOKS REAL GOOD ON YOU. IT'S *DISTINGUISHING.*
OH, DON'T BE RIDICULOUS.
BESIDES, MINE'S THE ONLY *OPINION* YOU SHOULD BE WORRIED ABOUT.

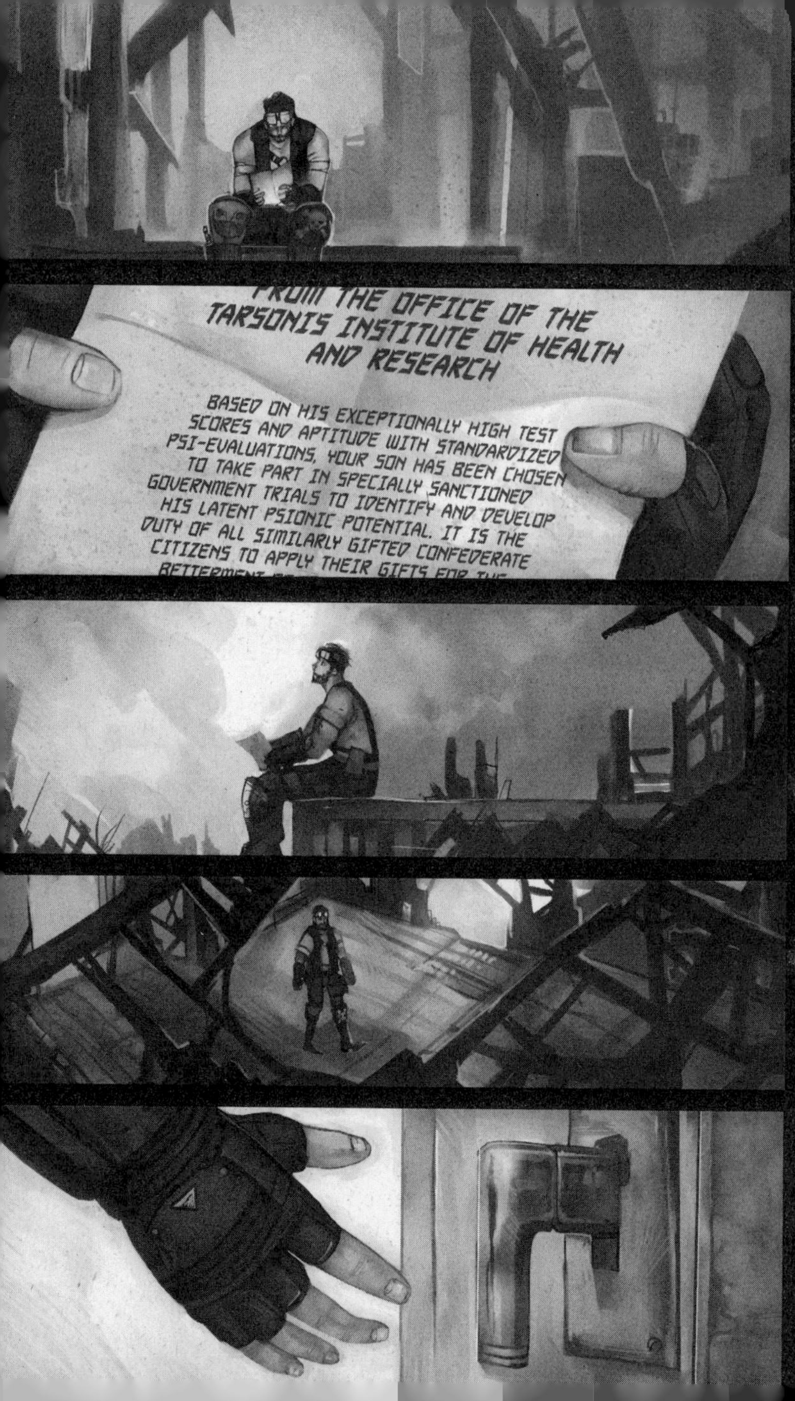
FROM THE OFFICE OF THE
TARSONIS INSTITUTE OF HEALTH
AND RESEARCH
BASED ON HIS EXCEPTIONALLY HIGH TEST SCORES AND APTITUDE WITH STANDARDIZED PSI-EVALUATIONS, YOUR SON HAS BEEN CHOSEN TO TAKE PART IN SPECIALLY SANCTIONED GOVERNMENT TRIALS TO IDENTIFY AND DEVELOP HIS LATENT PSIONIC POTENTIAL. IT IS THE DUTY OF ALL SIMILARLY GIFTED CONFEDERATE CITIZENS TO APPLY THEIR GIFTS FOR THE

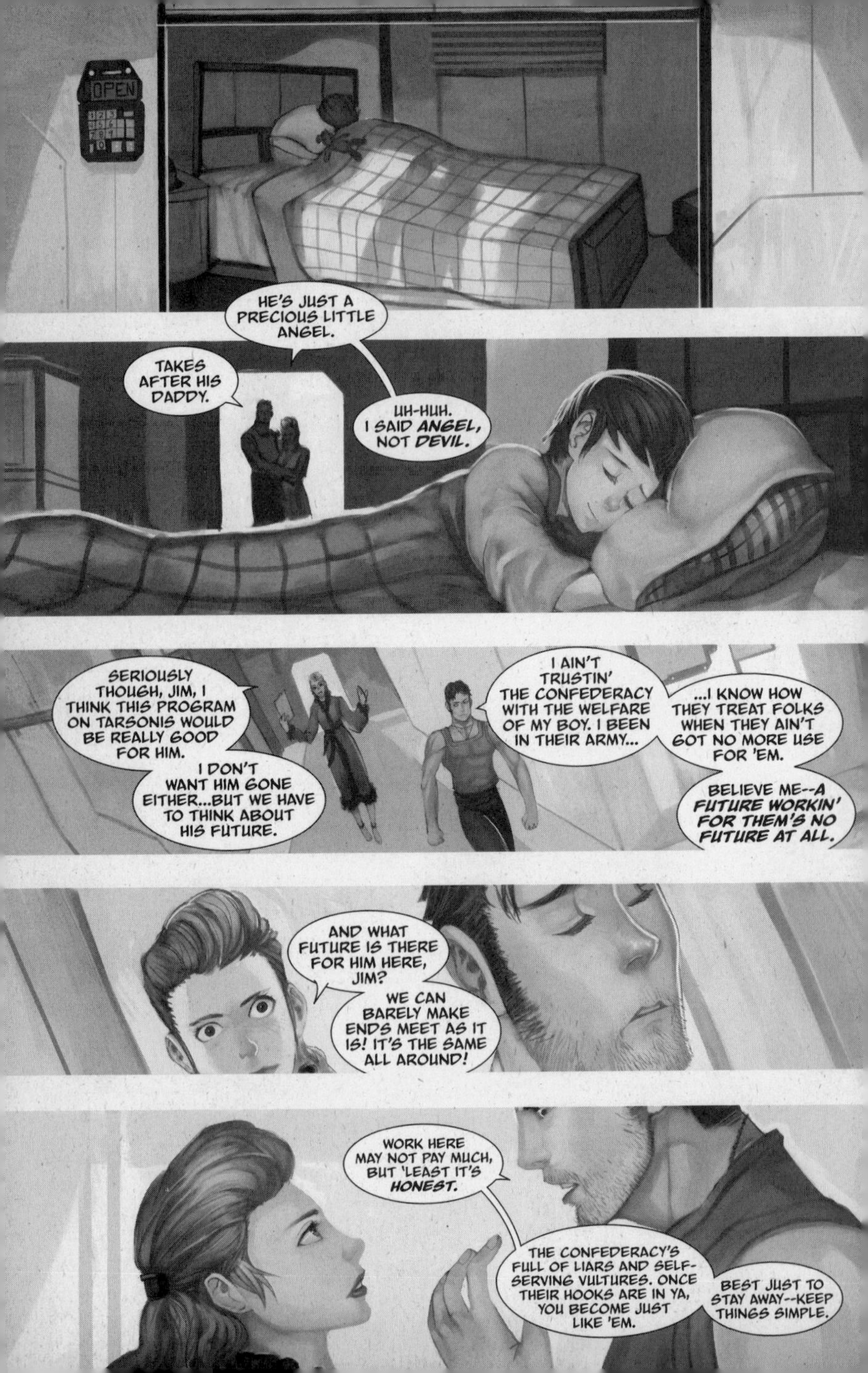
OPEN
HE'S JUST A PRECIOUS LITTLE ANGEL.
TAKES AFTER HIS DADDY.
UH-HUH. I SAID *ANGEL*, NOT *DEVIL*.
SERIOUSLY THOUGH, JIM, I THINK THIS PROGRAM ON TARSONIS WOULD BE REALLY GOOD FOR HIM.
I DON'T WANT HIM GONE EITHER...BUT WE HAVE TO THINK ABOUT HIS FUTURE.
I AIN'T TRUSTIN' THE CONFEDERACY WITH THE WELFARE OF MY BOY. I BEEN IN THEIR ARMY...
...I KNOW HOW THEY TREAT FOLKS WHEN THEY AIN'T GOT NO MORE USE FOR 'EM.
BELIEVE ME--A *FUTURE WORKIN' FOR THEM'S NO FUTURE AT ALL.*
AND WHAT FUTURE IS THERE FOR HIM HERE, JIM?
WE CAN BARELY MAKE ENDS MEET AS IT IS! IT'S THE SAME ALL AROUND!
WORK HERE MAY NOT PAY MUCH, BUT 'LEAST IT'S *HONEST*.
THE CONFEDERACY'S FULL OF LIARS AND SELF-SERVING VULTURES. ONCE THEIR HOOKS ARE IN YA, YOU BECOME JUST LIKE 'EM.
BEST JUST TO STAY AWAY--KEEP THINGS SIMPLE.

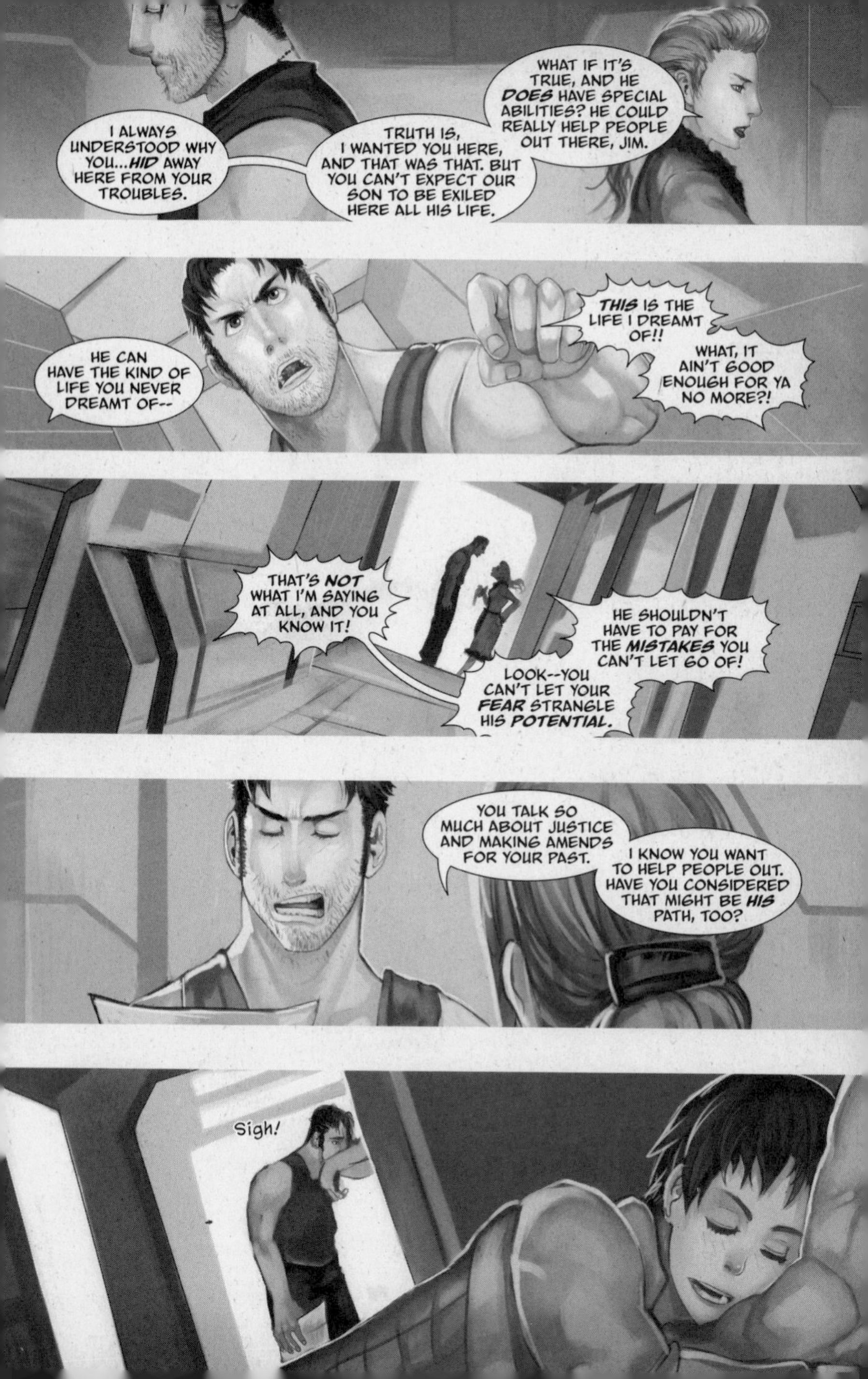
I ALWAYS UNDERSTOOD WHY YOU...HID AWAY HERE FROM YOUR TROUBLES.
TRUTH IS, I WANTED YOU HERE, AND THAT WAS THAT. BUT YOU CAN'T EXPECT OUR SON TO BE EXILED HERE ALL HIS LIFE.
WHAT IF IT'S TRUE, AND HE DOES HAVE SPECIAL ABILITIES? HE COULD REALLY HELP PEOPLE OUT THERE, JIM.
HE CAN HAVE THE KIND OF LIFE YOU NEVER DREAMT OF--
THIS IS THE LIFE I DREAMT OF!!
WHAT, IT AIN'T GOOD ENOUGH FOR YA NO MORE?!
THAT'S NOT WHAT I'M SAYING AT ALL, AND YOU KNOW IT!
HE SHOULDN'T HAVE TO PAY FOR THE MISTAKES YOU CAN'T LET GO OF!
LOOK--YOU CAN'T LET YOUR FEAR STRANGLE HIS POTENTIAL.
YOU TALK SO MUCH ABOUT JUSTICE AND MAKING AMENDS FOR YOUR PAST.
I KNOW YOU WANT TO HELP PEOPLE OUT. HAVE YOU CONSIDERED THAT MIGHT BE HIS PATH, TOO?
Sigh!

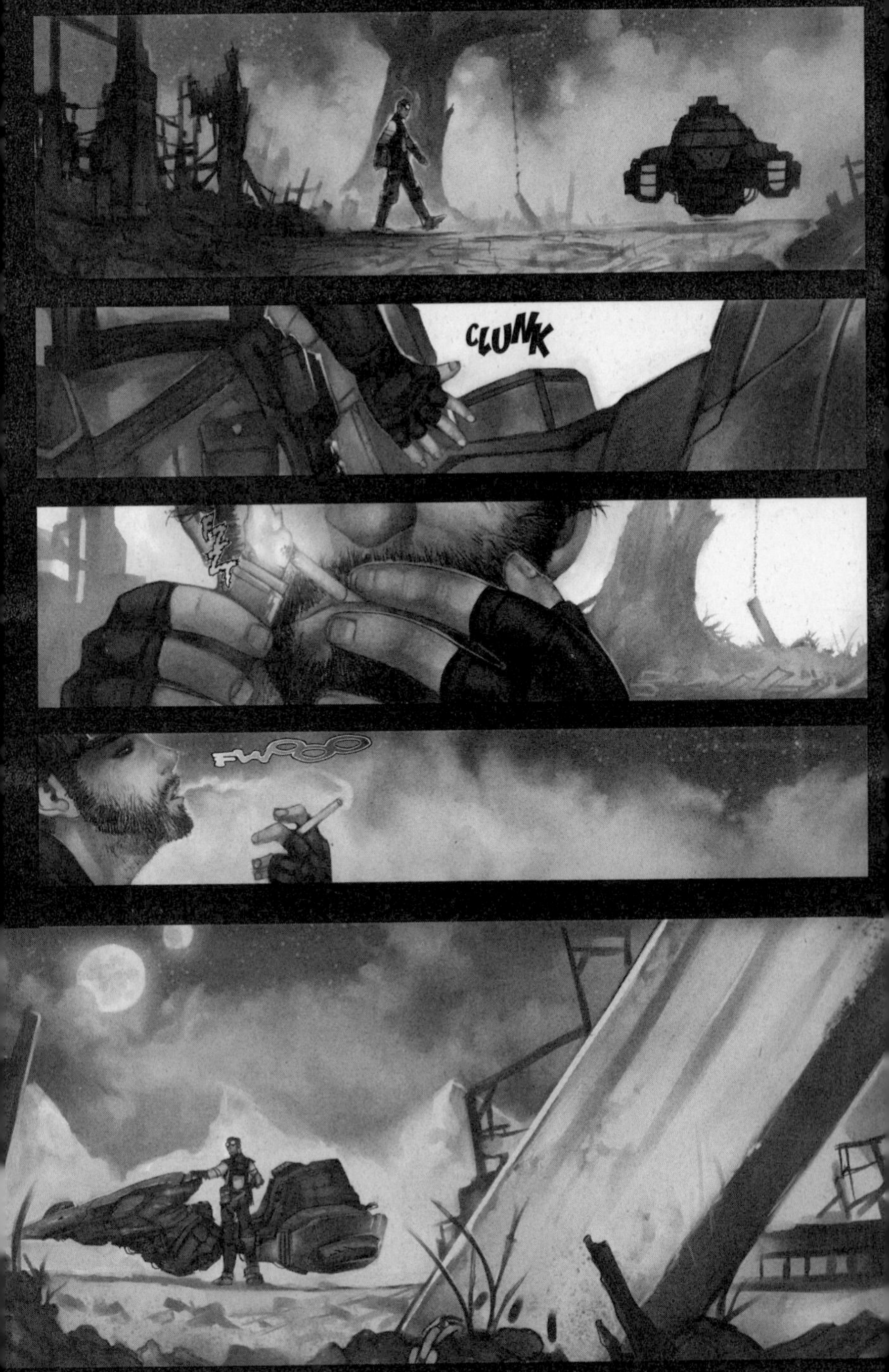
CLUNK
FZZT
FWOOO

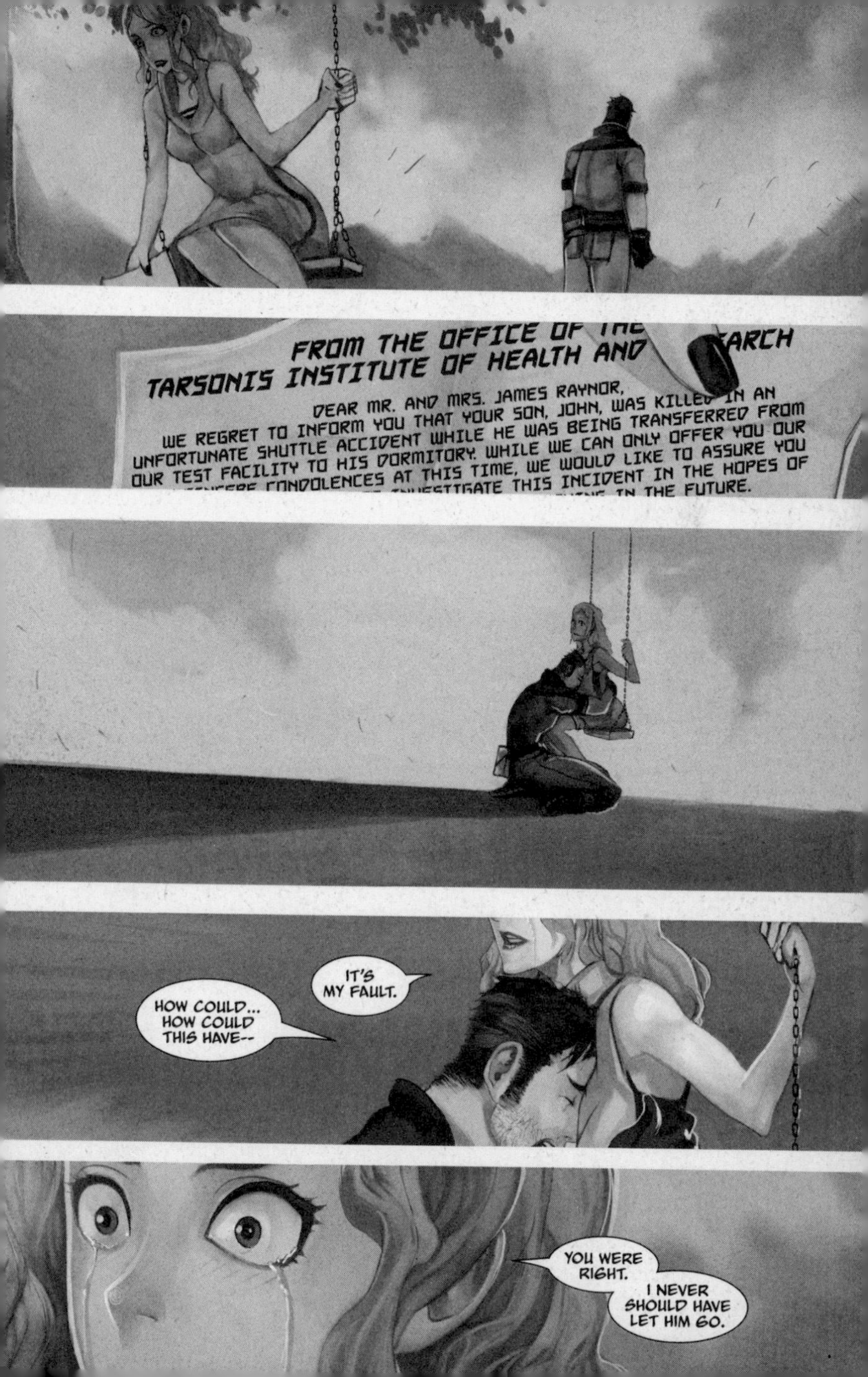
FROM THE OFFICE OF THE
TARSONIS INSTITUTE OF HEALTH AND
ARCH
DEAR MR. AND MRS. JAMES RAYNOR,
WE REGRET TO INFORM YOU THAT YOUR SON, JOHN, WAS KILLED IN AN
UNFORTUNATE SHUTTLE ACCIDENT WHILE HE WAS BEING TRANSFERRED FROM
OUR TEST FACILITY TO HIS DORMITORY. WHILE WE CAN ONLY OFFER YOU OUR
CONDOLENCES AT THIS TIME, WE WOULD LIKE TO ASSURE YOU
INVESTIGATE THIS INCIDENT IN THE HOPES OF
IN THE FUTURE.
HOW COULD... HOW COULD THIS HAVE--
IT'S MY FAULT.
YOU WERE RIGHT.
I NEVER SHOULD HAVE LET HIM GO.

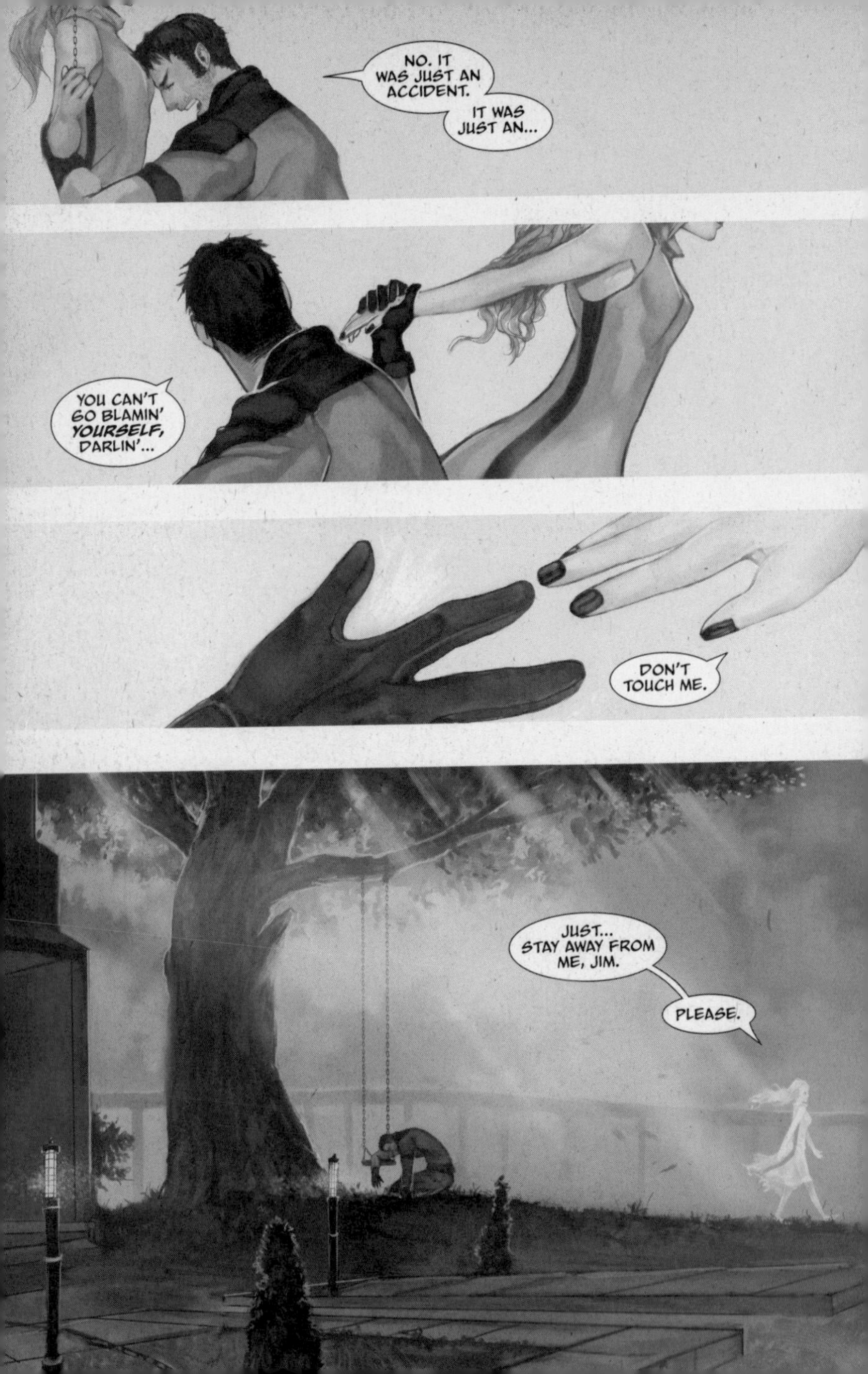
NO. IT WAS JUST AN ACCIDENT.
IT WAS JUST AN...
YOU CAN'T GO BLAMIN' *YOURSELF*, DARLIN'...
DON'T TOUCH ME.
JUST... STAY AWAY FROM ME, JIM.
PLEASE.

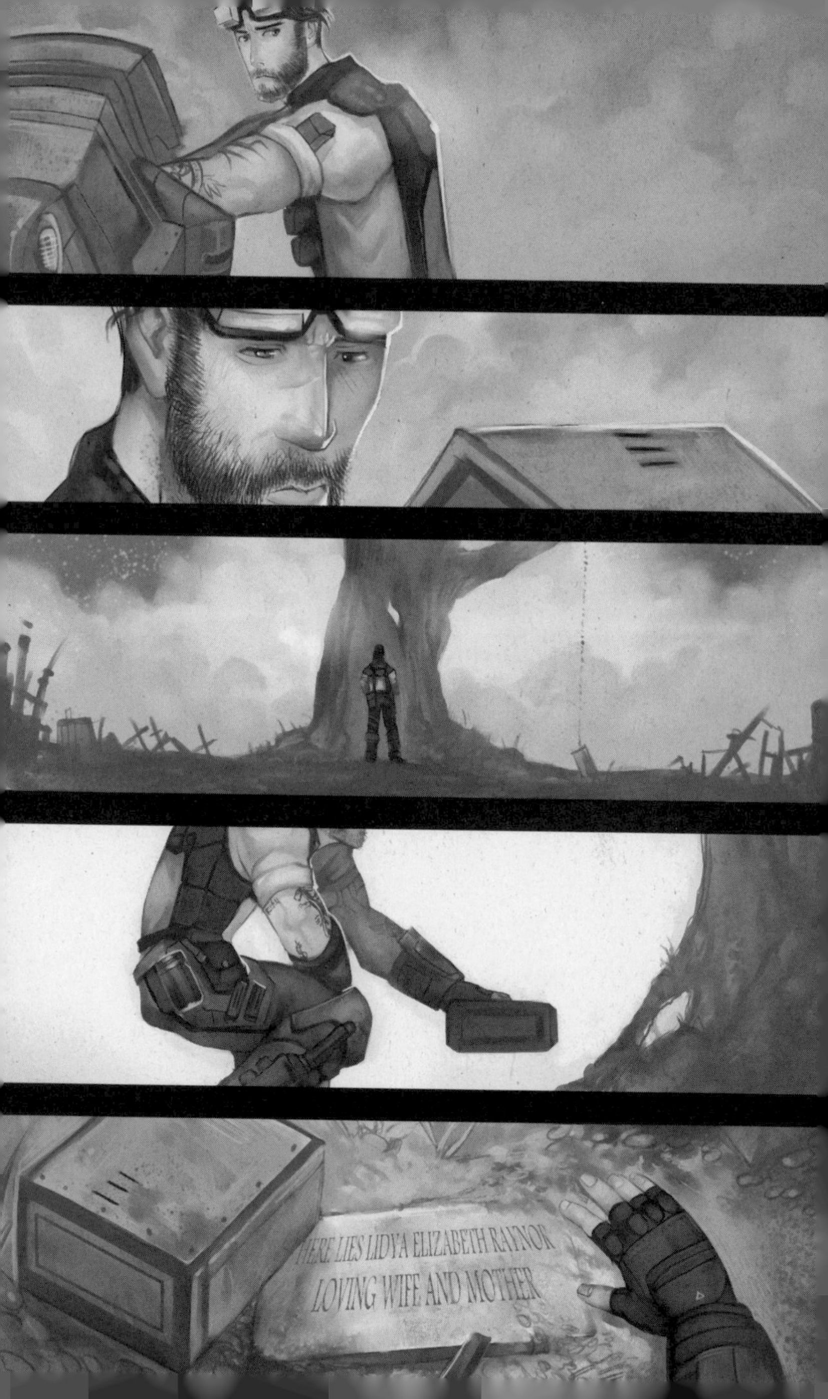
HERE LIES LIDYA ELIZABETH RAYNOR
LOVING WIFE AND MOTHER

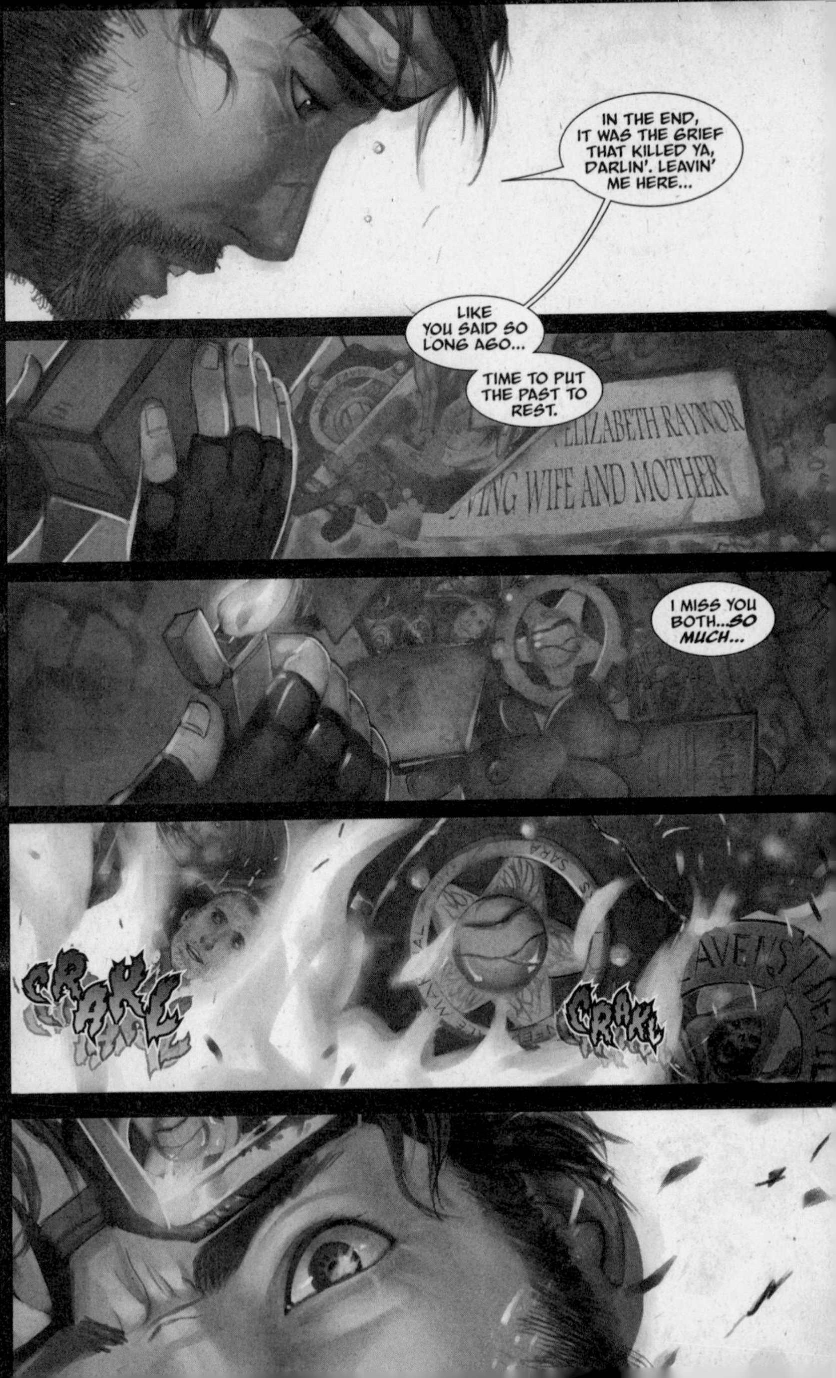
IN THE END, IT WAS THE GRIEF THAT KILLED YA, DARLIN'. LEAVIN' ME HERE...
LIKE YOU SAID SO LONG AGO...
TIME TO PUT THE PAST TO REST.
ELIZABETH RAYNOR
VING WIFE AND MOTHER
I MISS YOU BOTH...SO MUCH...
CRAKL
CRAKL

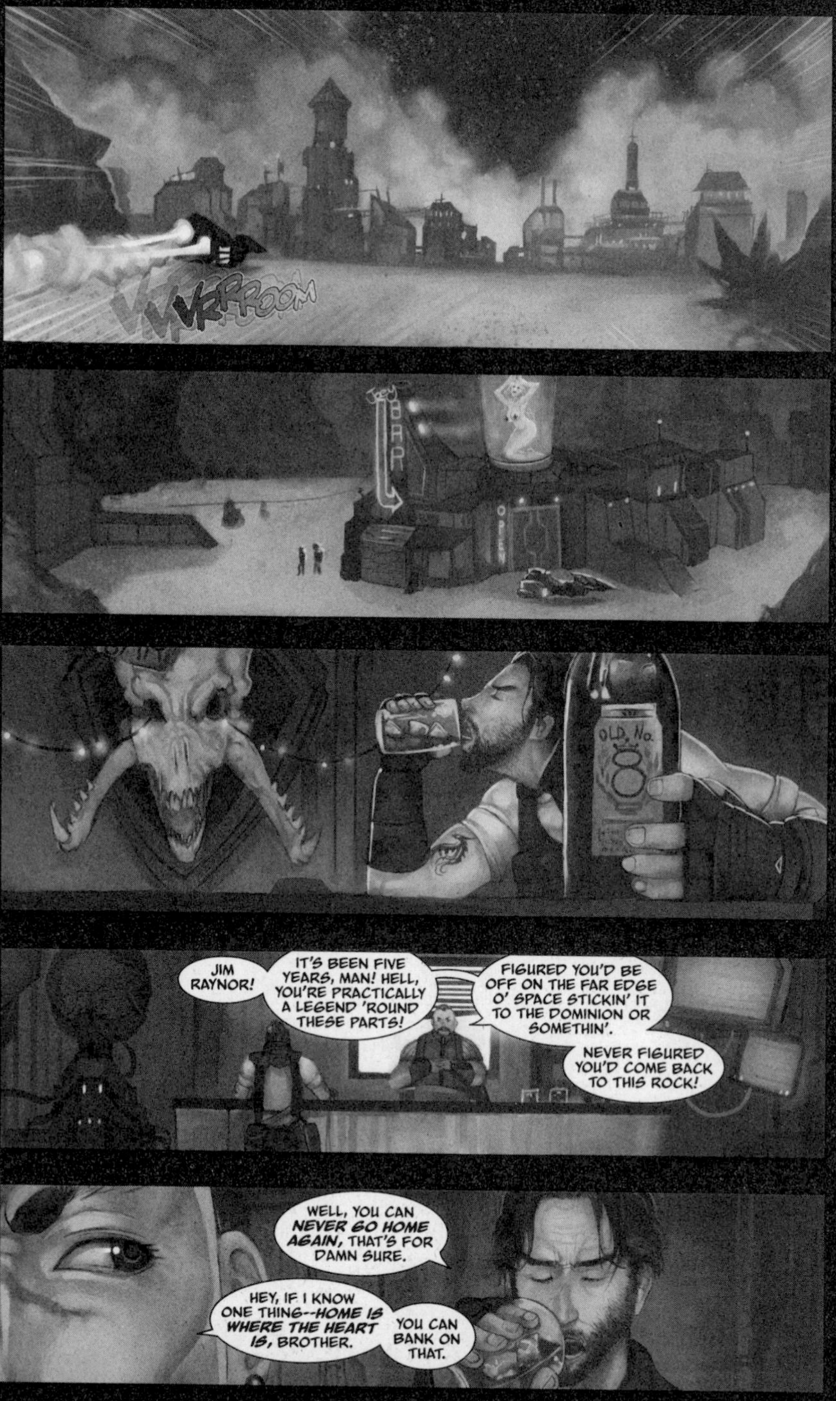
VVVRROOM
Joey
BAR
OPEN
OLD No. 8
JIM RAYNOR!
IT'S BEEN FIVE YEARS, MAN! HELL, YOU'RE PRACTICALLY A LEGEND 'ROUND THESE PARTS!
FIGURED YOU'D BE OFF ON THE FAR EDGE O' SPACE STICKIN' IT TO THE DOMINION OR SOMETHIN'.
NEVER FIGURED YOU'D COME BACK TO THIS ROCK!
WELL, YOU CAN *NEVER GO HOME AGAIN,* THAT'S FOR DAMN SURE.
HEY, IF I KNOW ONE THING--*HOME IS WHERE THE HEART IS,* BROTHER.
YOU CAN BANK ON THAT.

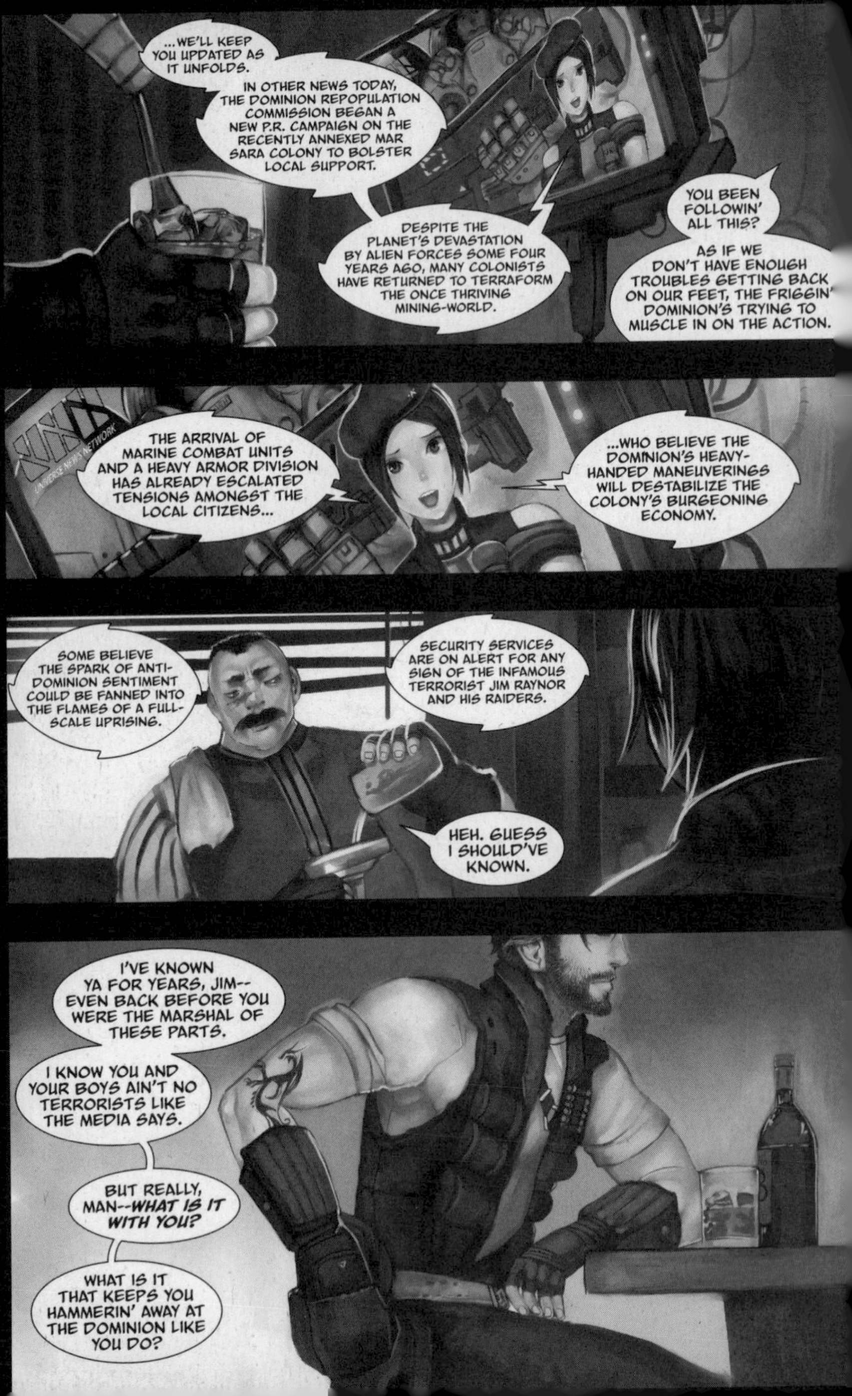
...WE'LL KEEP YOU UPDATED AS IT UNFOLDS.
IN OTHER NEWS TODAY, THE DOMINION REPOPULATION COMMISSION BEGAN A NEW P.R. CAMPAIGN ON THE RECENTLY ANNEXED MAR SARA COLONY TO BOLSTER LOCAL SUPPORT.
DESPITE THE PLANET'S DEVASTATION BY ALIEN FORCES SOME FOUR YEARS AGO, MANY COLONISTS HAVE RETURNED TO TERRAFORM THE ONCE THRIVING MINING-WORLD.
YOU BEEN FOLLOWIN' ALL THIS?
AS IF WE DON'T HAVE ENOUGH TROUBLES GETTING BACK ON OUR FEET, THE FRIGGIN' DOMINION'S TRYING TO MUSCLE IN ON THE ACTION.
UNIVERSE NEWS NETWORK
THE ARRIVAL OF MARINE COMBAT UNITS AND A HEAVY ARMOR DIVISION HAS ALREADY ESCALATED TENSIONS AMONGST THE LOCAL CITIZENS...
...WHO BELIEVE THE DOMINION'S HEAVY-HANDED MANEUVERINGS WILL DESTABILIZE THE COLONY'S BURGEONING ECONOMY.
SOME BELIEVE THE SPARK OF ANTI-DOMINION SENTIMENT COULD BE FANNED INTO THE FLAMES OF A FULL-SCALE UPRISING.
SECURITY SERVICES ARE ON ALERT FOR ANY SIGN OF THE INFAMOUS TERRORIST JIM RAYNOR AND HIS RAIDERS.
HEH. GUESS I SHOULD'VE KNOWN.
I'VE KNOWN YA FOR YEARS, JIM--EVEN BACK BEFORE YOU WERE THE MARSHAL OF THESE PARTS.
I KNOW YOU AND YOUR BOYS AIN'T NO TERRORISTS LIKE THE MEDIA SAYS.
BUT REALLY, MAN--*WHAT IS IT WITH YOU?*
WHAT IS IT THAT KEEPS YOU HAMMERIN' AWAY AT THE DOMINION LIKE YOU DO?

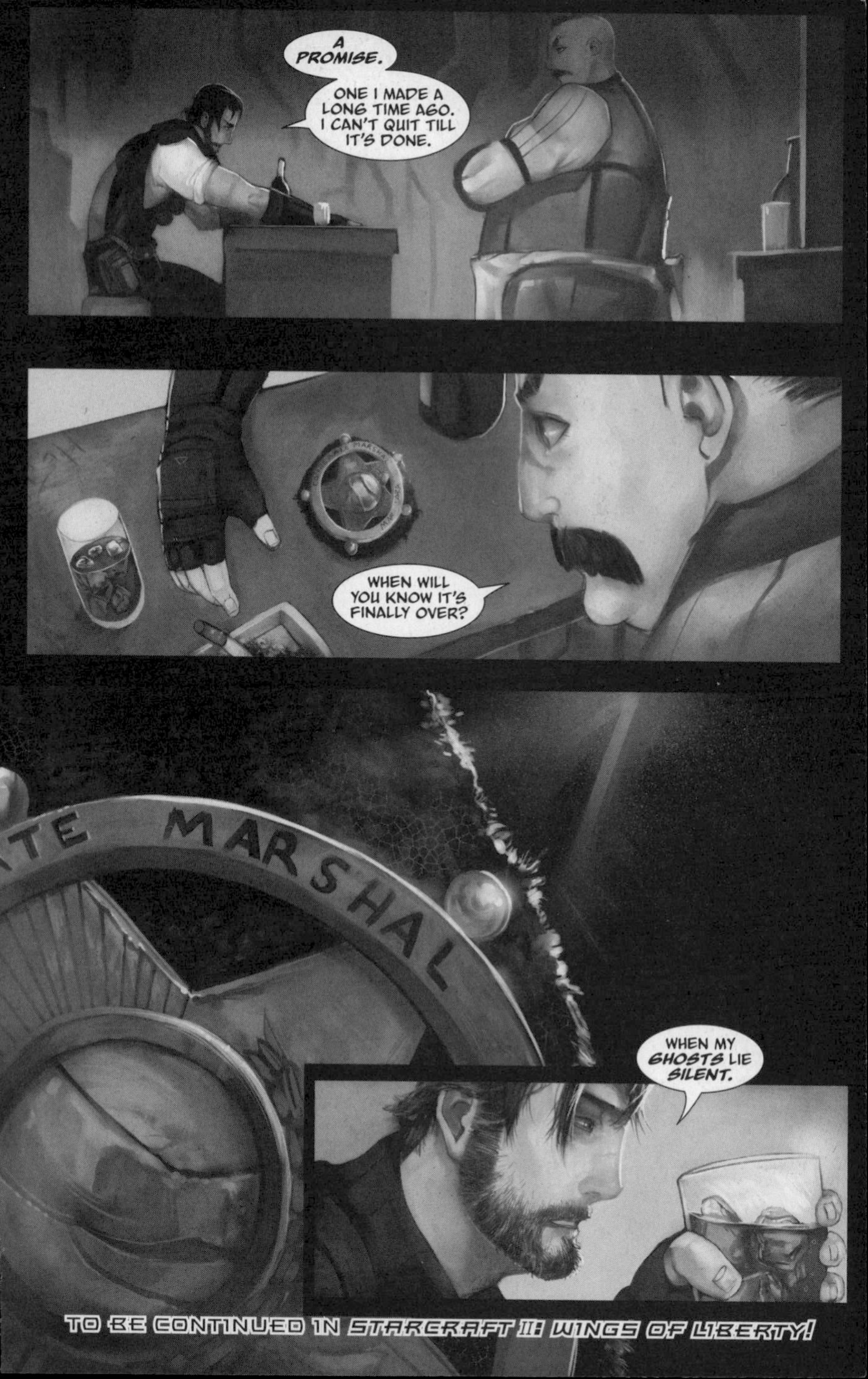
A PROMISE.
ONE I MADE A LONG TIME AGO. I CAN'T QUIT TILL IT'S DONE.
WHEN WILL YOU KNOW IT'S FINALLY OVER?
MARSHAL
WHEN MY GHOSTS LIE SILENT.
TO BE CONTINUED IN STARCRAFT II: WINGS OF LIBERTY!

# StarCraft

## Frontline
### Volume 4

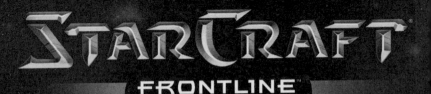

# Fear the Reaper

Written by David Gerrold

Pencils by Ruben de Vela
Inks by Dan Borgonos
Tones by Gonzalo Duarte

Letterer: Michael Paolilli

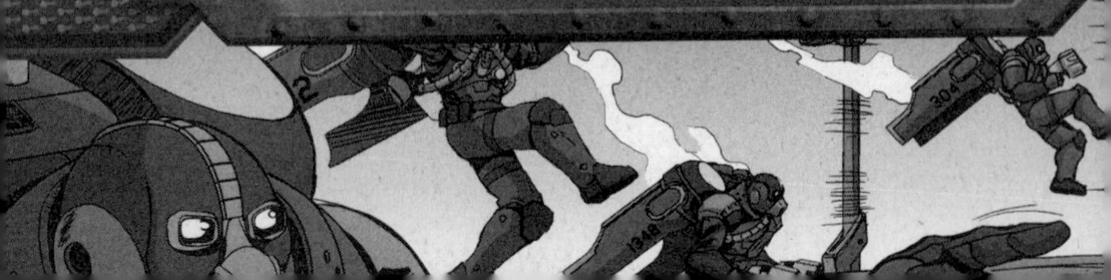

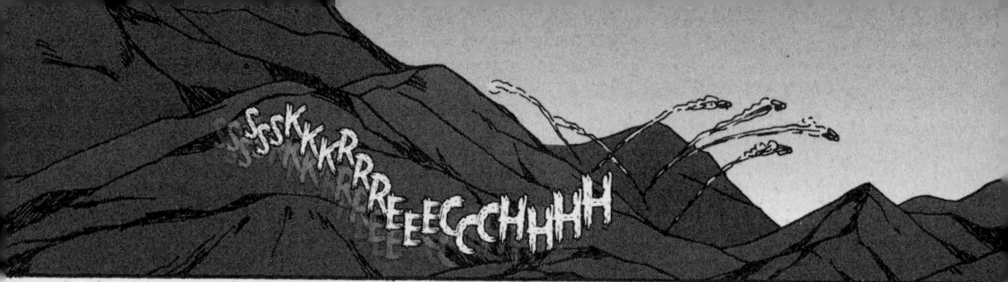
SSSKKKRRREEECCCHHHH

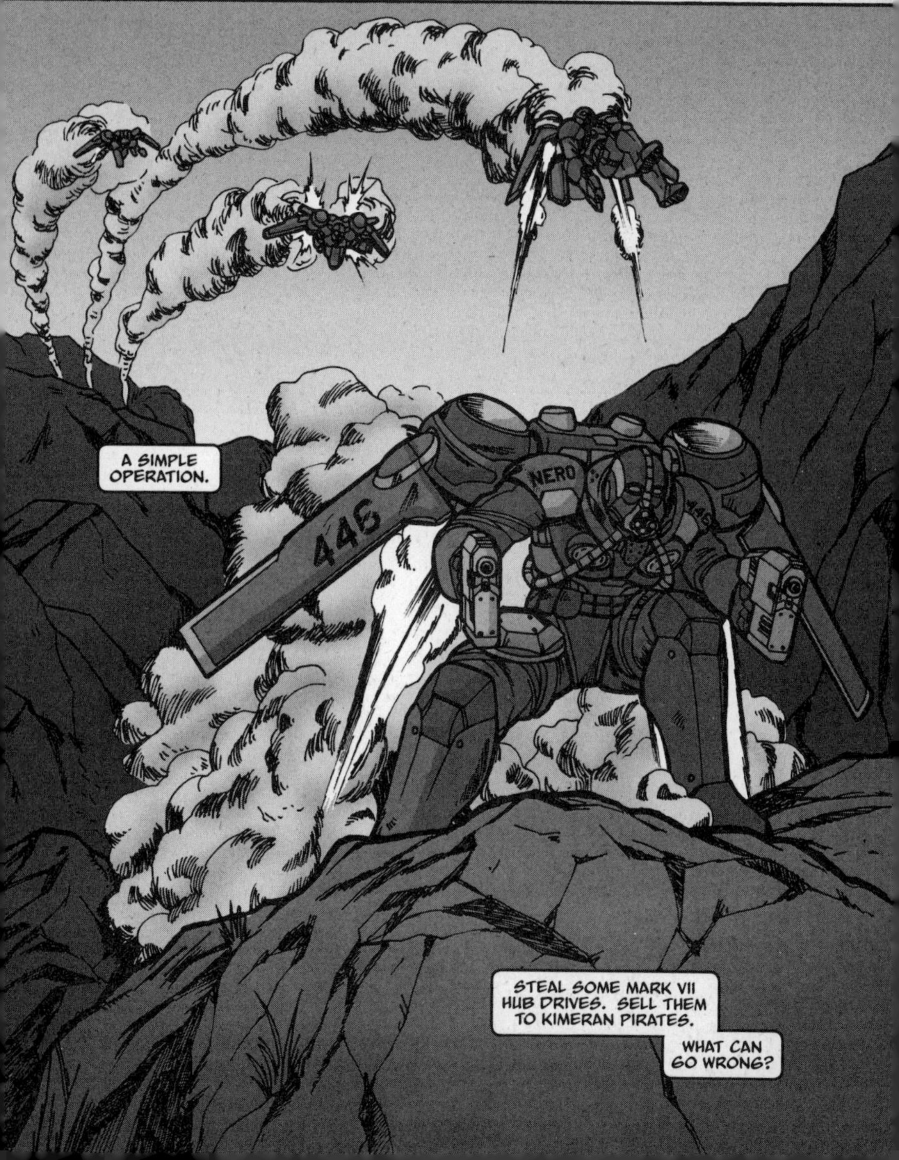
A SIMPLE OPERATION.
NERO
446
STEAL SOME MARK VII HUB DRIVES. SELL THEM TO KIMERAN PIRATES.
WHAT CAN GO WRONG?

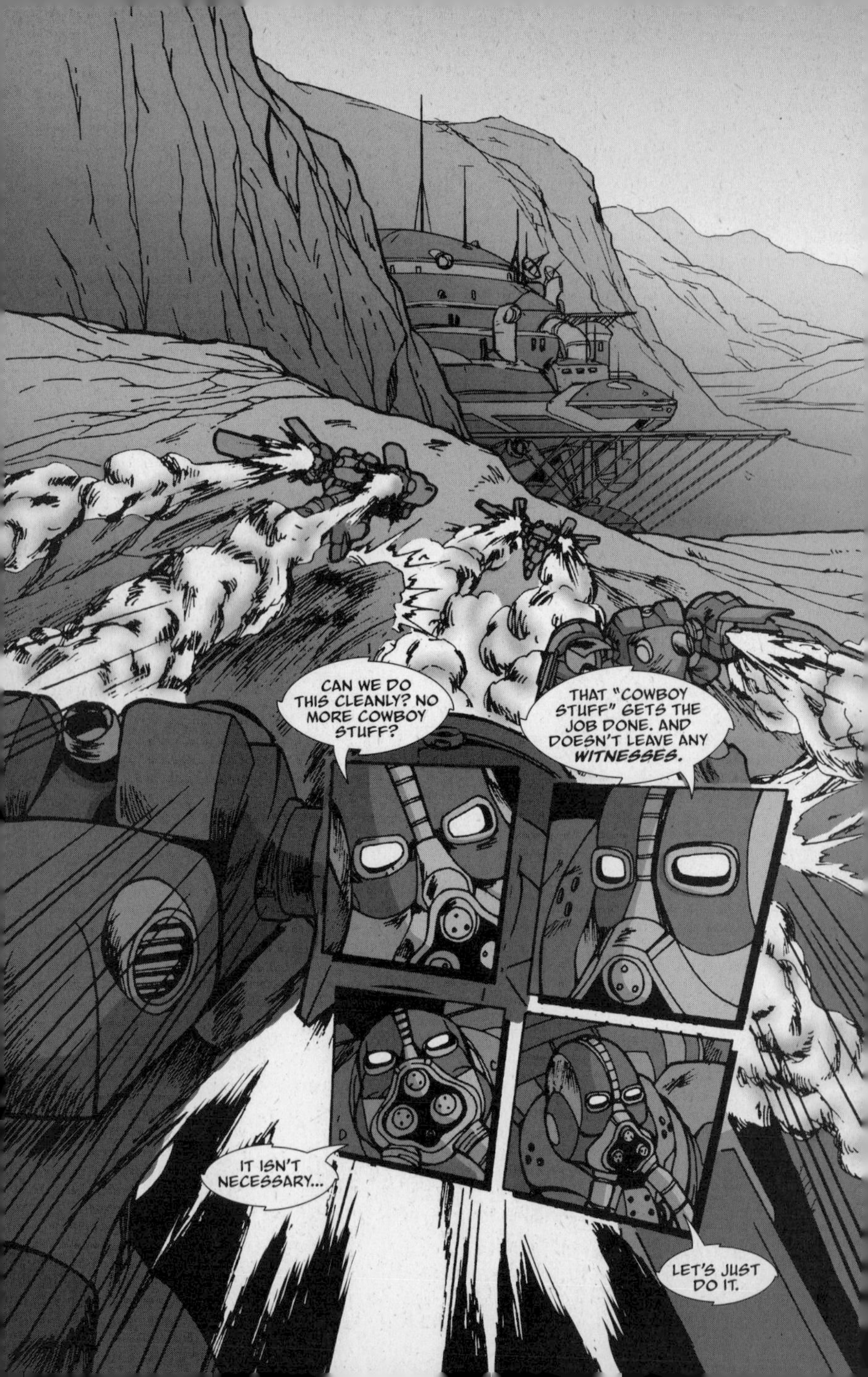
CAN WE DO THIS CLEANLY? NO MORE COWBOY STUFF?
THAT "COWBOY STUFF" GETS THE JOB DONE. AND DOESN'T LEAVE ANY *WITNESSES.*
IT ISN'T NECESSARY...
LET'S JUST DO IT.

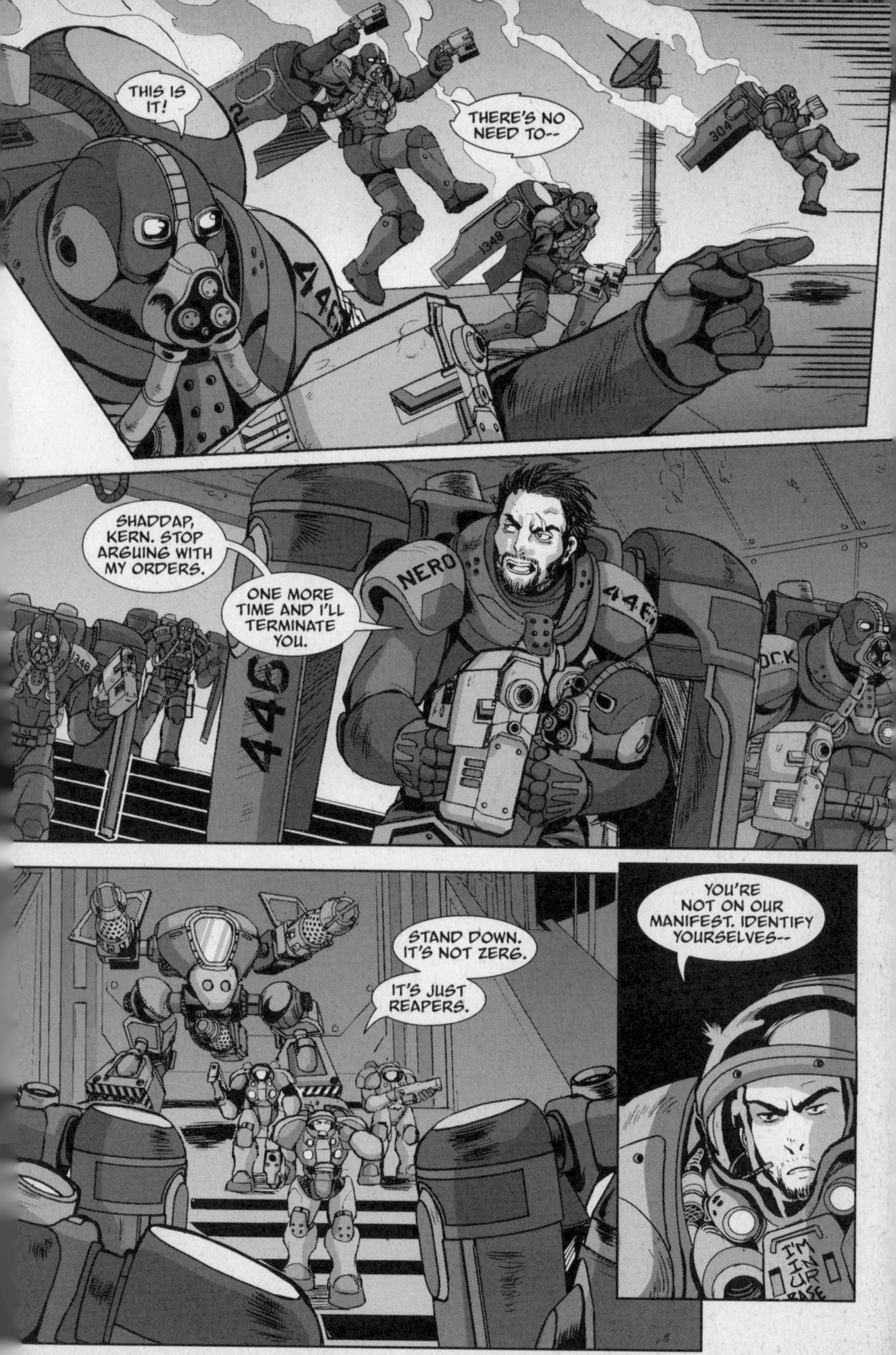
THIS IS IT!
THERE'S NO NEED TO--
SHADDAP, KERN. STOP ARGUING WITH MY ORDERS.
ONE MORE TIME AND I'LL TERMINATE YOU.
STAND DOWN. IT'S NOT ZERG.
IT'S JUST REAPERS.
YOU'RE NOT ON OUR MANIFEST. IDENTIFY YOURSELVES--

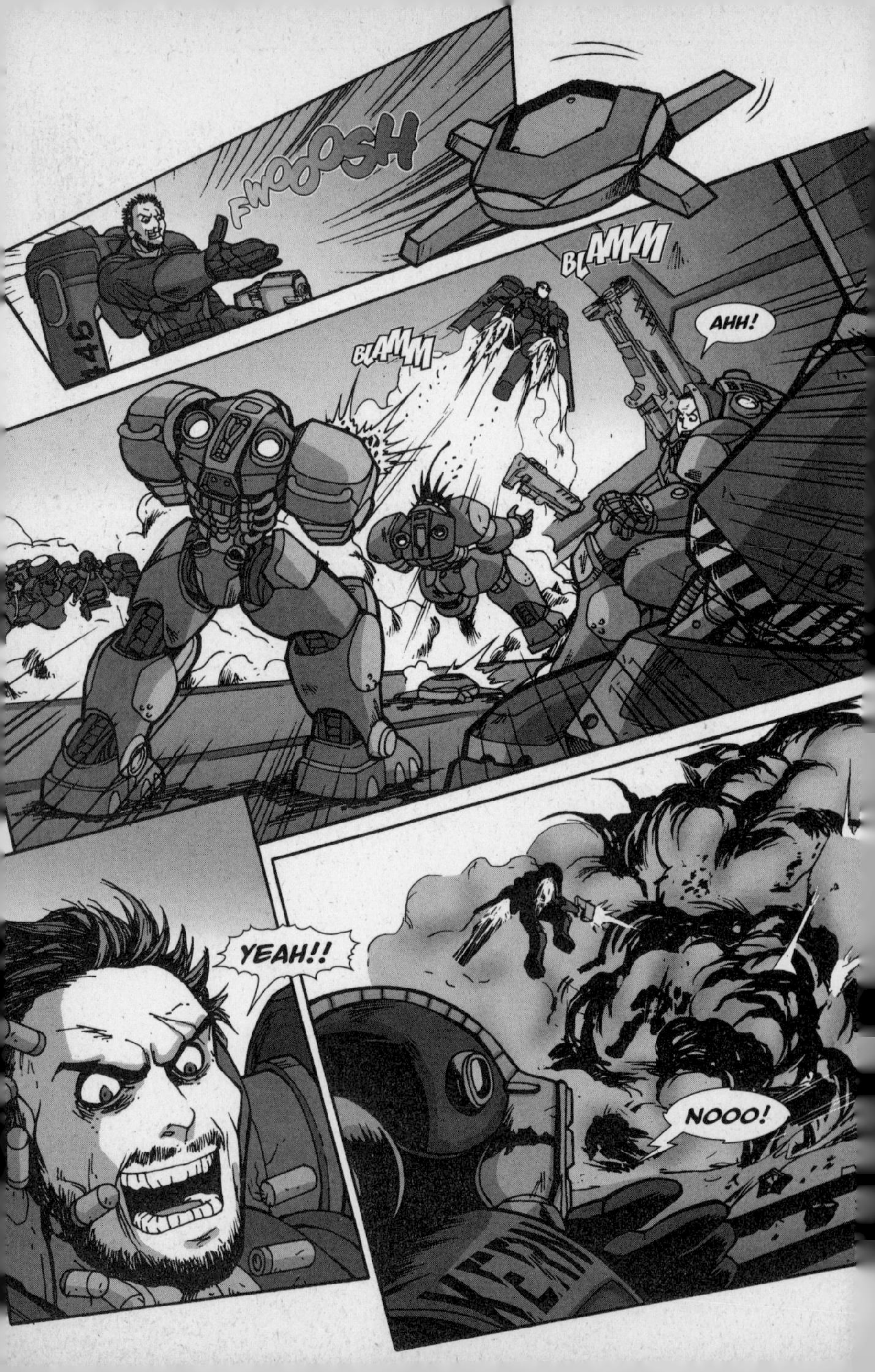
FWOOOSH
BLAMMM
BLAMMM
AHH!
YEAH!!
NOOO!

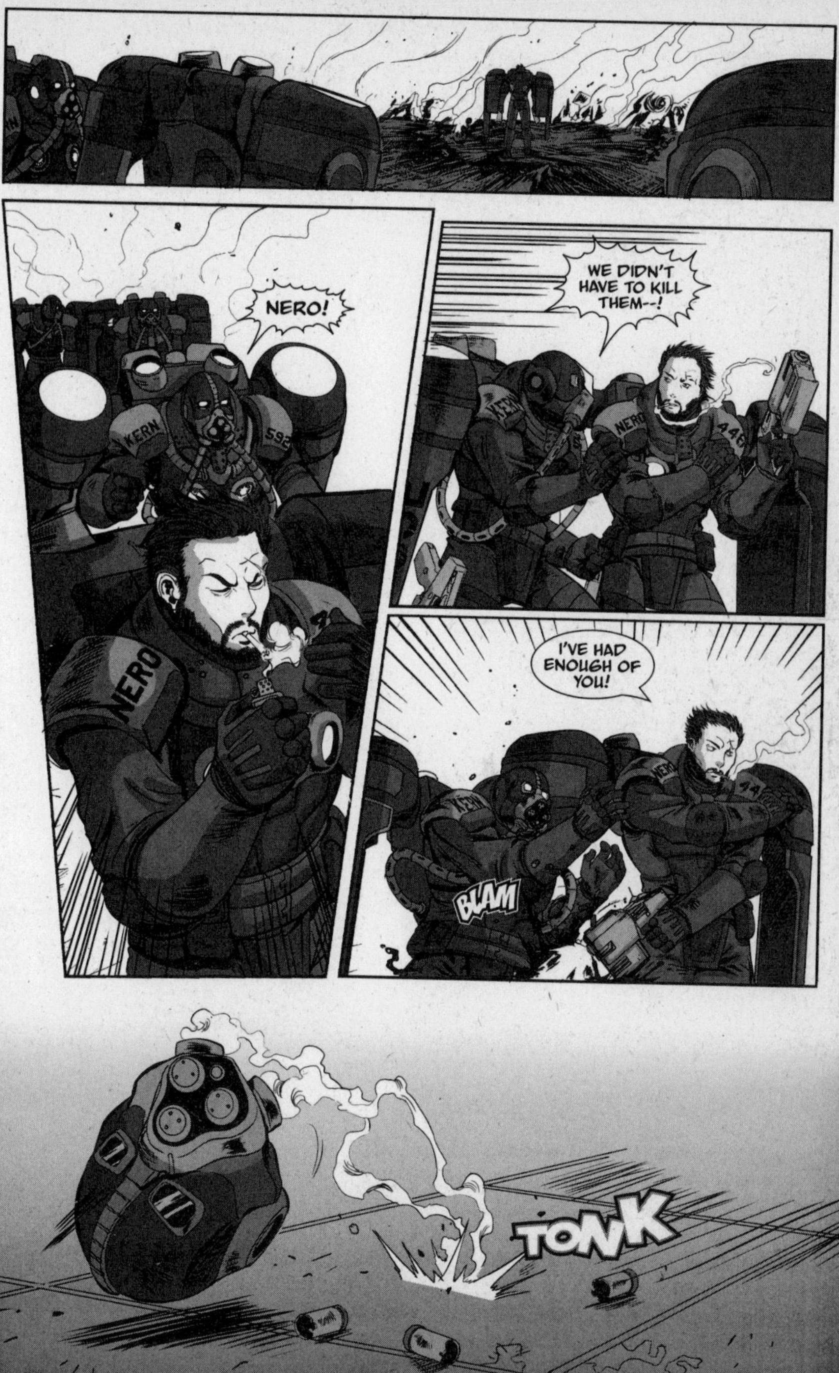
KERN
NERO!
KERN
592
NERO
WE DIDN'T HAVE TO KILL THEM--!
KERN
NERO
I'VE HAD ENOUGH OF YOU!
KERN
NERO
BLAM
TONK

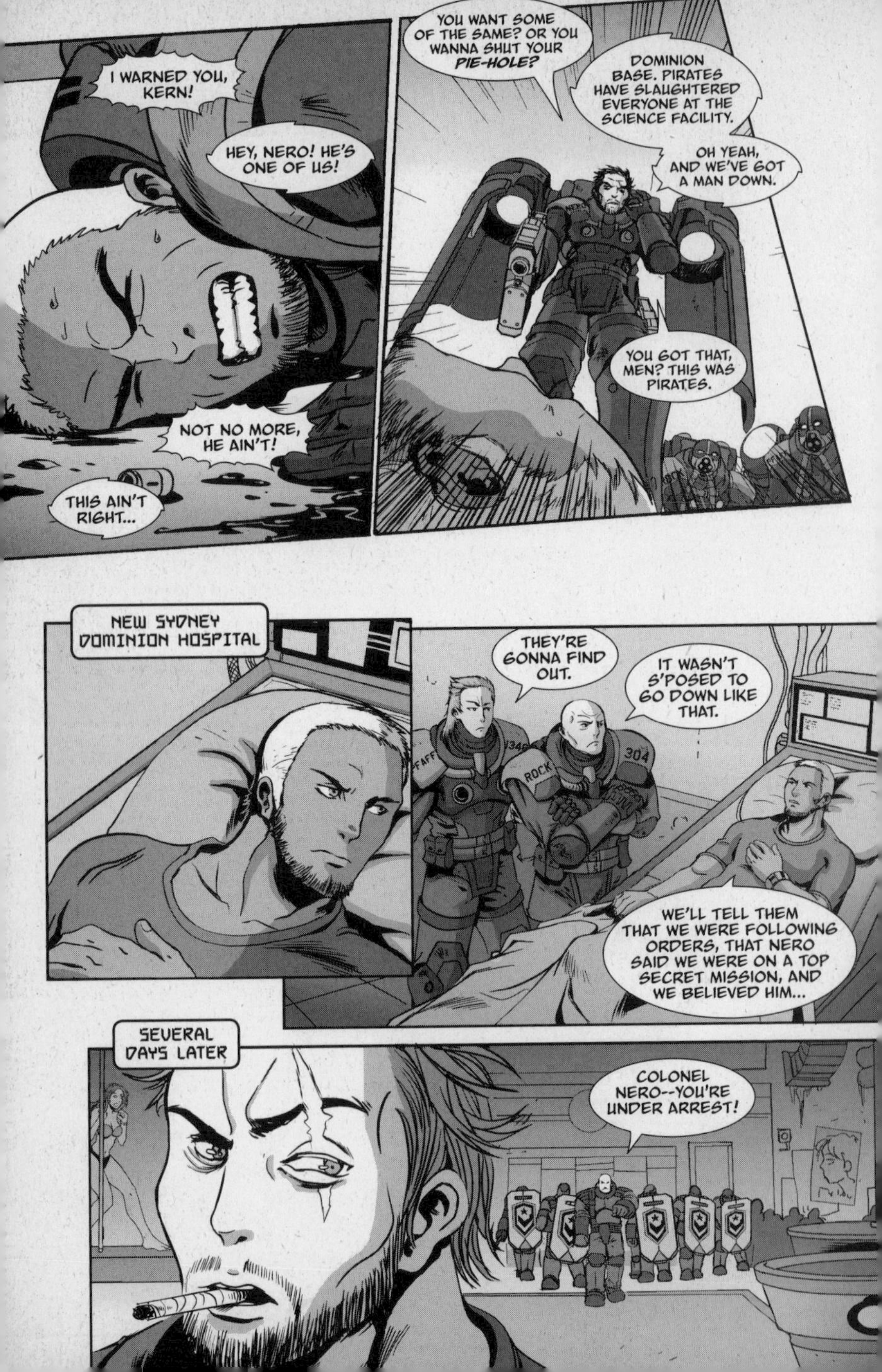
I WARNED YOU, KERN!
HEY, NERO! HE'S ONE OF US!
NOT NO MORE, HE AIN'T!
THIS AIN'T RIGHT...
YOU WANT SOME OF THE SAME? OR YOU WANNA SHUT YOUR *PIE-HOLE?*
DOMINION BASE. PIRATES HAVE SLAUGHTERED EVERYONE AT THE SCIENCE FACILITY.
OH YEAH, AND WE'VE GOT A MAN DOWN.
YOU GOT THAT, MEN? THIS WAS PIRATES.
NEW SYDNEY DOMINION HOSPITAL
THEY'RE GONNA FIND OUT.
IT WASN'T S'POSED TO GO DOWN LIKE THAT.
WE'LL TELL THEM THAT WE WERE FOLLOWING ORDERS, THAT NERO SAID WE WERE ON A TOP SECRET MISSION, AND WE BELIEVED HIM...
SEVERAL DAYS LATER
COLONEL NERO--YOU'RE UNDER ARREST!

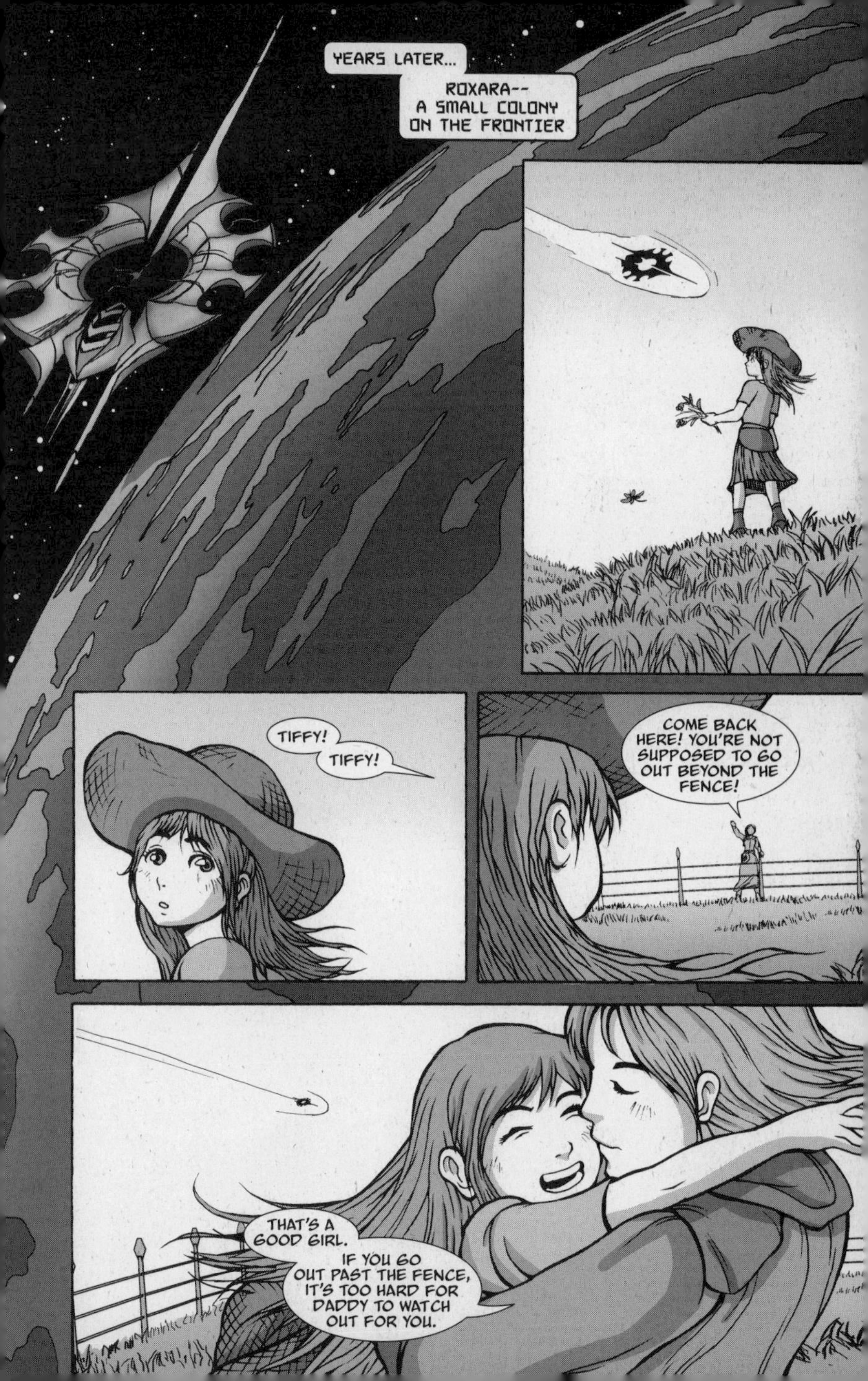
YEARS LATER...
ROXARA-- A SMALL COLONY ON THE FRONTIER
TIFFY!
TIFFY!
COME BACK HERE! YOU'RE NOT SUPPOSED TO GO OUT BEYOND THE FENCE!
THAT'S A GOOD GIRL.
IF YOU GO OUT PAST THE FENCE, IT'S TOO HARD FOR DADDY TO WATCH OUT FOR YOU.

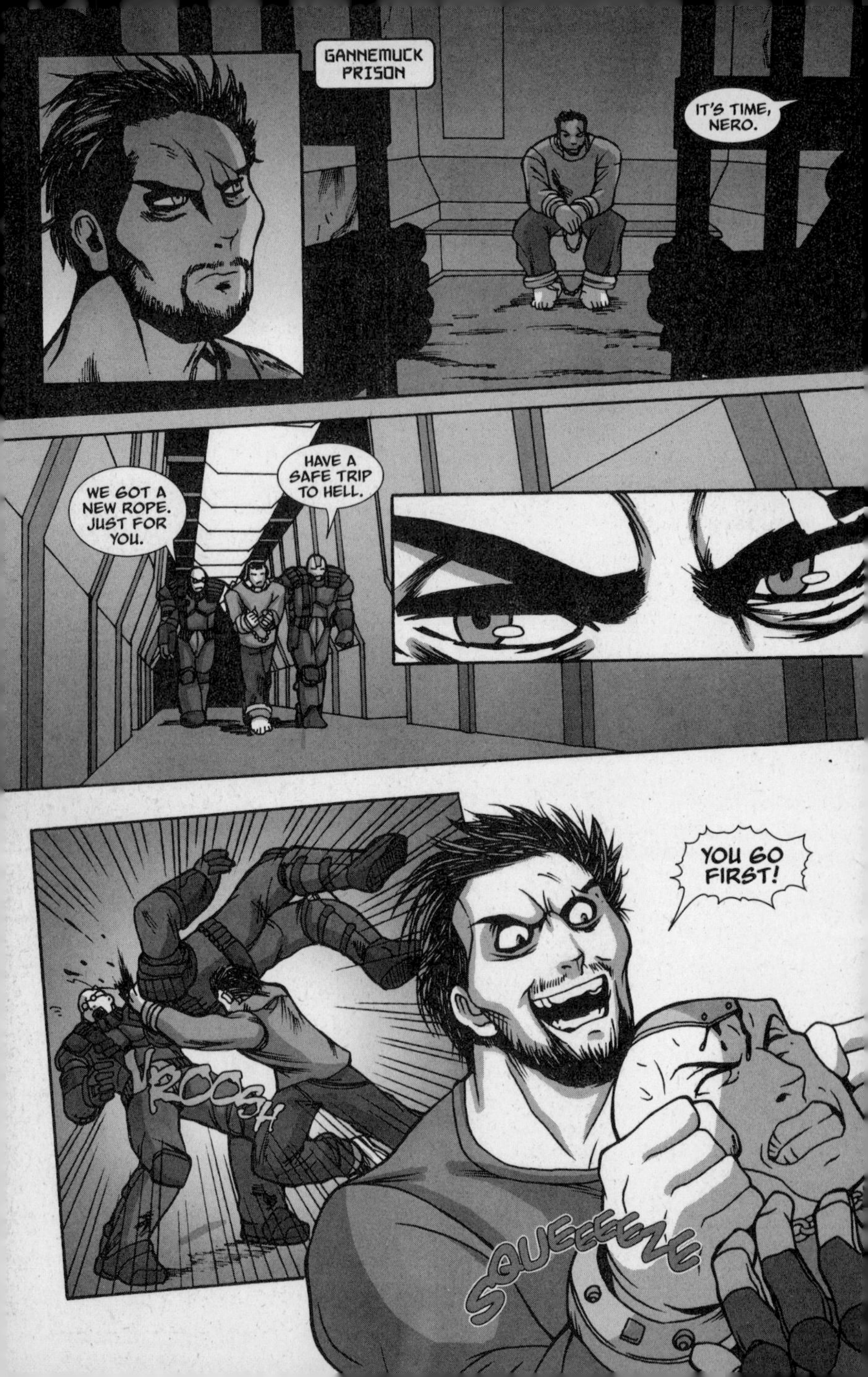
GANNEMUCK PRISON
IT'S TIME, NERO.
WE GOT A NEW ROPE. JUST FOR YOU.
HAVE A SAFE TRIP TO HELL.
YOU GO FIRST!
VROOSH
SQUEEEEZE

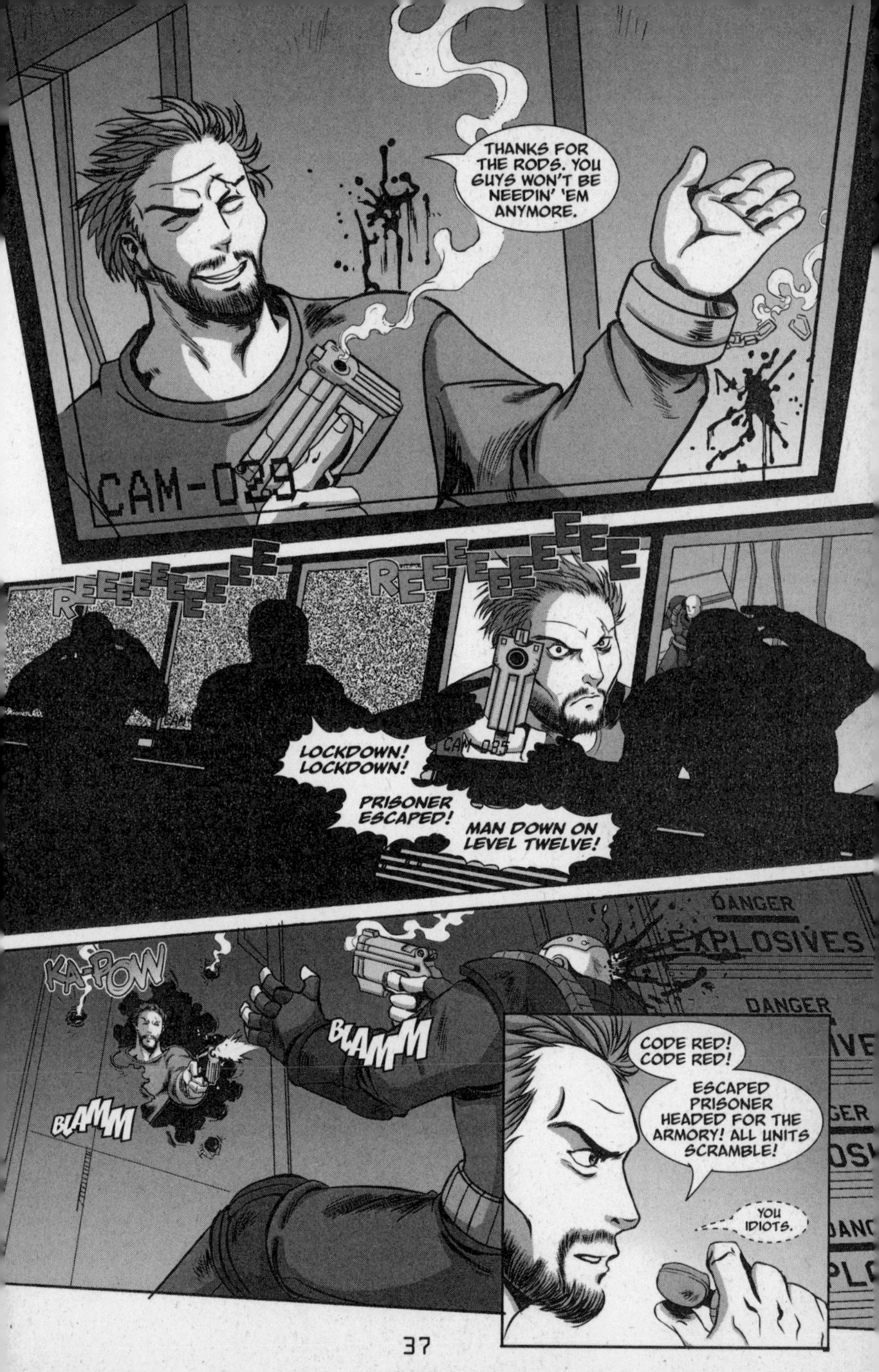
THANKS FOR THE RODS. YOU GUYS WON'T BE NEEDIN' 'EM ANYMORE.
CAM-029
REEEEEEEEEE
REEEEEEEEEEEE
CAM-085
LOCKDOWN! LOCKDOWN!
PRISONER ESCAPED!
MAN DOWN ON LEVEL TWELVE!
KA-POW
BLAMM
BLAMMM
DANGER
EXPLOSIVES
DANGER
CODE RED! CODE RED!
ESCAPED PRISONER HEADED FOR THE ARMORY! ALL UNITS SCRAMBLE!
YOU IDIOTS.

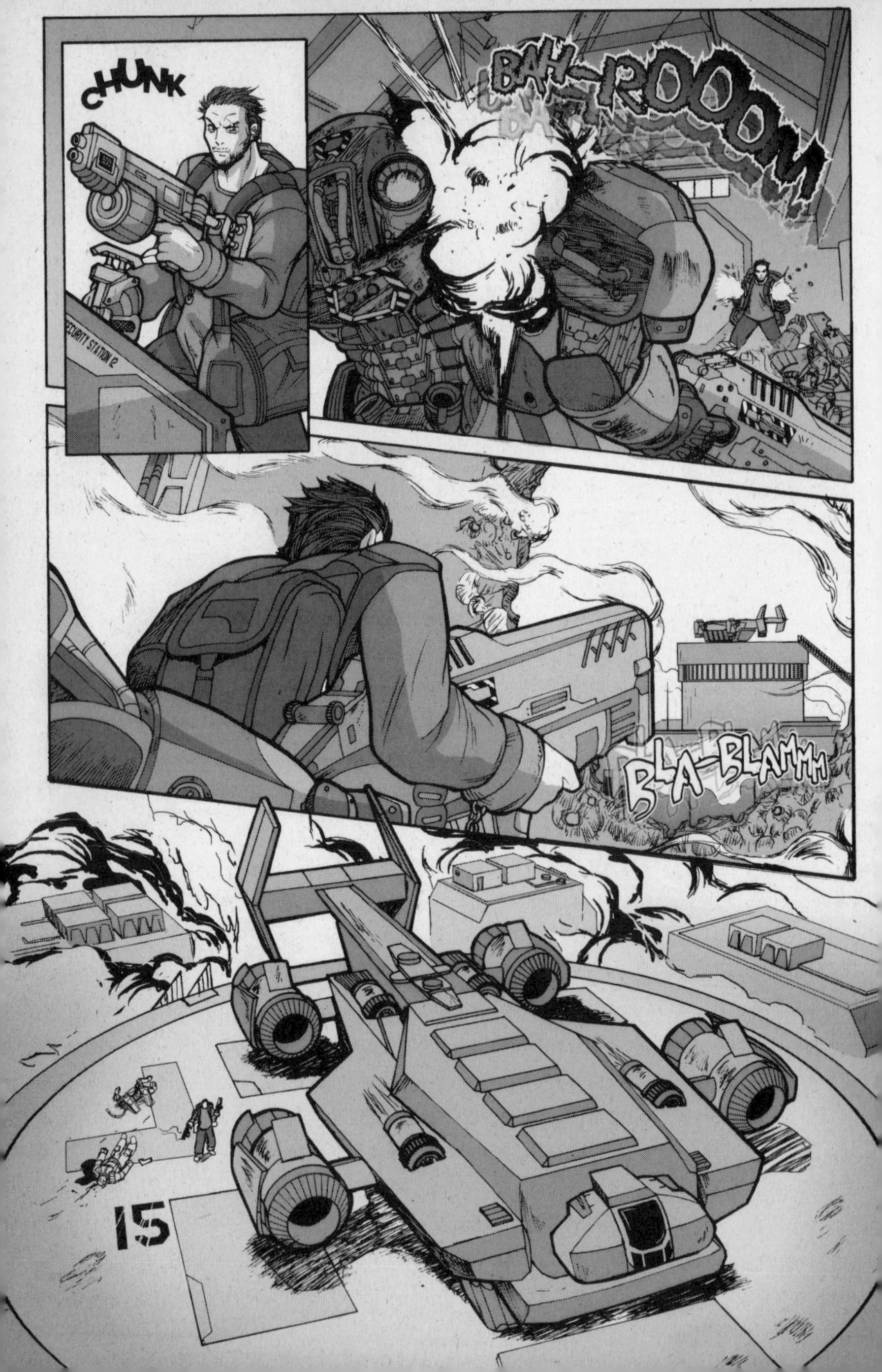
CHUNK
SECURITY STATION 12
BAH-ROOOM
BLA-BLAMMM
15

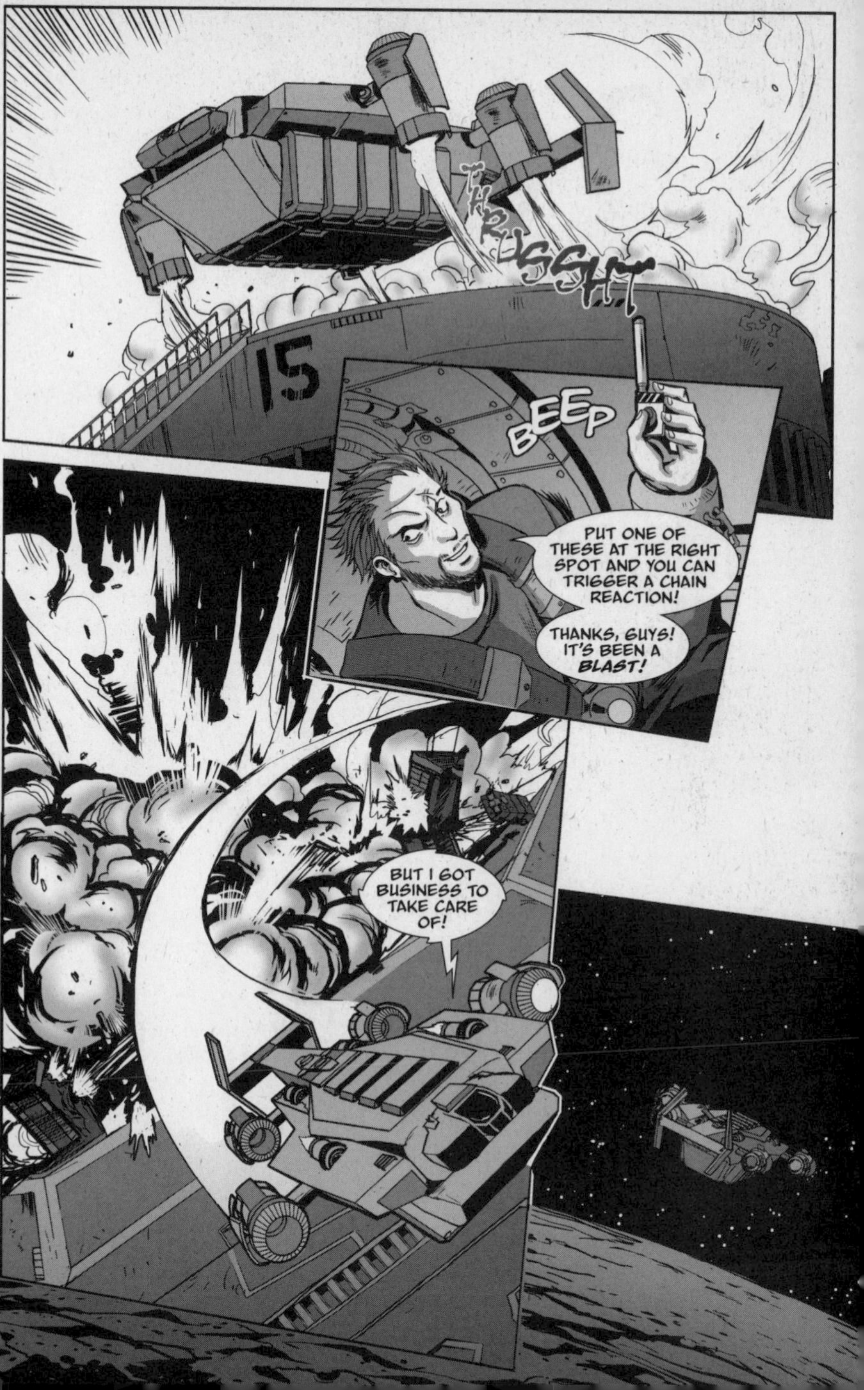
THRUSSHT
BEEP
PUT ONE OF THESE AT THE RIGHT SPOT AND YOU CAN TRIGGER A CHAIN REACTION!
THANKS, GUYS! IT'S BEEN A BLAST!
BUT I GOT BUSINESS TO TAKE CARE OF!

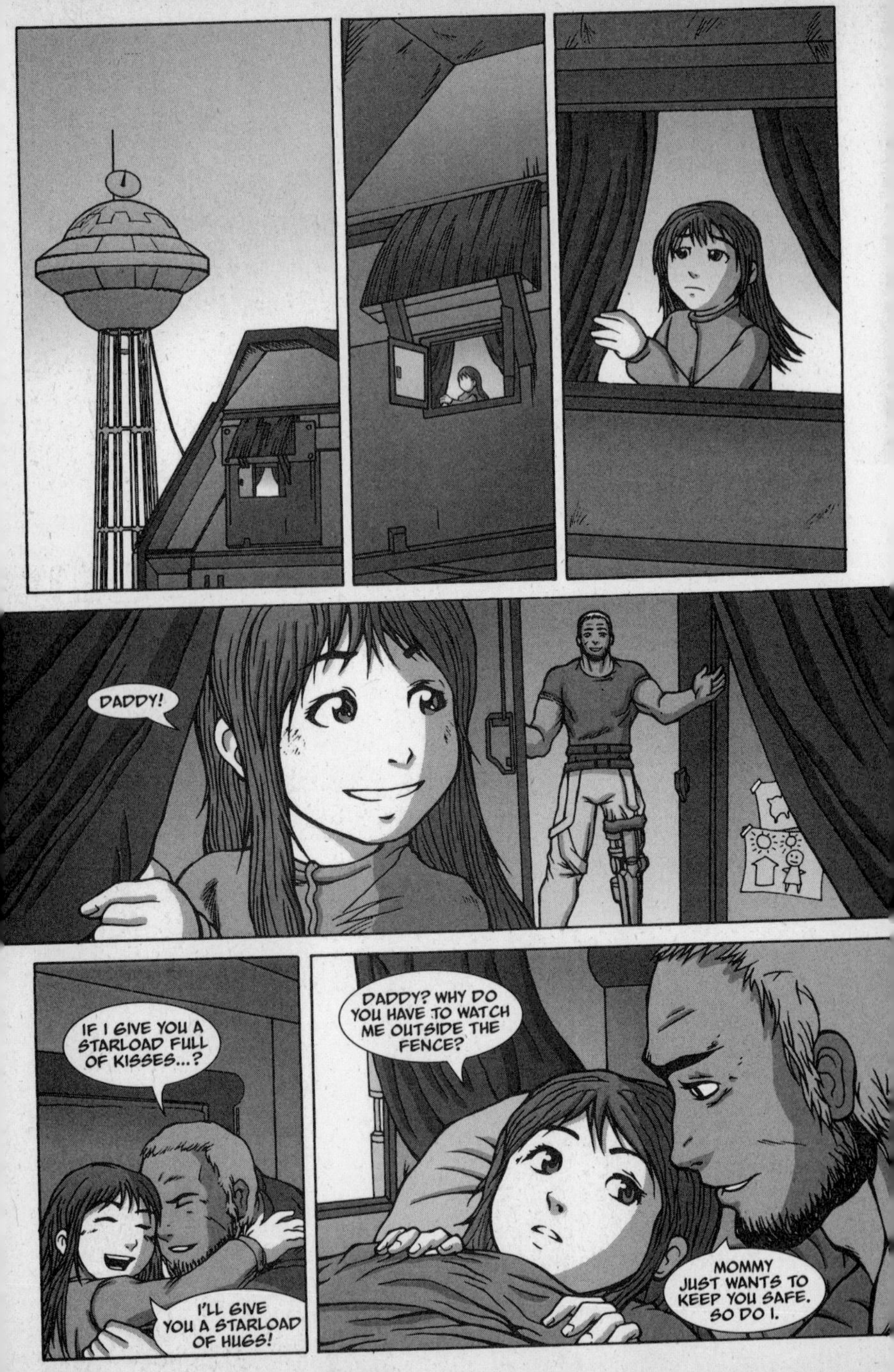
DADDY!
IF I GIVE YOU A STARLOAD FULL OF KISSES...?
I'LL GIVE YOU A STARLOAD OF HUGS!
DADDY? WHY DO YOU HAVE TO WATCH ME OUTSIDE THE FENCE?
MOMMY JUST WANTS TO KEEP YOU SAFE. SO DO I.

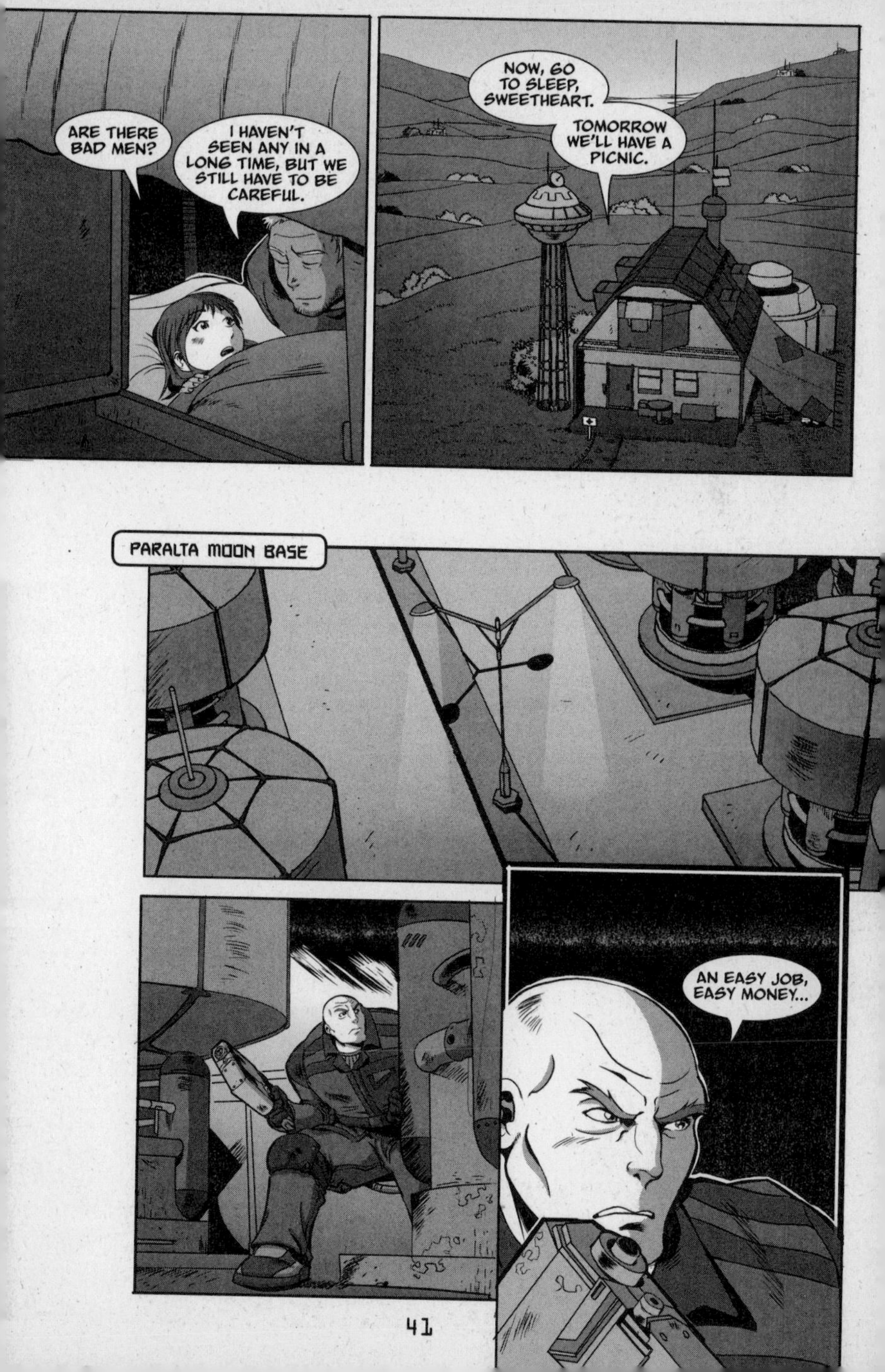
ARE THERE BAD MEN?
I HAVEN'T SEEN ANY IN A LONG TIME, BUT WE STILL HAVE TO BE CAREFUL.
NOW, GO TO SLEEP, SWEETHEART.
TOMORROW WE'LL HAVE A PICNIC.
PARALTA MOON BASE
AN EASY JOB, EASY MONEY...

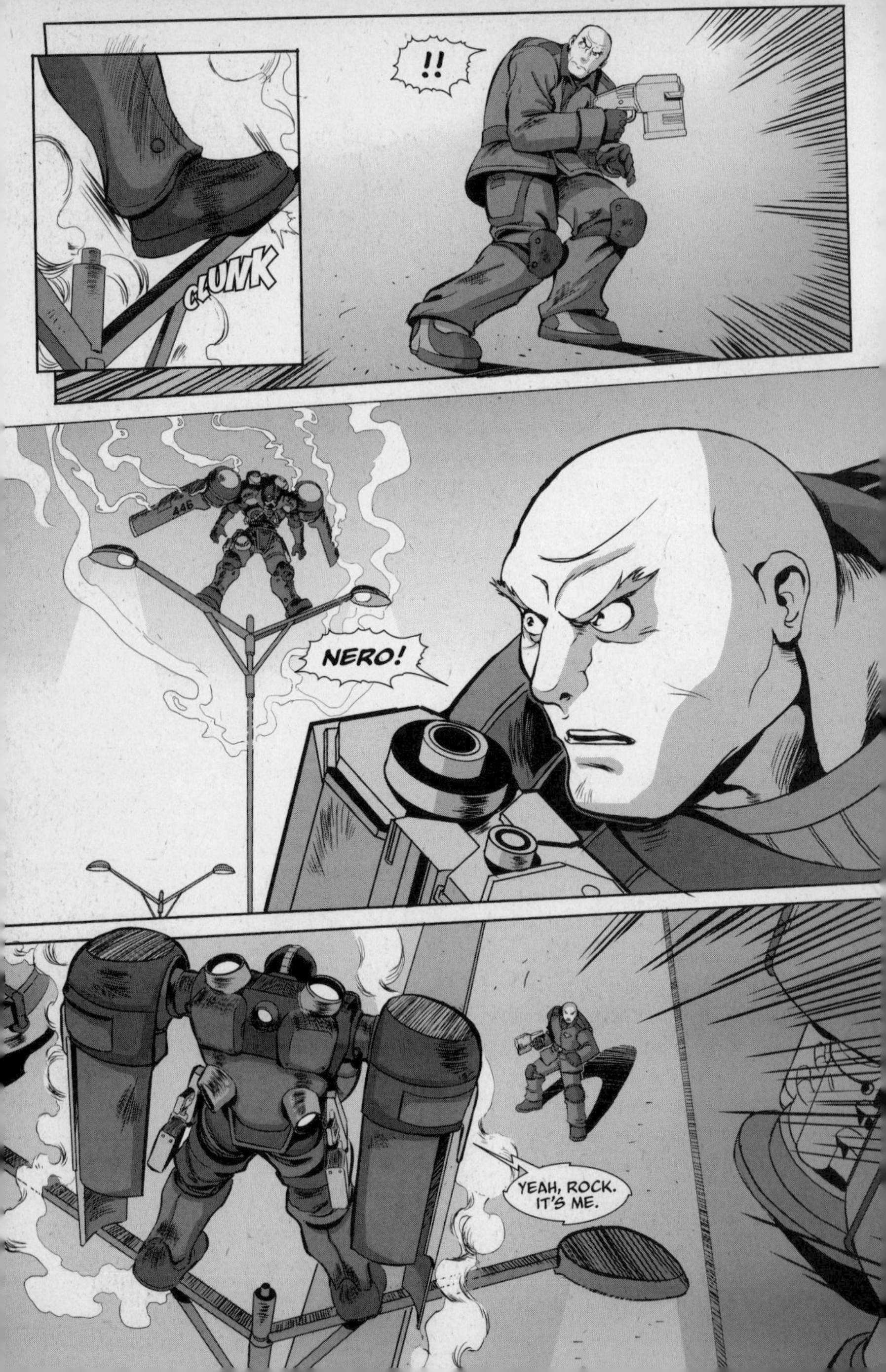
CLUNK
!!
NERO!
YEAH, ROCK.
IT'S ME.

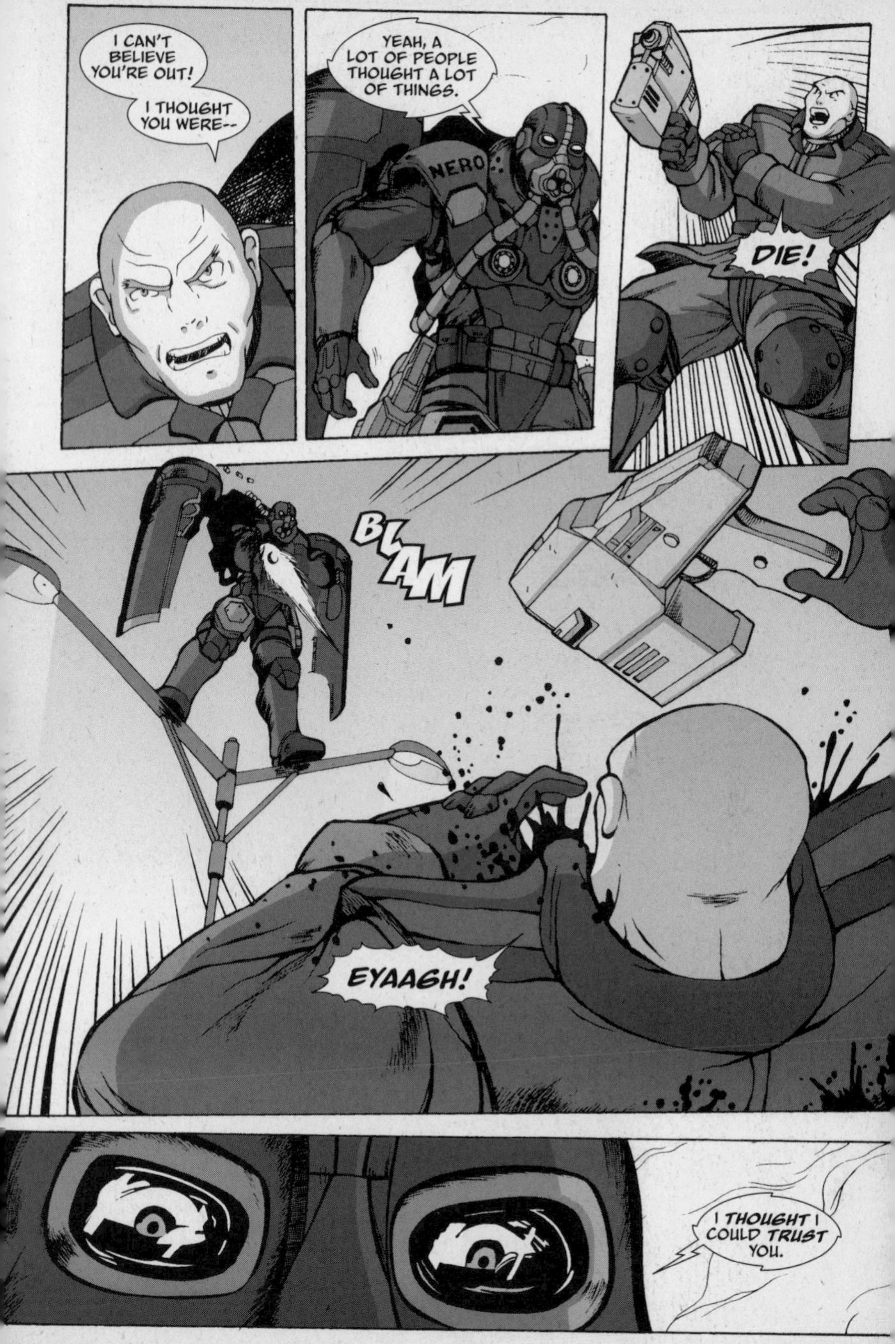
I CAN'T BELIEVE YOU'RE OUT!
I THOUGHT YOU WERE--
YEAH, A LOT OF PEOPLE THOUGHT A LOT OF THINGS.
NERO
DIE!
BLAM
EYAAGH!
I THOUGHT I COULD TRUST YOU.

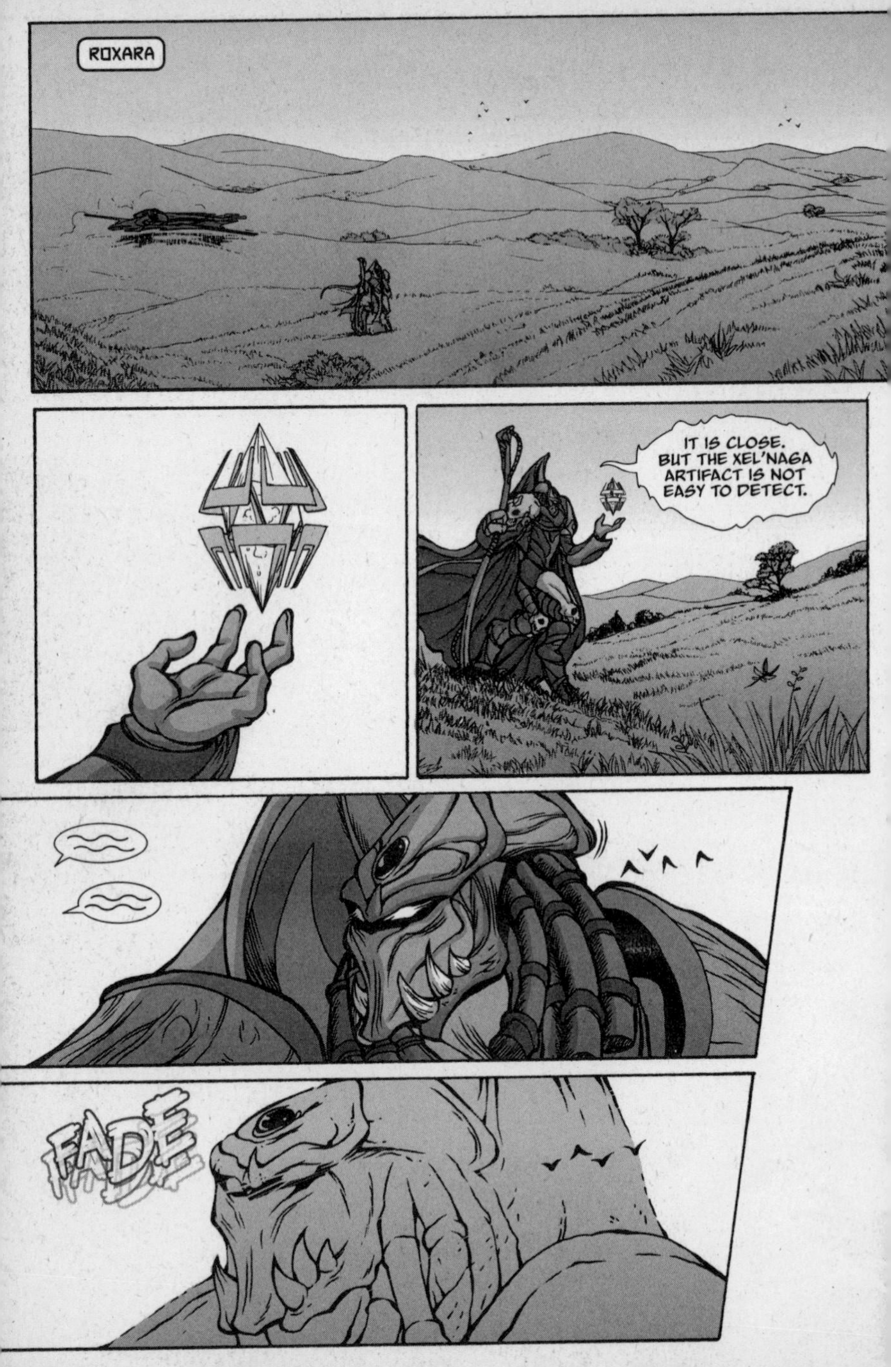
ROXARA
IT IS CLOSE. BUT THE XEL'NAGA ARTIFACT IS NOT EASY TO DETECT.
FADE

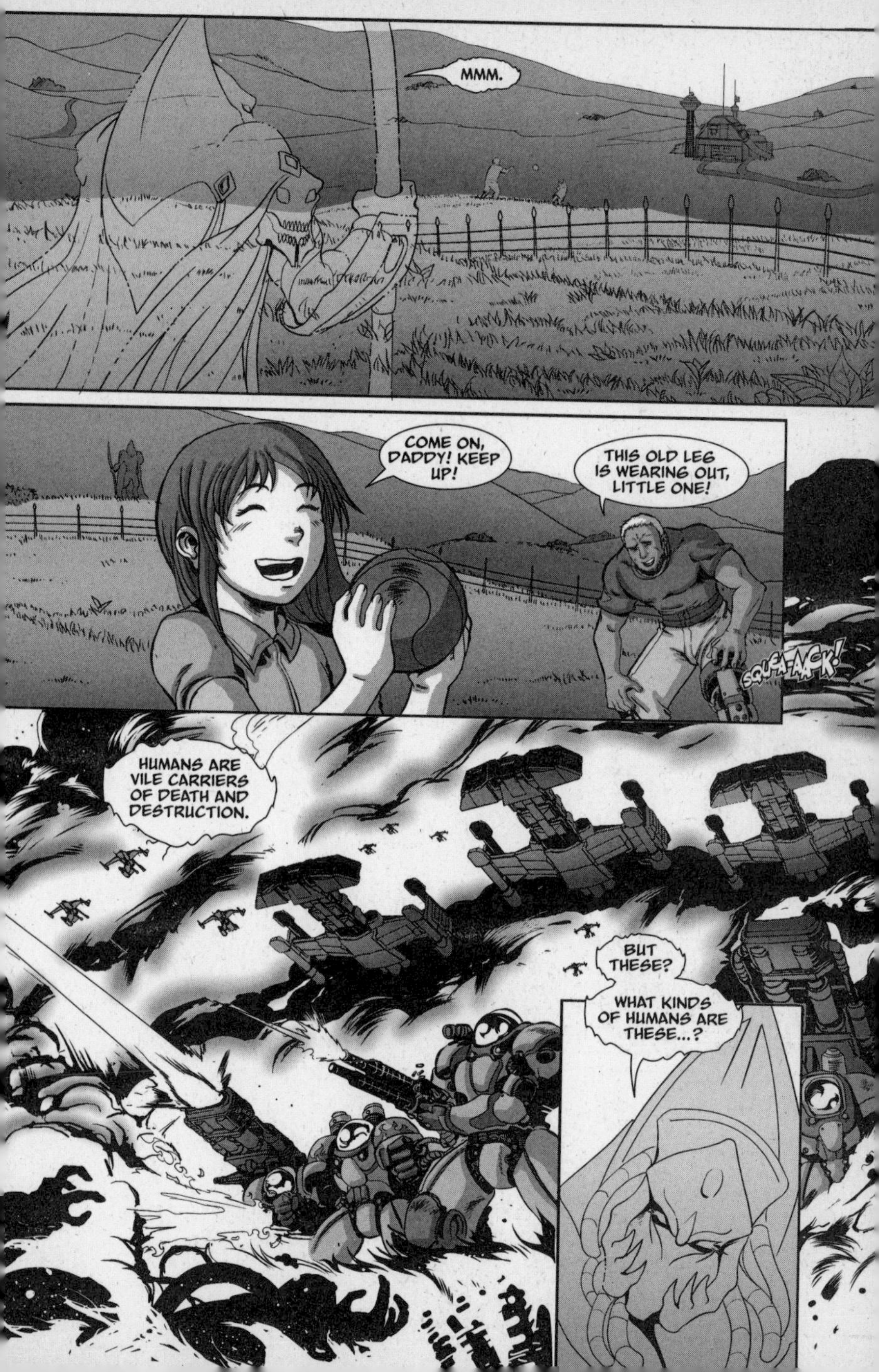
MMM.
COME ON, DADDY! KEEP UP!
THIS OLD LEG IS WEARING OUT, LITTLE ONE!
SQUEAAACK!
HUMANS ARE VILE CARRIERS OF DEATH AND DESTRUCTION.
BUT THESE?
WHAT KINDS OF HUMANS ARE THESE...?

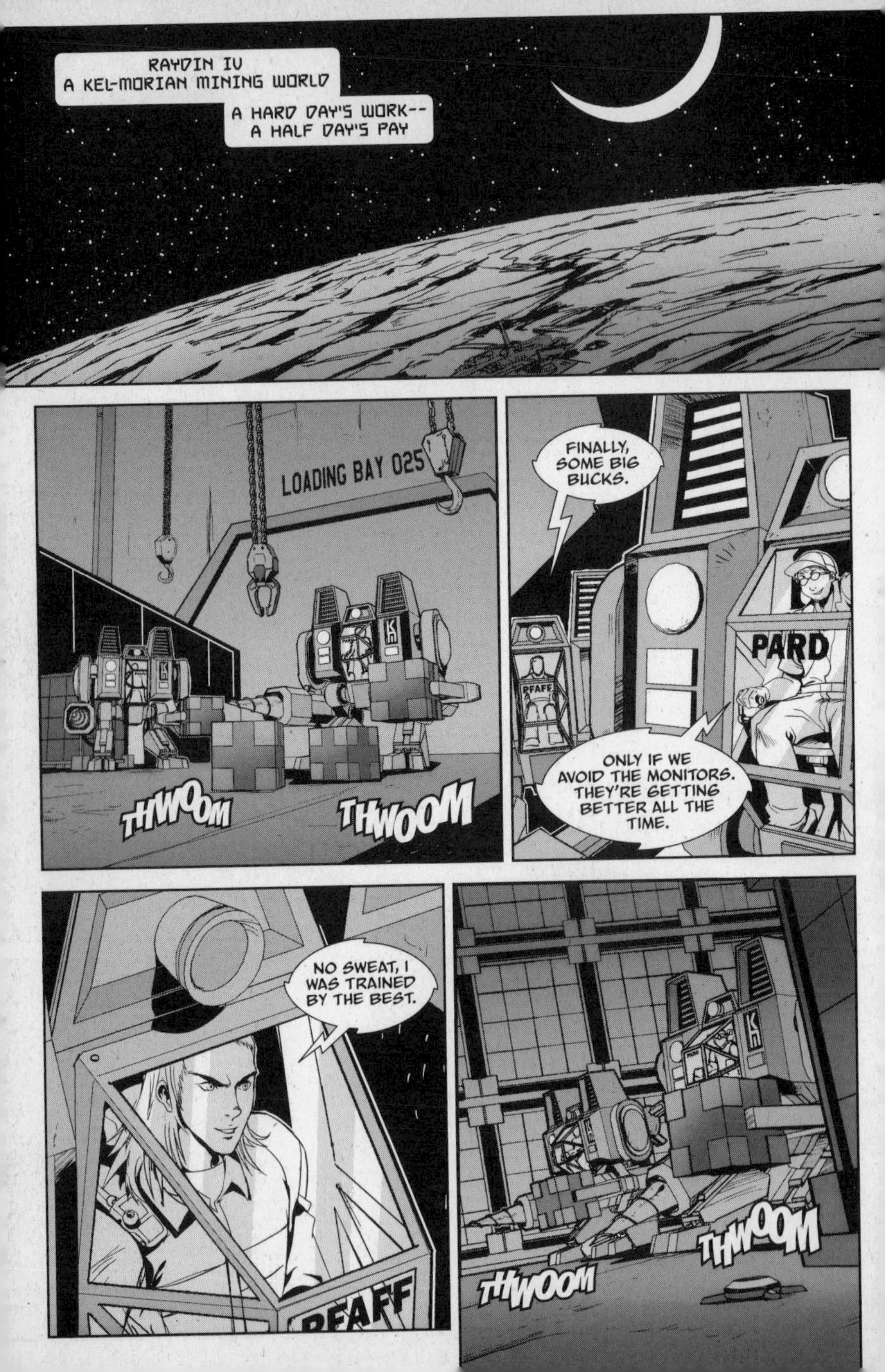
RAYDIN IV
A KEL-MORIAN MINING WORLD
A HARD DAY'S WORK--
A HALF DAY'S PAY
LOADING BAY 025
THWOOM
THWOOM
FINALLY, SOME BIG BUCKS.
PARD
PFAFF
ONLY IF WE AVOID THE MONITORS. THEY'RE GETTING BETTER ALL THE TIME.
NO SWEAT, I WAS TRAINED BY THE BEST.
PFAFF
PARD
THWOOM
THWOOM

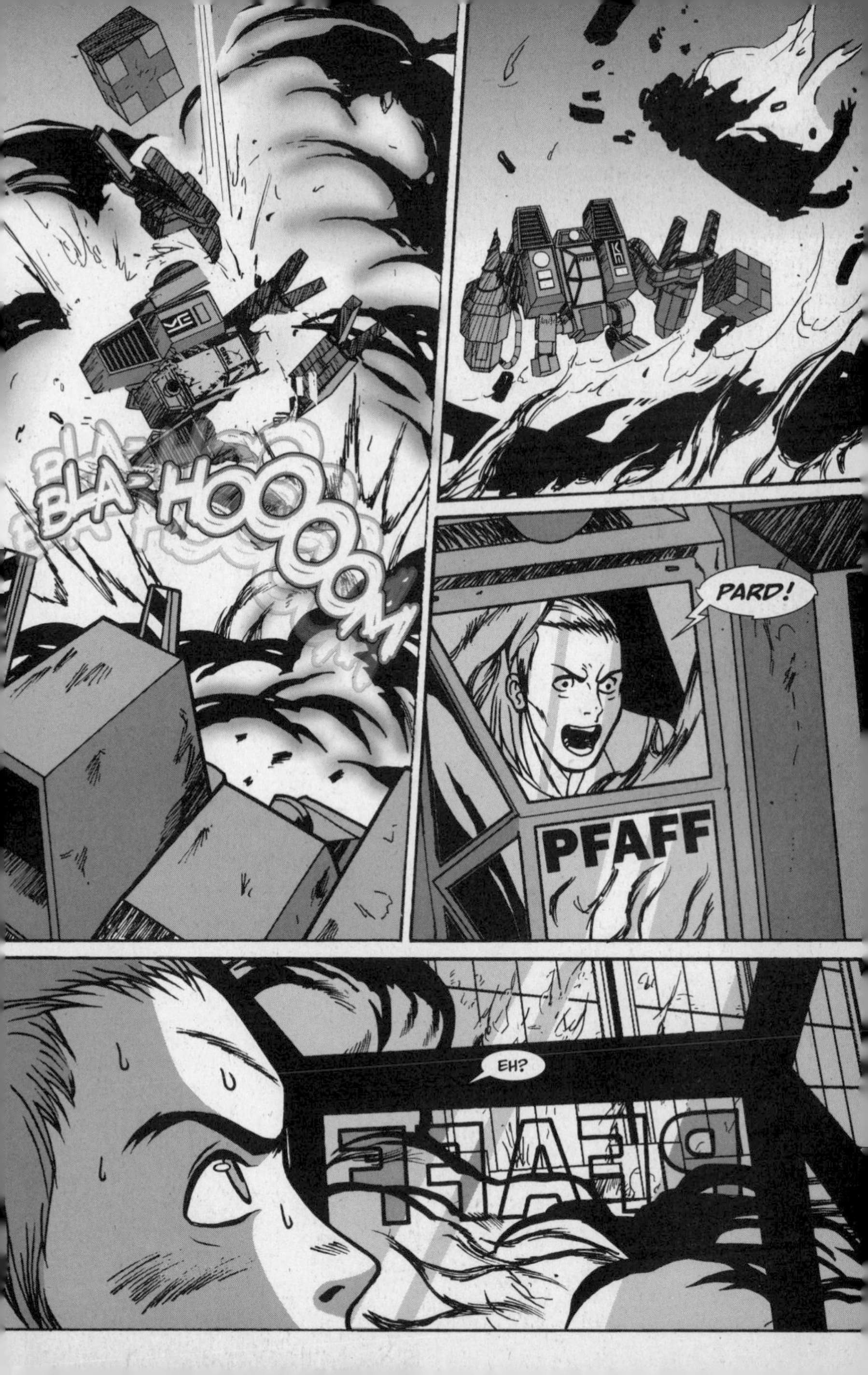
BLA-HOOOOOM
PFAFF
PARD!
EH?

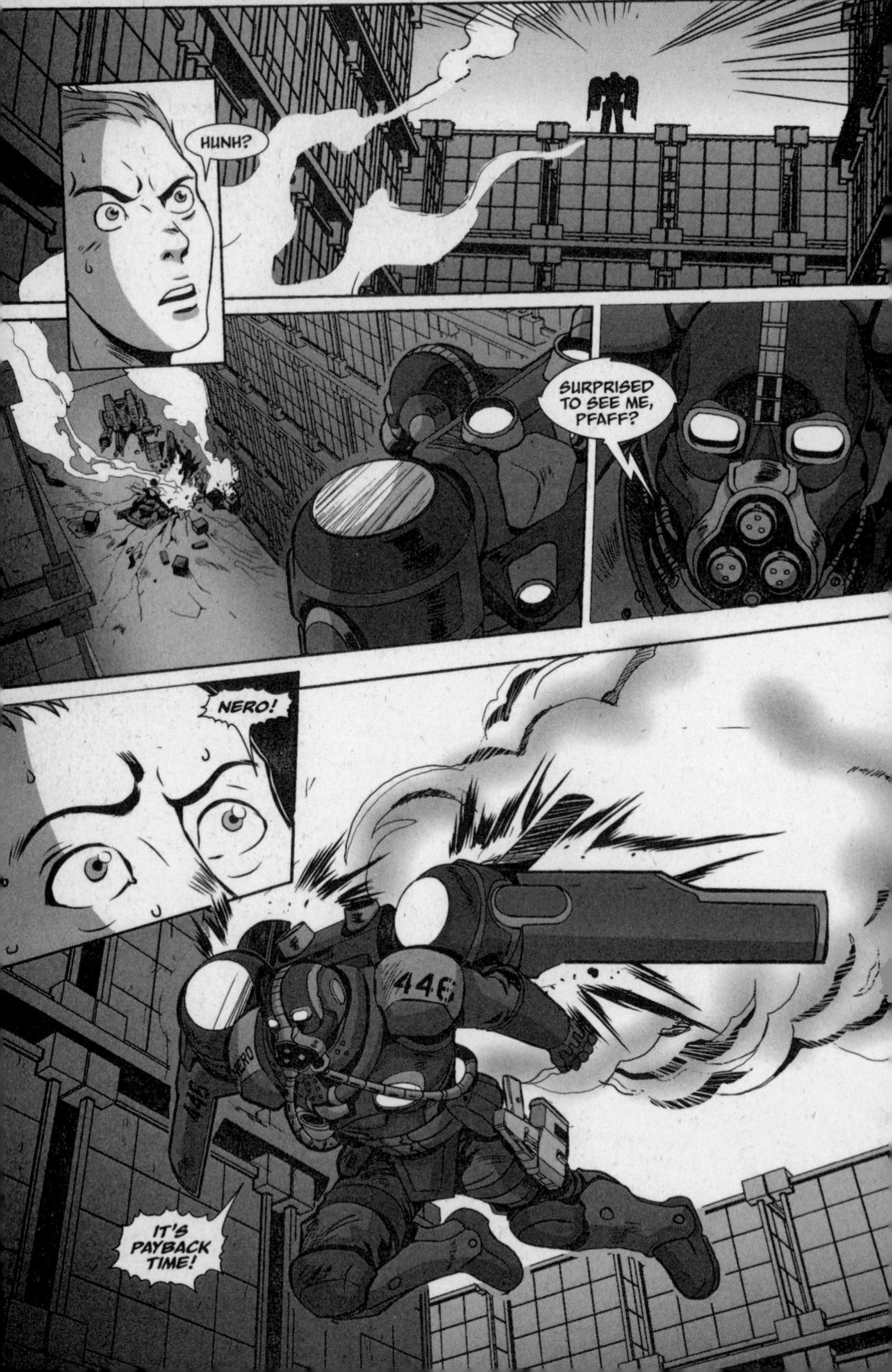
HUNH?
SURPRISED TO SEE ME, PFAFF?
NERO!
IT'S PAYBACK TIME!

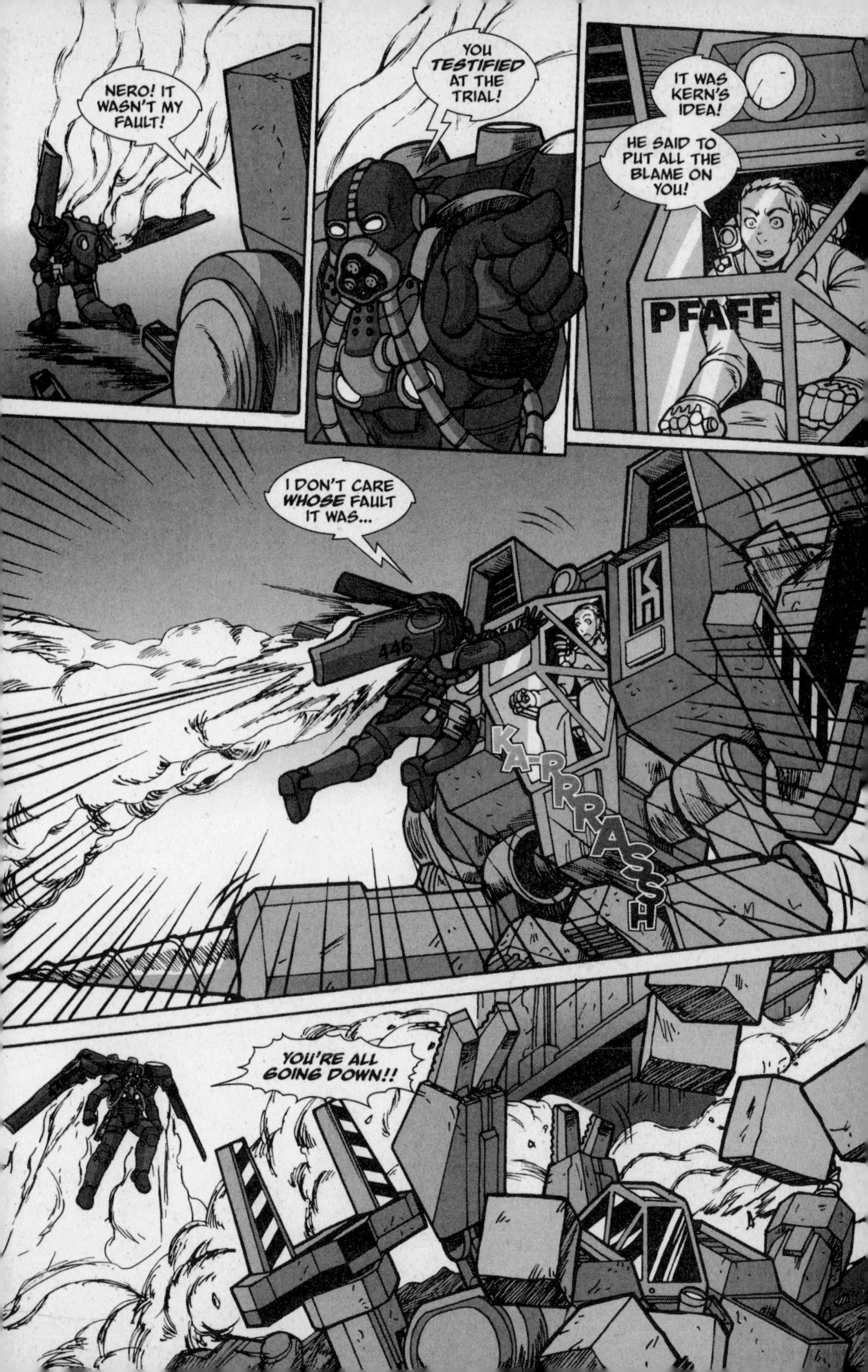
NERO! IT WASN'T MY FAULT!
YOU TESTIFIED AT THE TRIAL!
IT WAS KERN'S IDEA!
HE SAID TO PUT ALL THE BLAME ON YOU!
PFAFF
I DON'T CARE WHOSE FAULT IT WAS...
446
KA-RRRASSSH
YOU'RE ALL GOING DOWN!!

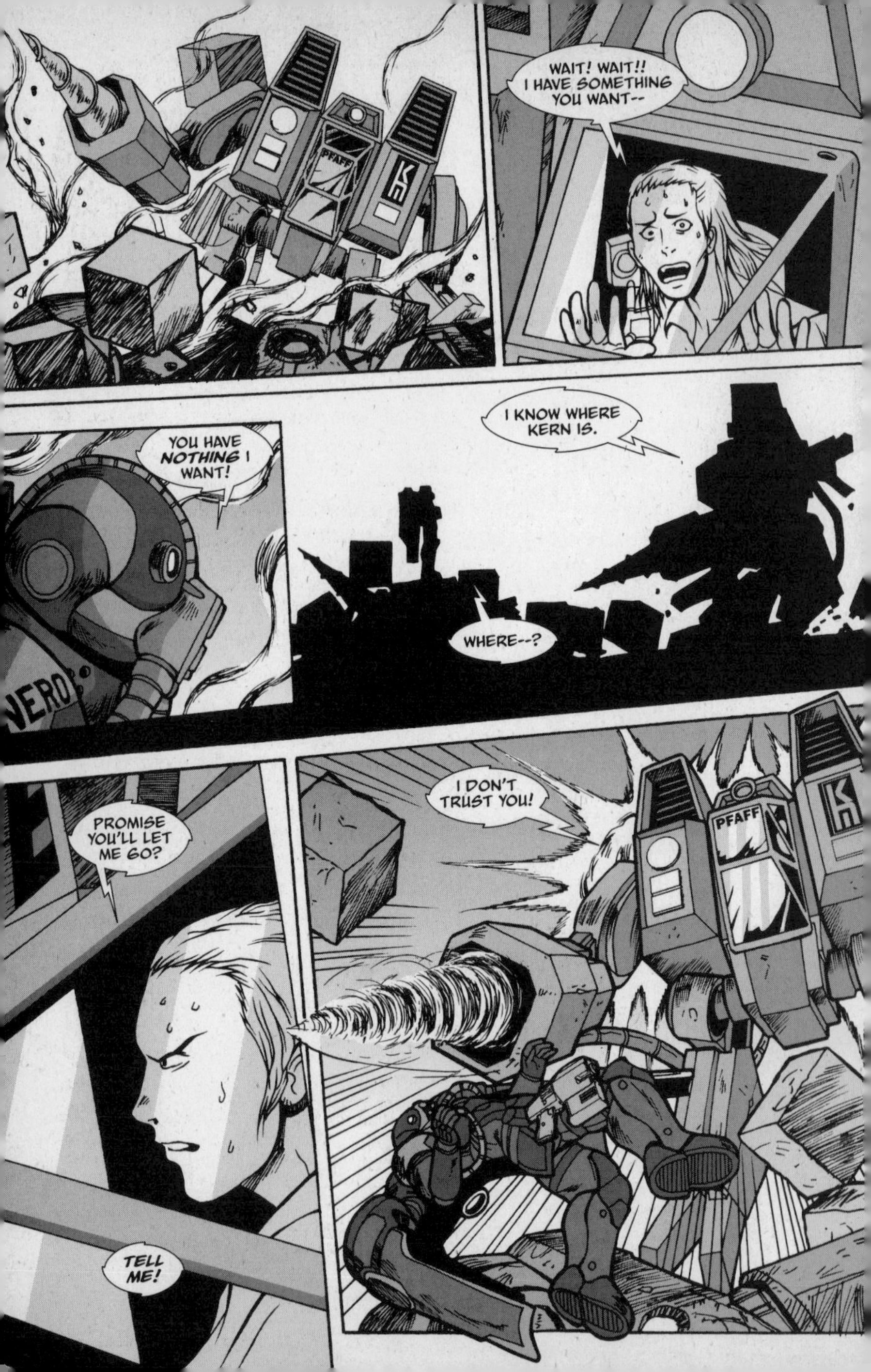
PFAFF
WAIT! WAIT!! I HAVE SOMETHING YOU WANT--
YOU HAVE ***NOTHING*** I WANT!
VERO
I KNOW WHERE KERN IS.
WHERE--?
PROMISE YOU'LL LET ME GO?
TELL ME!
I DON'T TRUST YOU!
PFAFF

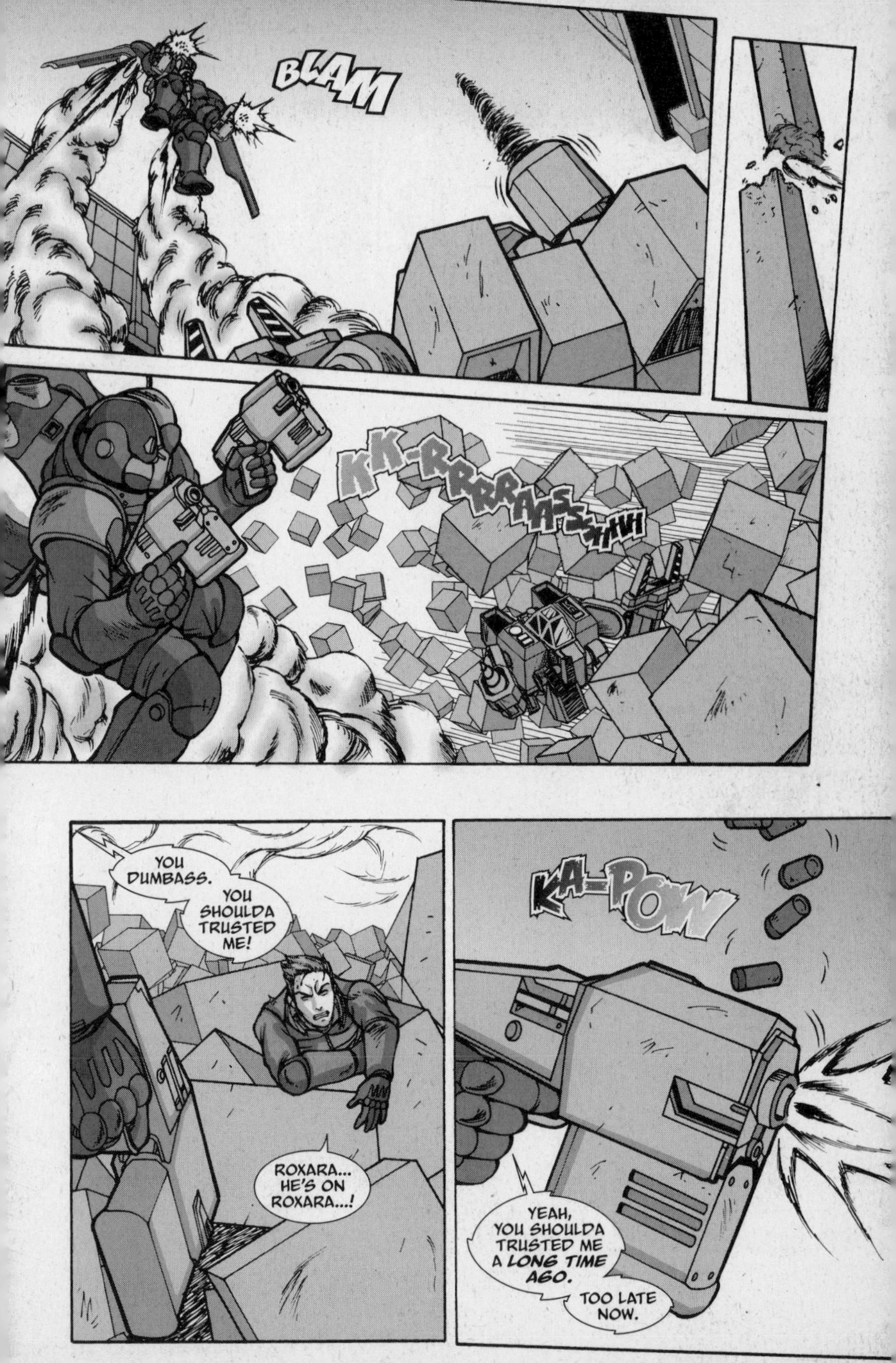
BLAM
KK-RRRRAASSSHH!!
YOU DUMBASS.
YOU SHOULDA TRUSTED ME!
ROXARA... HE'S ON ROXARA...!
KA-POW
YEAH, YOU SHOULDA TRUSTED ME A ***LONG TIME AGO.***
TOO LATE NOW.

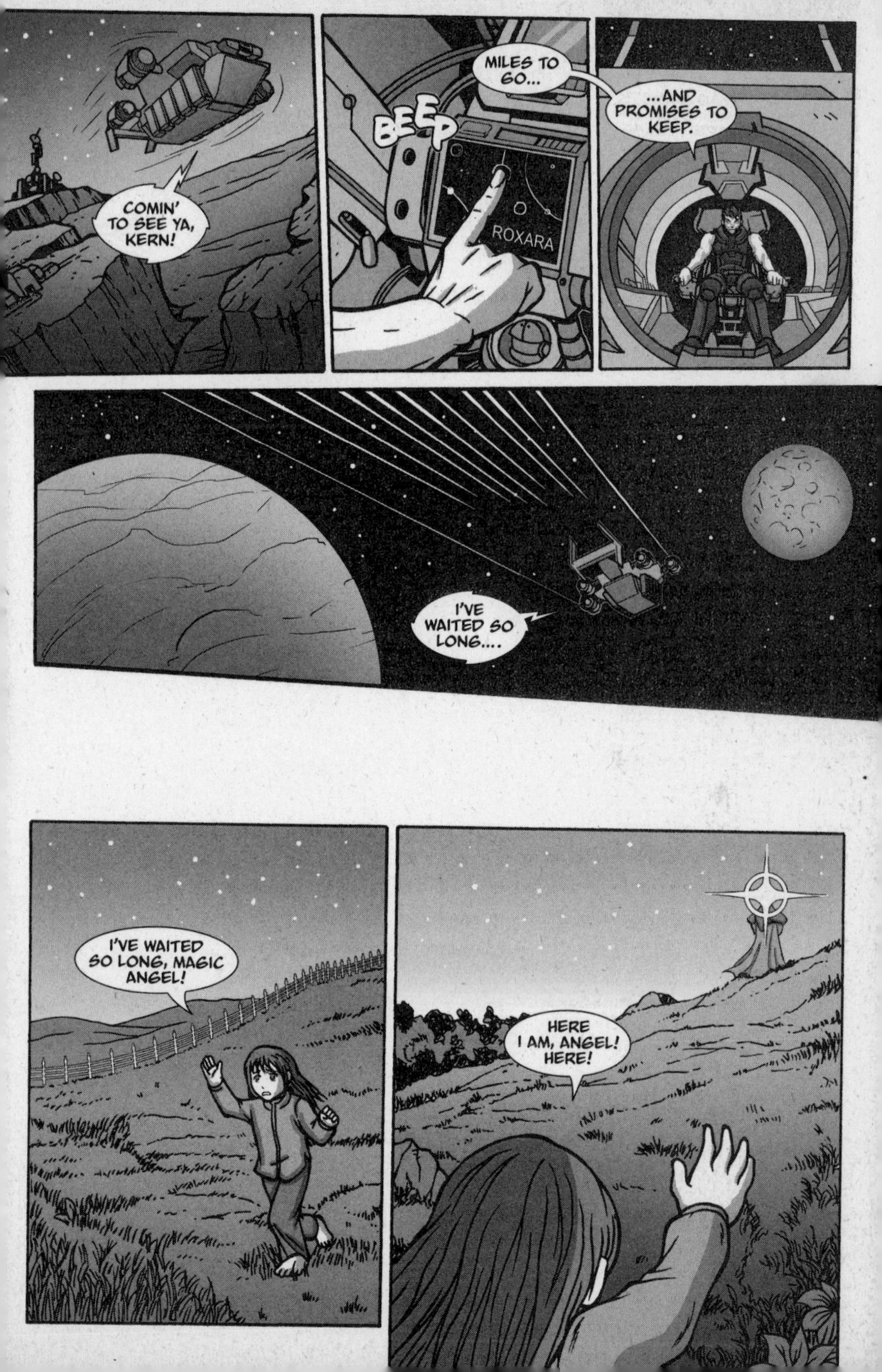
COMIN' TO SEE YA, KERN!
BEEP
ROXARA
MILES TO GO...
...AND PROMISES TO KEEP.
I'VE WAITED SO LONG....
I'VE WAITED SO LONG, MAGIC ANGEL!
HERE I AM, ANGEL! HERE!

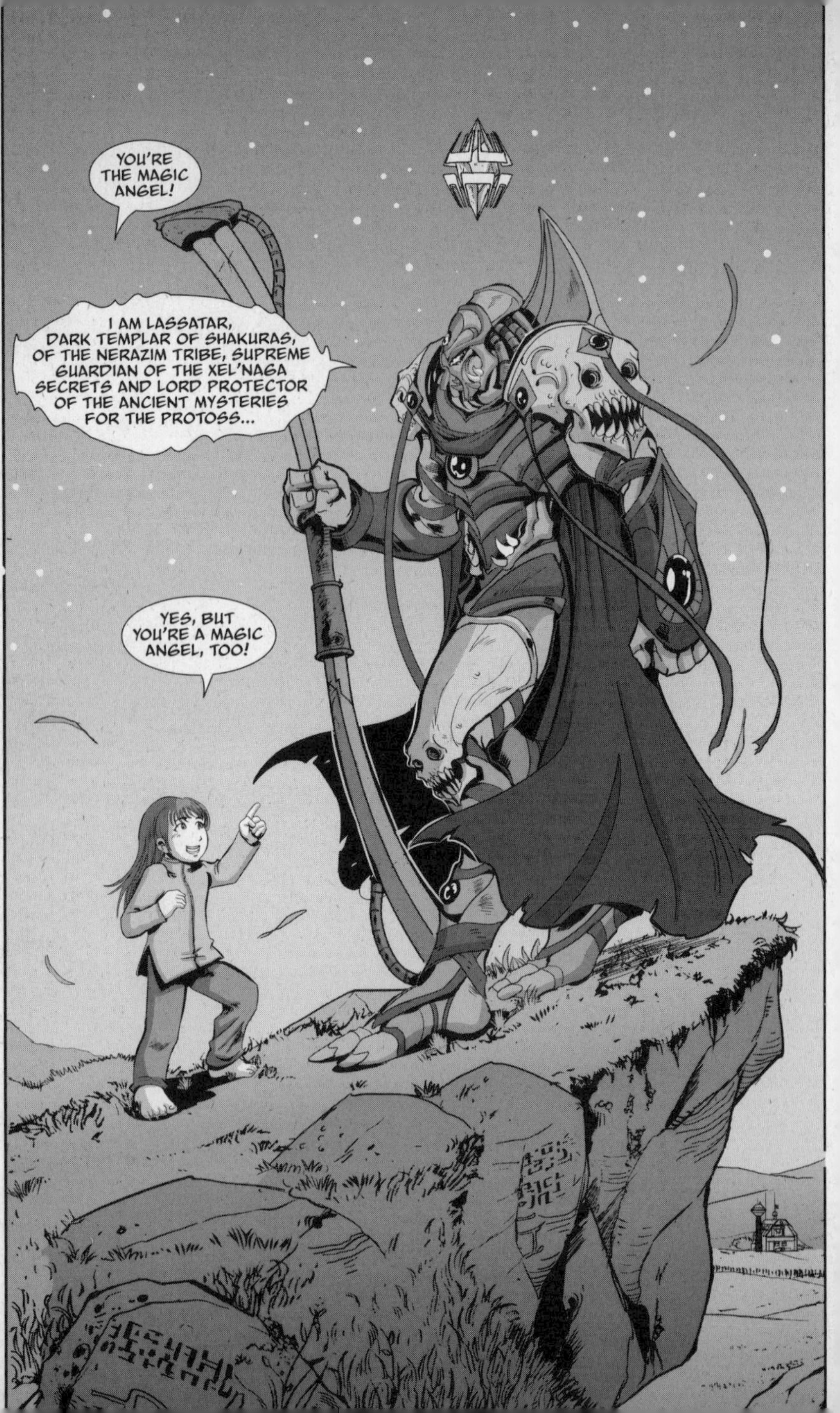
YOU'RE THE MAGIC ANGEL!
I AM LASSATAR, DARK TEMPLAR OF SHAKURAS, OF THE NERAZIM TRIBE, SUPREME GUARDIAN OF THE XEL'NAGA SECRETS AND LORD PROTECTOR OF THE ANCIENT MYSTERIES FOR THE PROTOSS...
YES, BUT YOU'RE A MAGIC ANGEL, TOO!

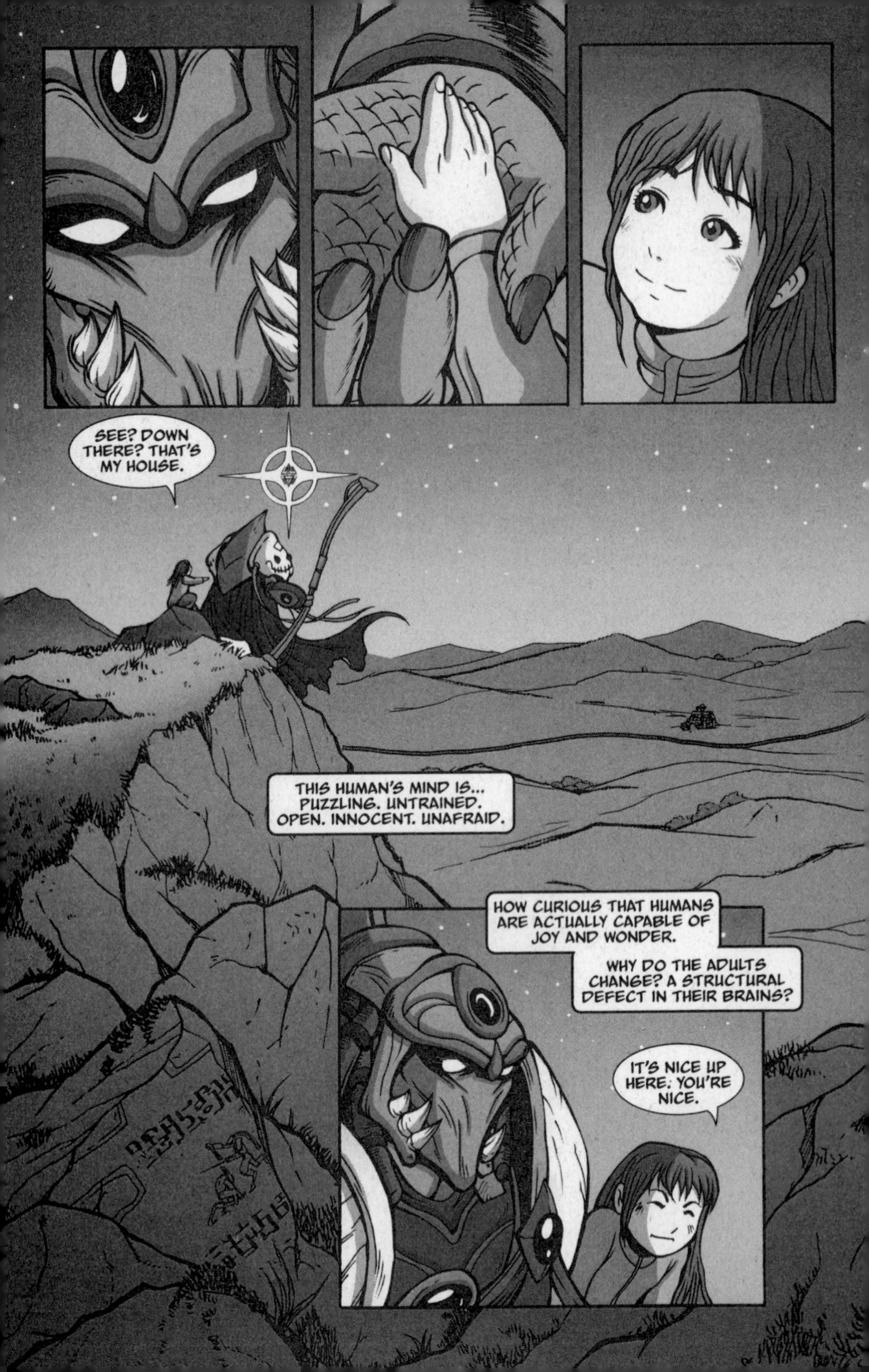
SEE? DOWN THERE? THAT'S MY HOUSE.
THIS HUMAN'S MIND IS... PUZZLING. UNTRAINED. OPEN. INNOCENT. UNAFRAID.
HOW CURIOUS THAT HUMANS ARE ACTUALLY CAPABLE OF JOY AND WONDER.
WHY DO THE ADULTS CHANGE? A STRUCTURAL DEFECT IN THEIR BRAINS?
IT'S NICE UP HERE. YOU'RE NICE.

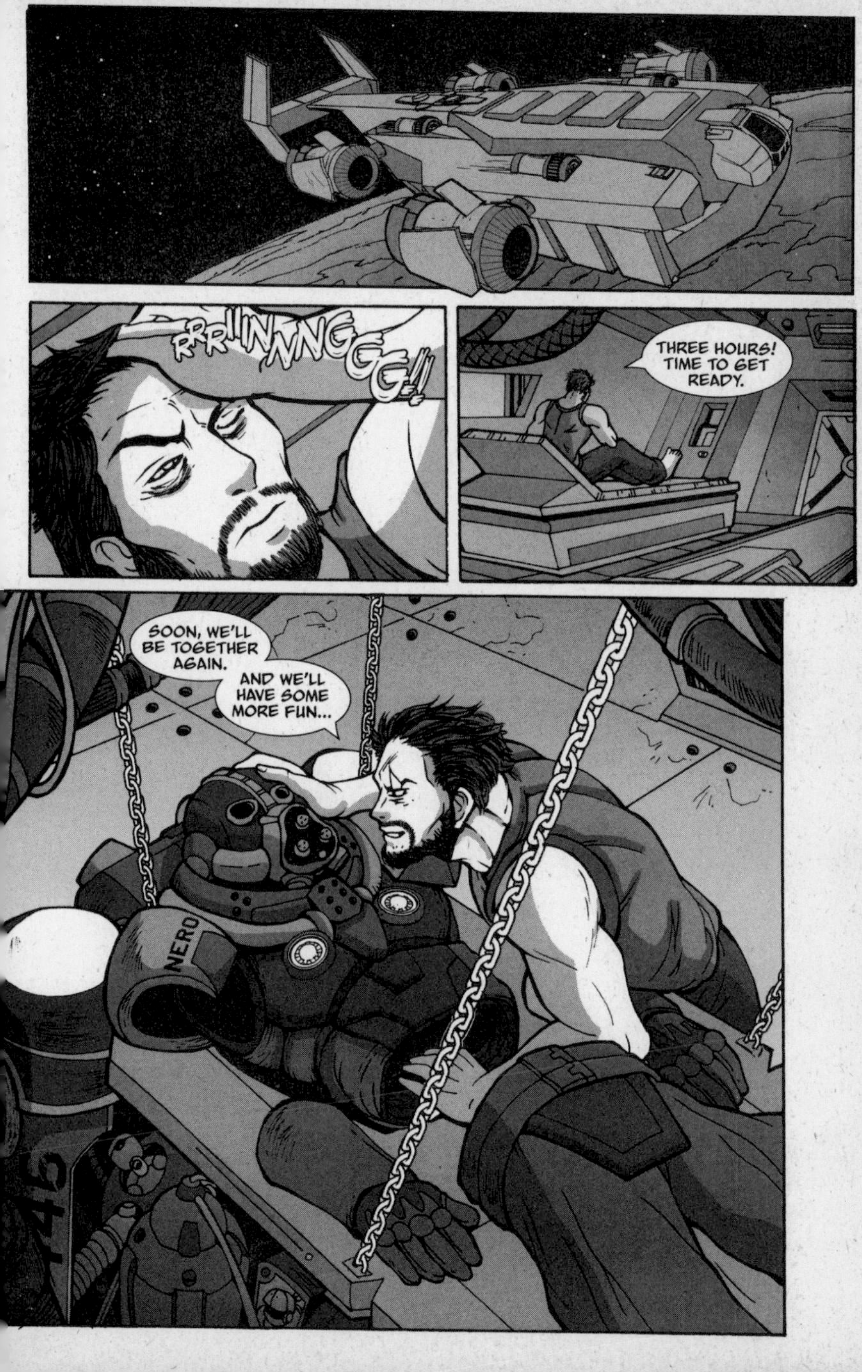
RRIINNNGGG!!
THREE HOURS! TIME TO GET READY.
SOON, WE'LL BE TOGETHER AGAIN.
AND WE'LL HAVE SOME MORE FUN...
NERO

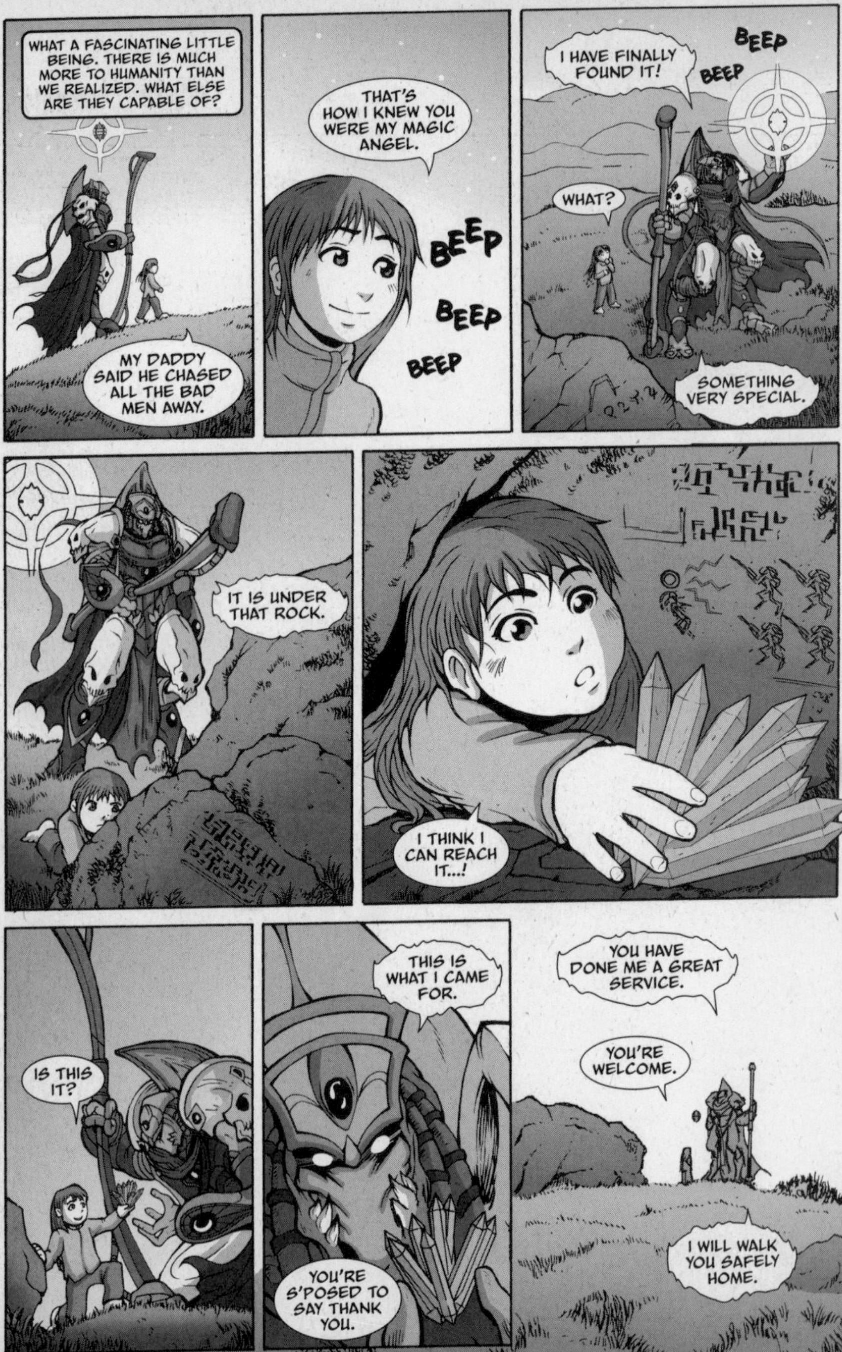
WHAT A FASCINATING LITTLE BEING. THERE IS MUCH MORE TO HUMANITY THAN WE REALIZED. WHAT ELSE ARE THEY CAPABLE OF?
MY DADDY SAID HE CHASED ALL THE BAD MEN AWAY.
THAT'S HOW I KNEW YOU WERE MY MAGIC ANGEL.
BEEP
BEEP
BEEP
I HAVE FINALLY FOUND IT!
BEEP
BEEP
WHAT?
SOMETHING VERY SPECIAL.
IT IS UNDER THAT ROCK.
I THINK I CAN REACH IT...!
IS THIS IT?
THIS IS WHAT I CAME FOR.
YOU'RE S'POSED TO SAY THANK YOU.
YOU HAVE DONE ME A GREAT SERVICE.
YOU'RE WELCOME.
I WILL WALK YOU SAFELY HOME.

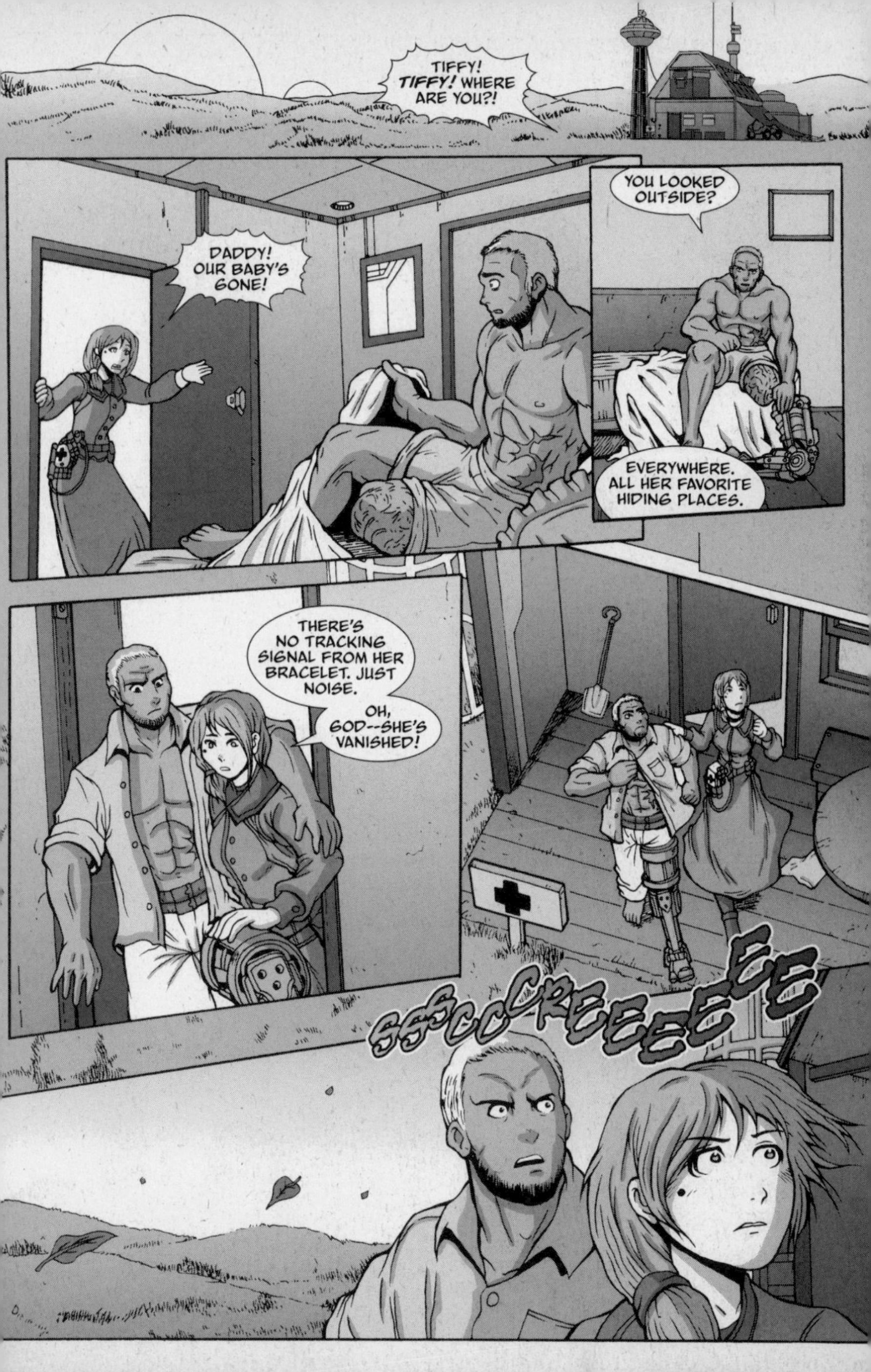
TIFFY! TIFFY! WHERE ARE YOU?!
DADDY! OUR BABY'S GONE!
YOU LOOKED OUTSIDE?
EVERYWHERE. ALL HER FAVORITE HIDING PLACES.
THERE'S NO TRACKING SIGNAL FROM HER BRACELET. JUST NOISE.
OH, GOD--SHE'S VANISHED!
SSSCCCREEEEEEEEE

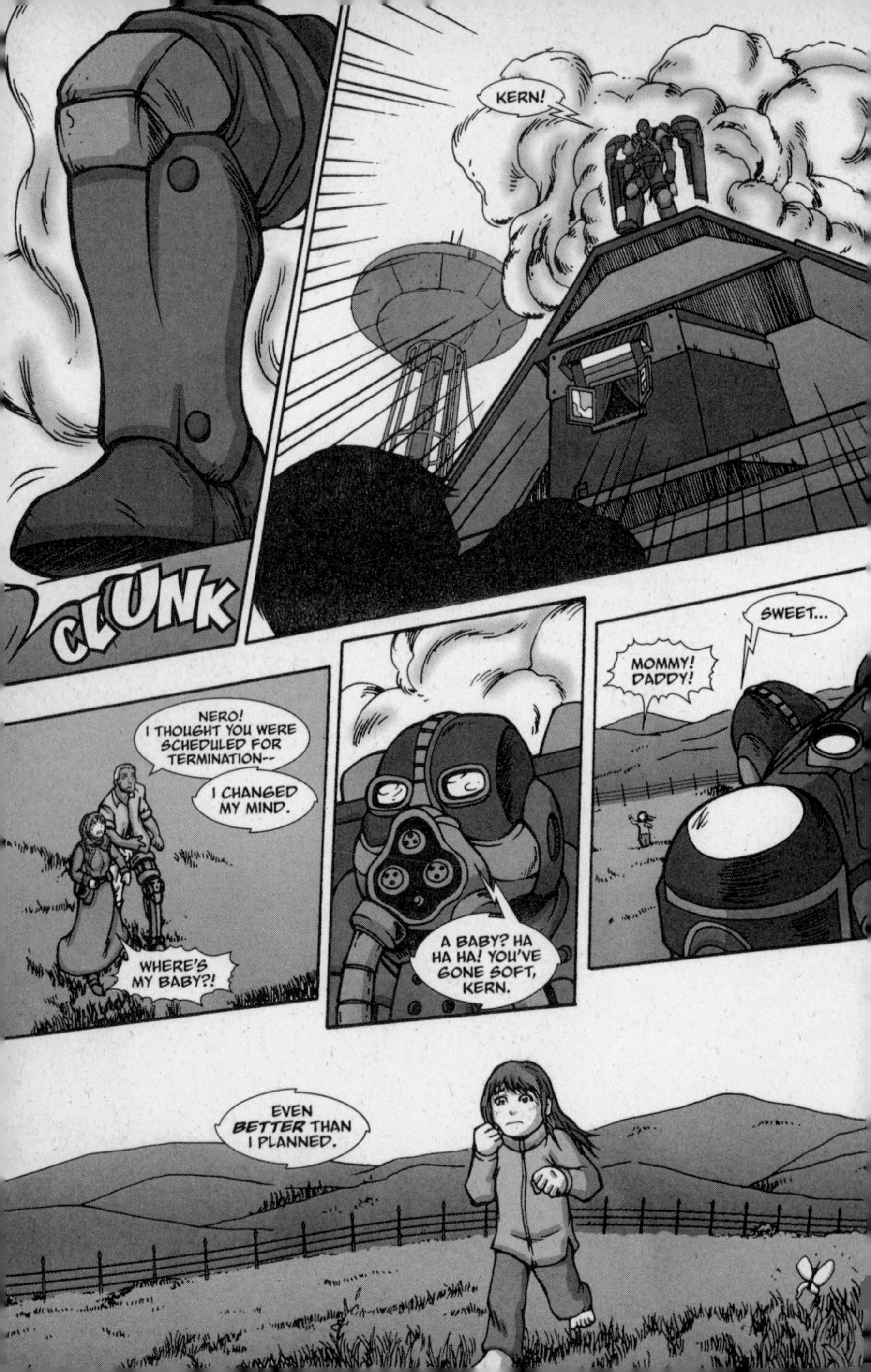
CLUNK
KERN!
NERO! I THOUGHT YOU WERE SCHEDULED FOR TERMINATION--
I CHANGED MY MIND.
WHERE'S MY BABY?!
A BABY? HA HA HA! YOU'VE GONE SOFT, KERN.
MOMMY! DADDY!
SWEET...
EVEN BETTER THAN I PLANNED.

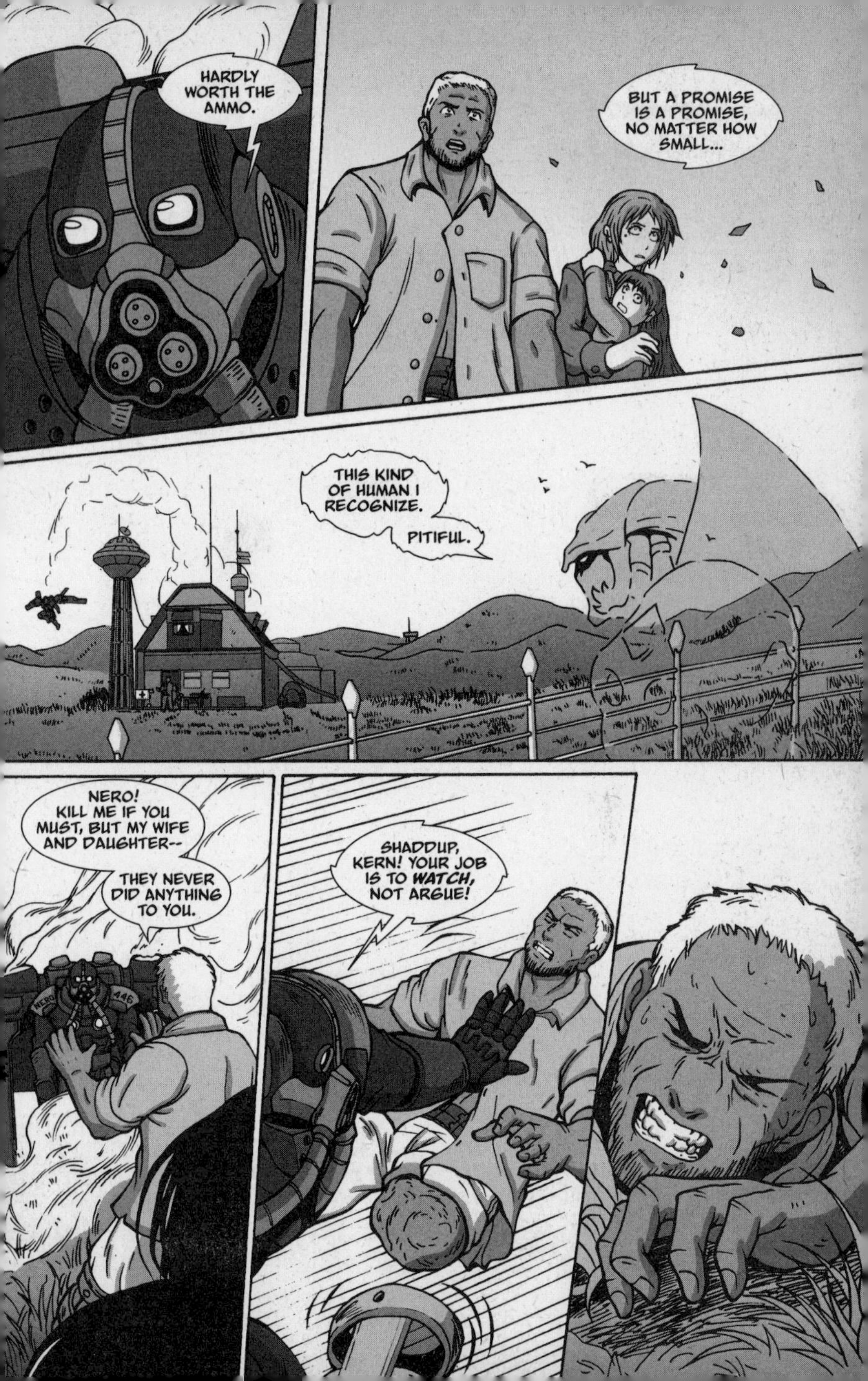
HARDLY WORTH THE AMMO.
BUT A PROMISE IS A PROMISE, NO MATTER HOW SMALL...
THIS KIND OF HUMAN I RECOGNIZE.
PITIFUL.
NERO! KILL ME IF YOU MUST, BUT MY WIFE AND DAUGHTER--
THEY NEVER DID ANYTHING TO YOU.
NERO
446
SHADDUP, KERN! YOUR JOB IS TO *WATCH*, NOT ARGUE!

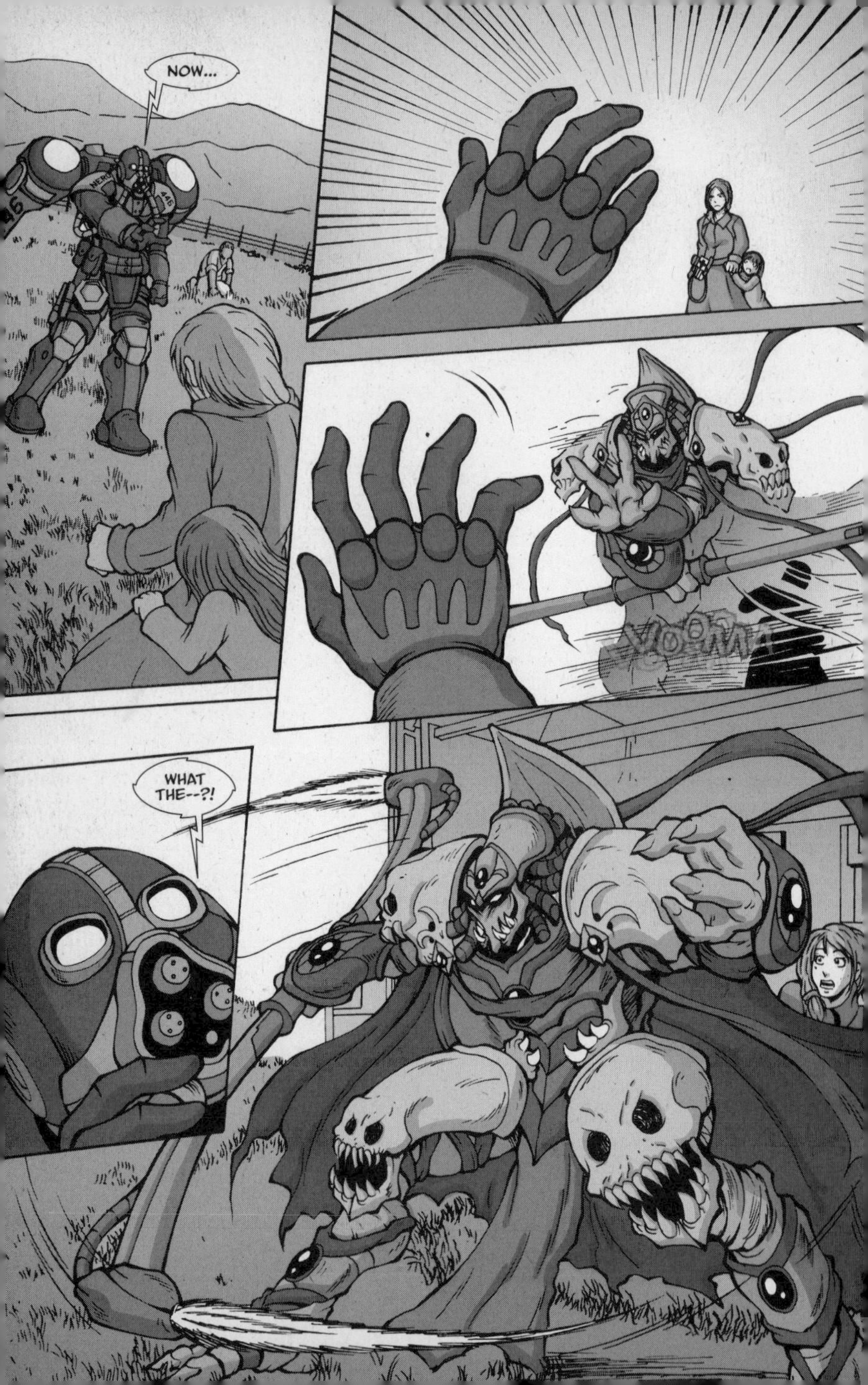
NOW...
WHAT THE--?!

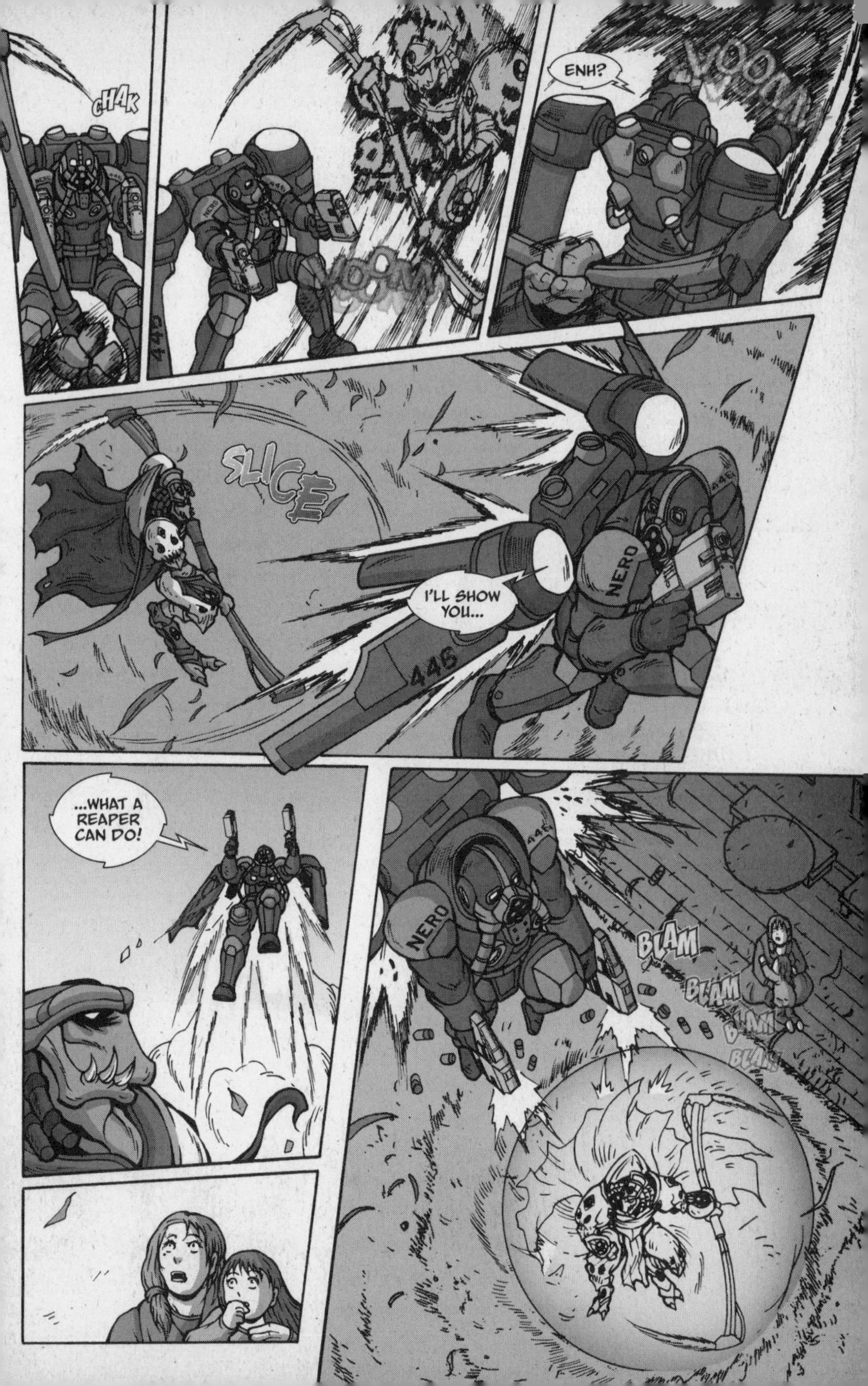
CHAK
ENH?
SLICE
I'LL SHOW YOU...
...WHAT A REAPER CAN DO!
BLAM
BLAM
BLAM
BLAM

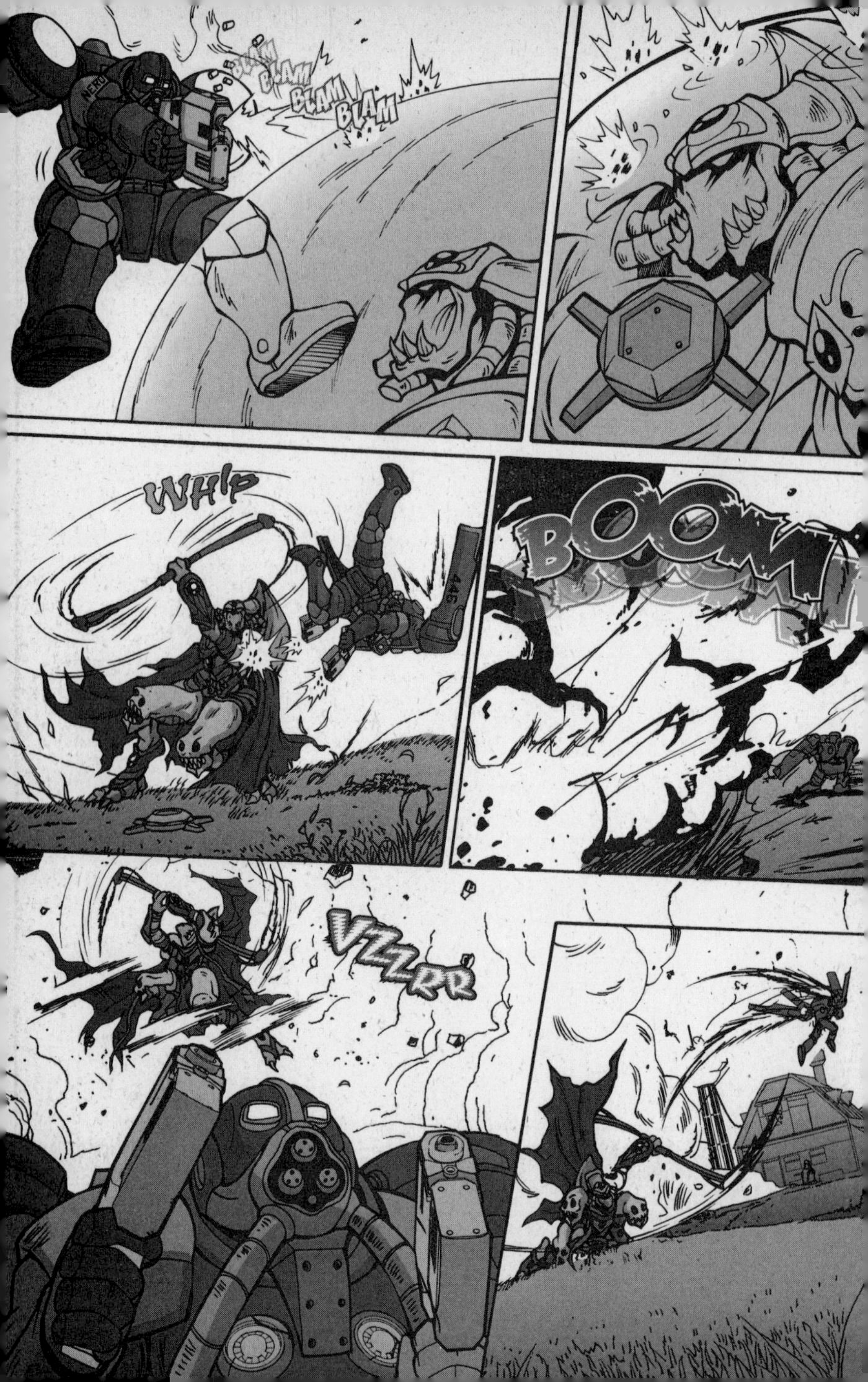
NERO
BLAM
BLAM
BLAM
BLAM
WHIP
446
BOOM
VZZRR

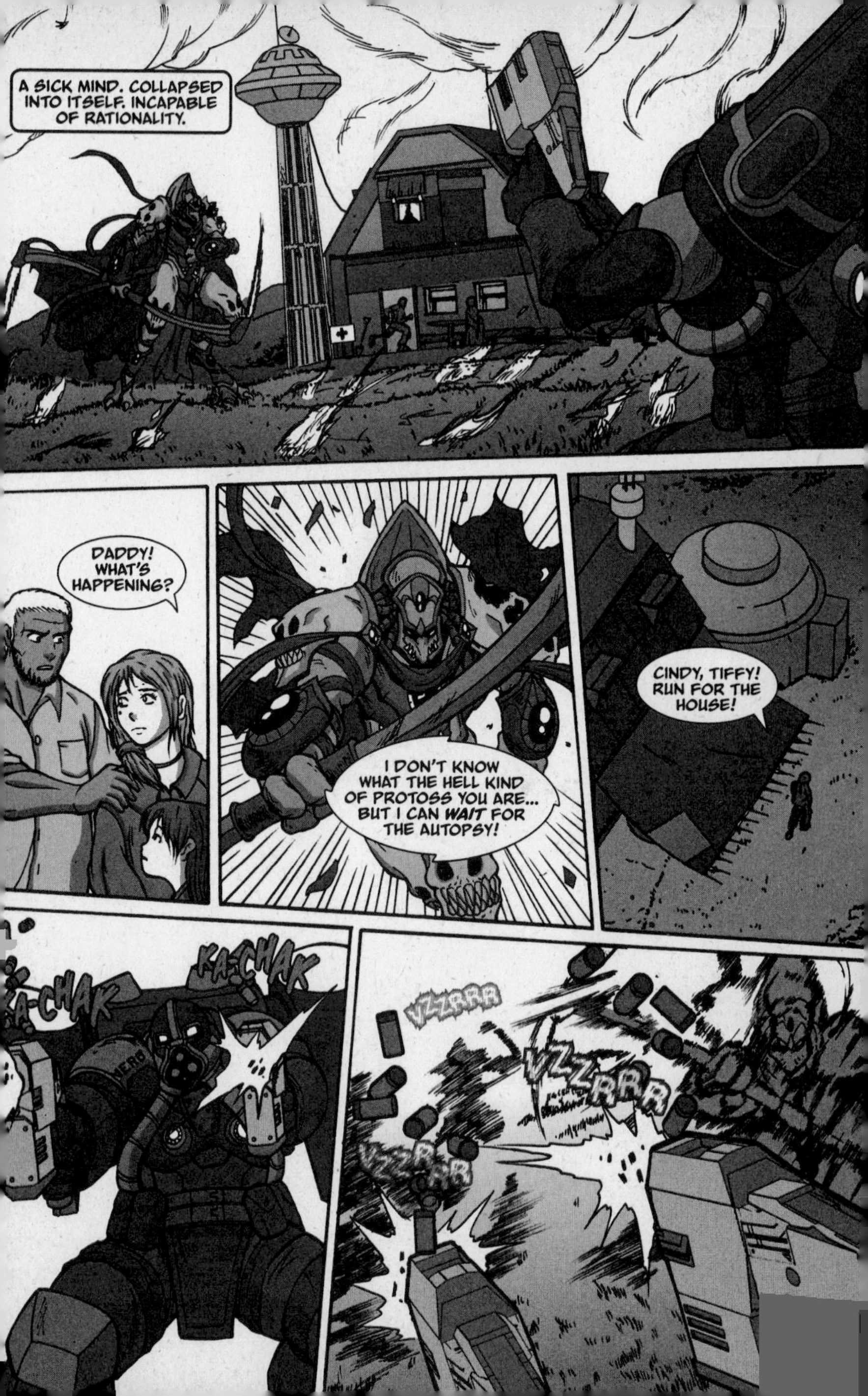
A SICK MIND. COLLAPSED INTO ITSELF. INCAPABLE OF RATIONALITY.
DADDY! WHAT'S HAPPENING?
I DON'T KNOW WHAT THE HELL KIND OF PROTOSS YOU ARE... BUT I CAN *WAIT* FOR THE AUTOPSY!
CINDY, TIFFY! RUN FOR THE HOUSE!
KA-CHAK
KA-CHAK
VZZRRR
VZZRRR
VZZRRR

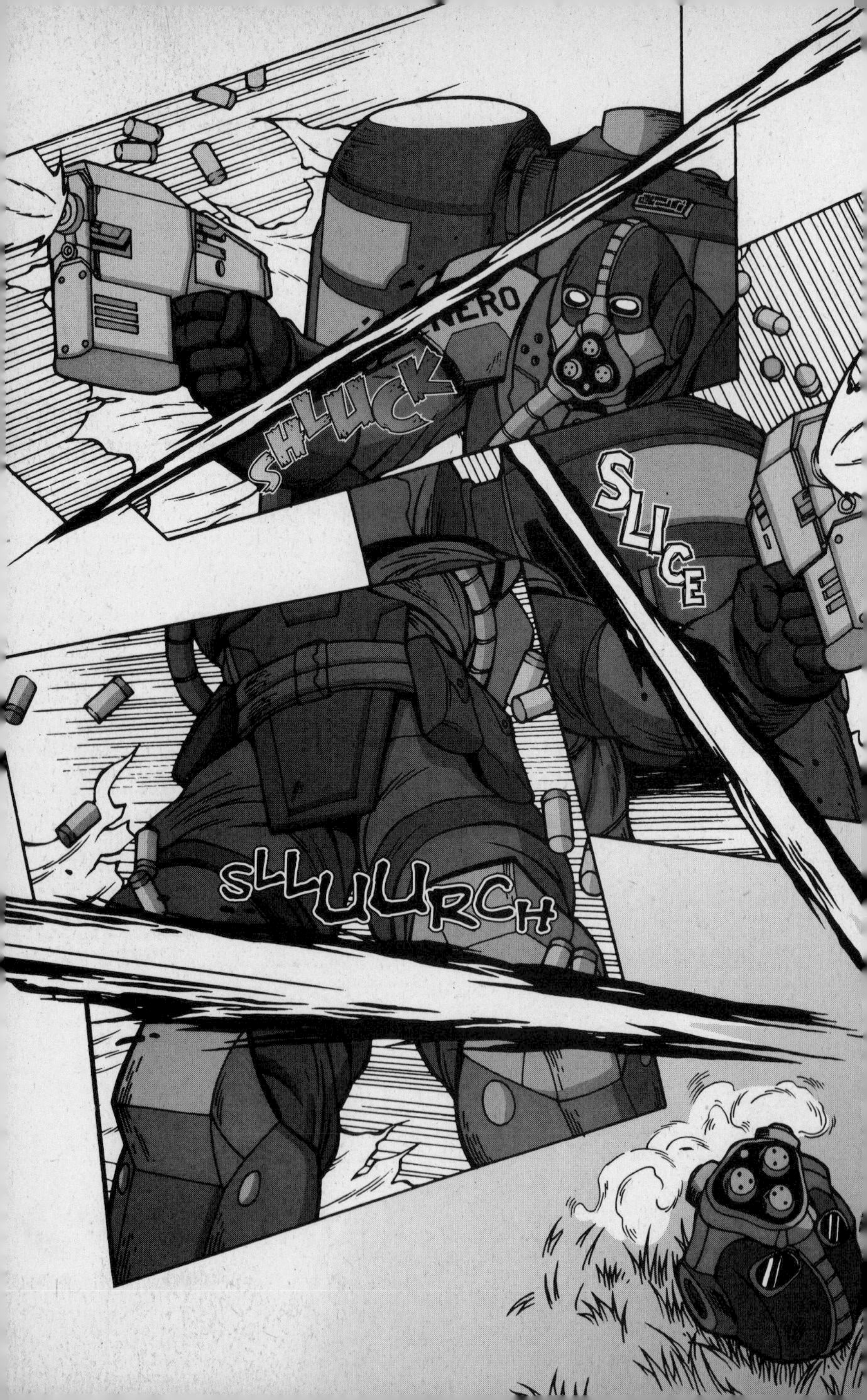
NERO
SHLUCK
SLICE
SLLUURCH

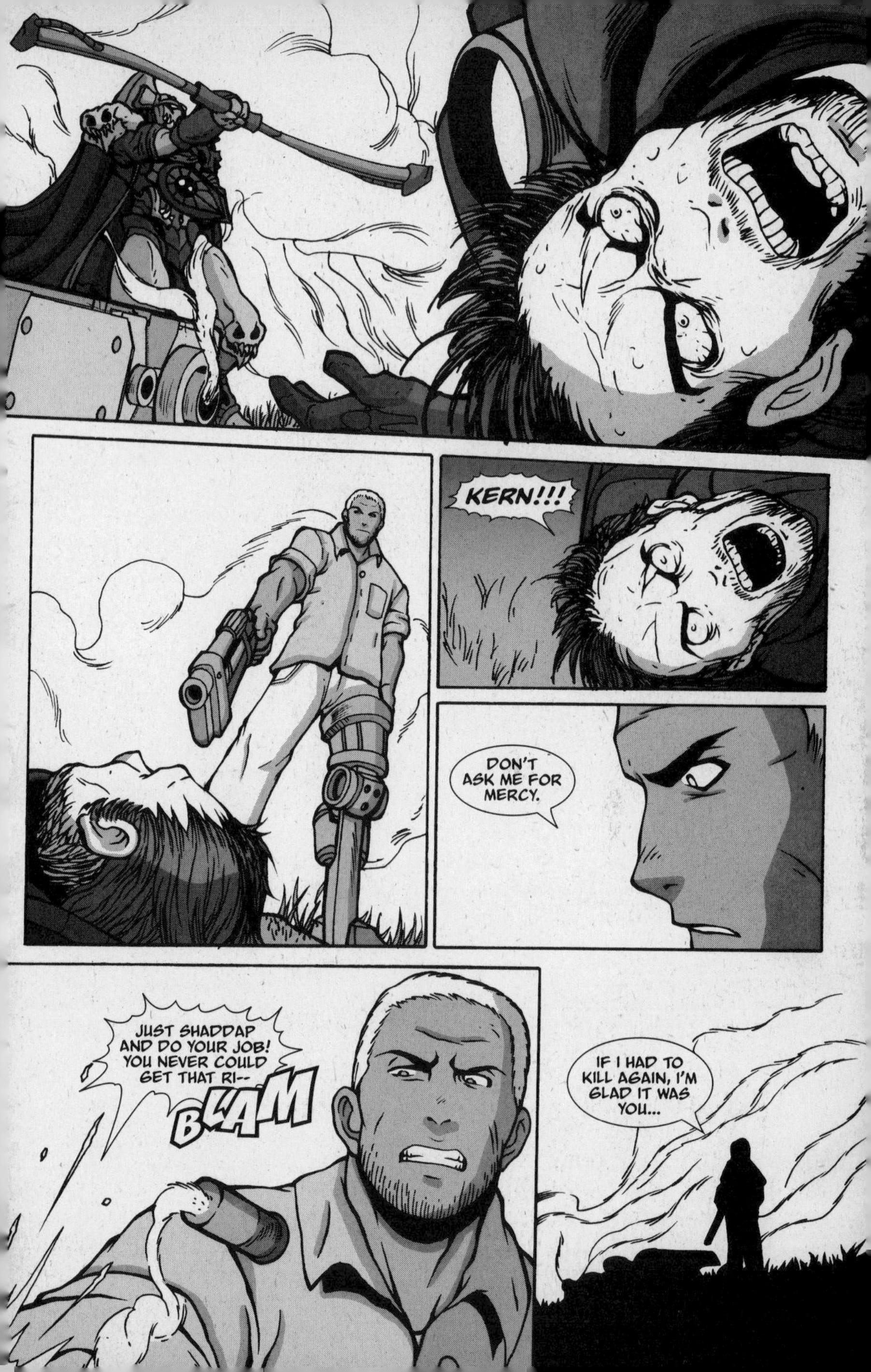
KERN!!!
DON'T ASK ME FOR MERCY.
JUST SHADDAP AND DO YOUR JOB! YOU NEVER COULD GET THAT RI--
BLAM
IF I HAD TO KILL AGAIN, I'M GLAD IT WAS YOU...

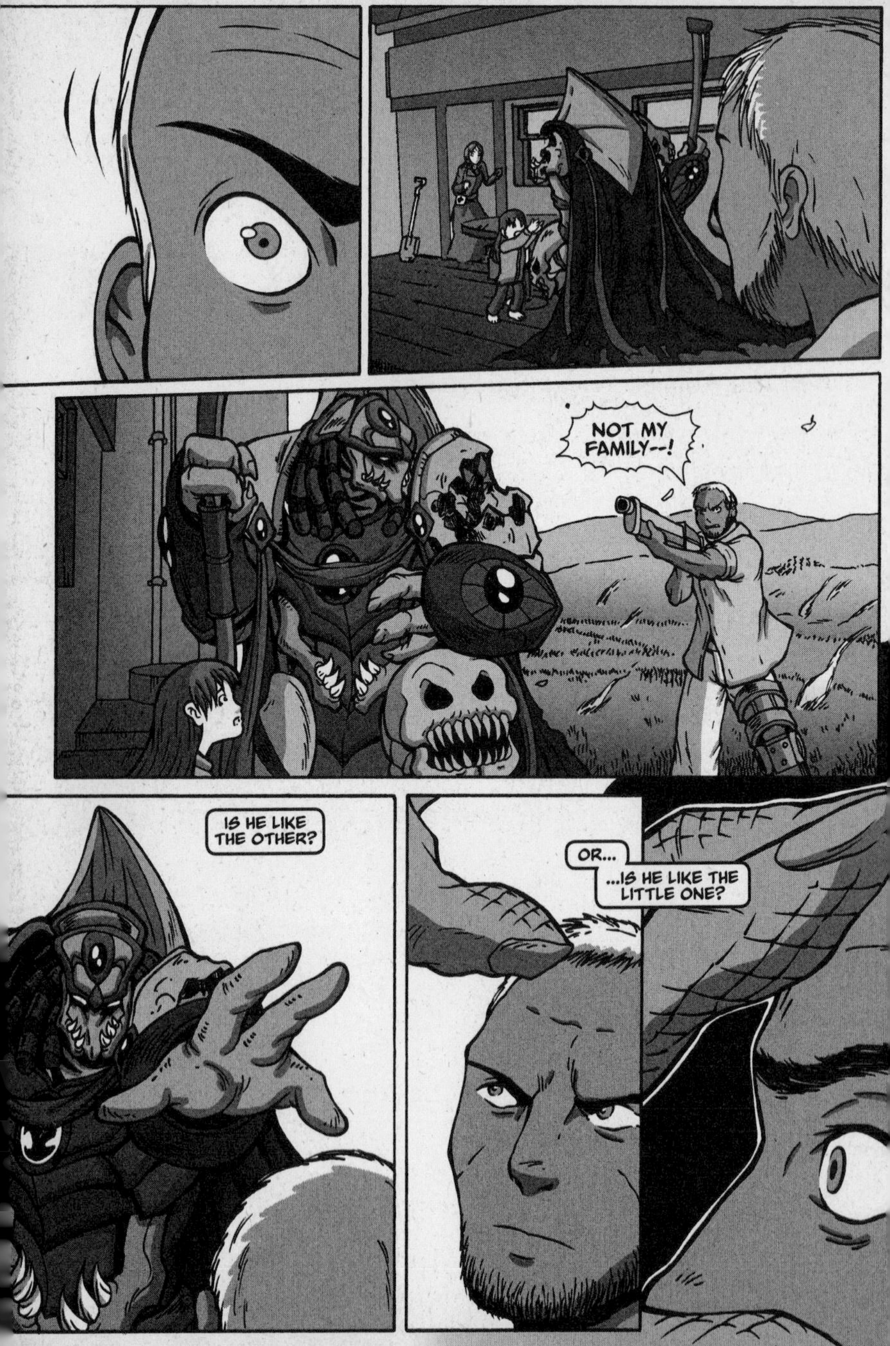
NOT MY FAMILY--!
IS HE LIKE THE OTHER?
OR...
...IS HE LIKE THE LITTLE ONE?

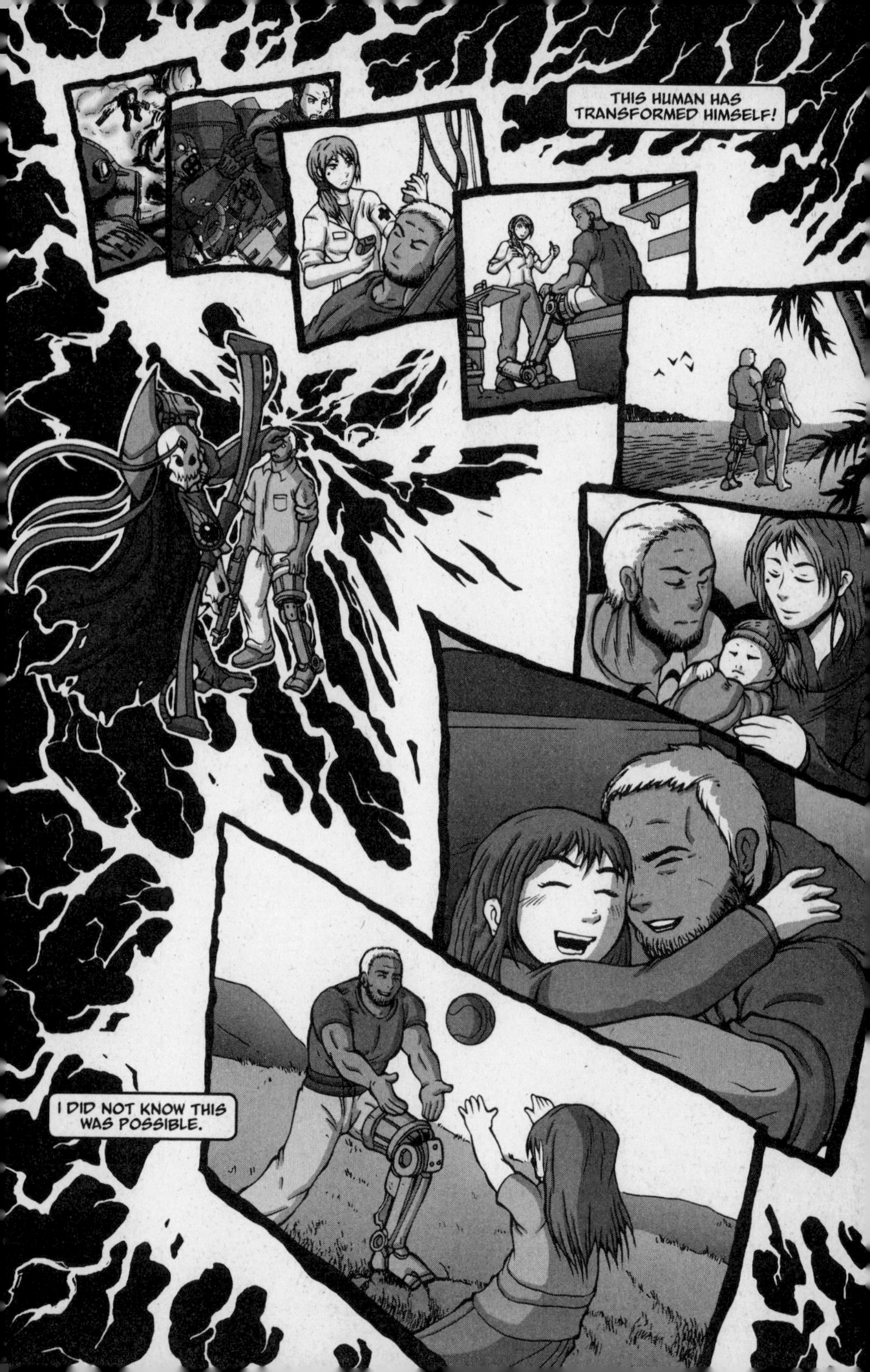
THIS HUMAN HAS TRANSFORMED HIMSELF!
I DID NOT KNOW THIS WAS POSSIBLE.

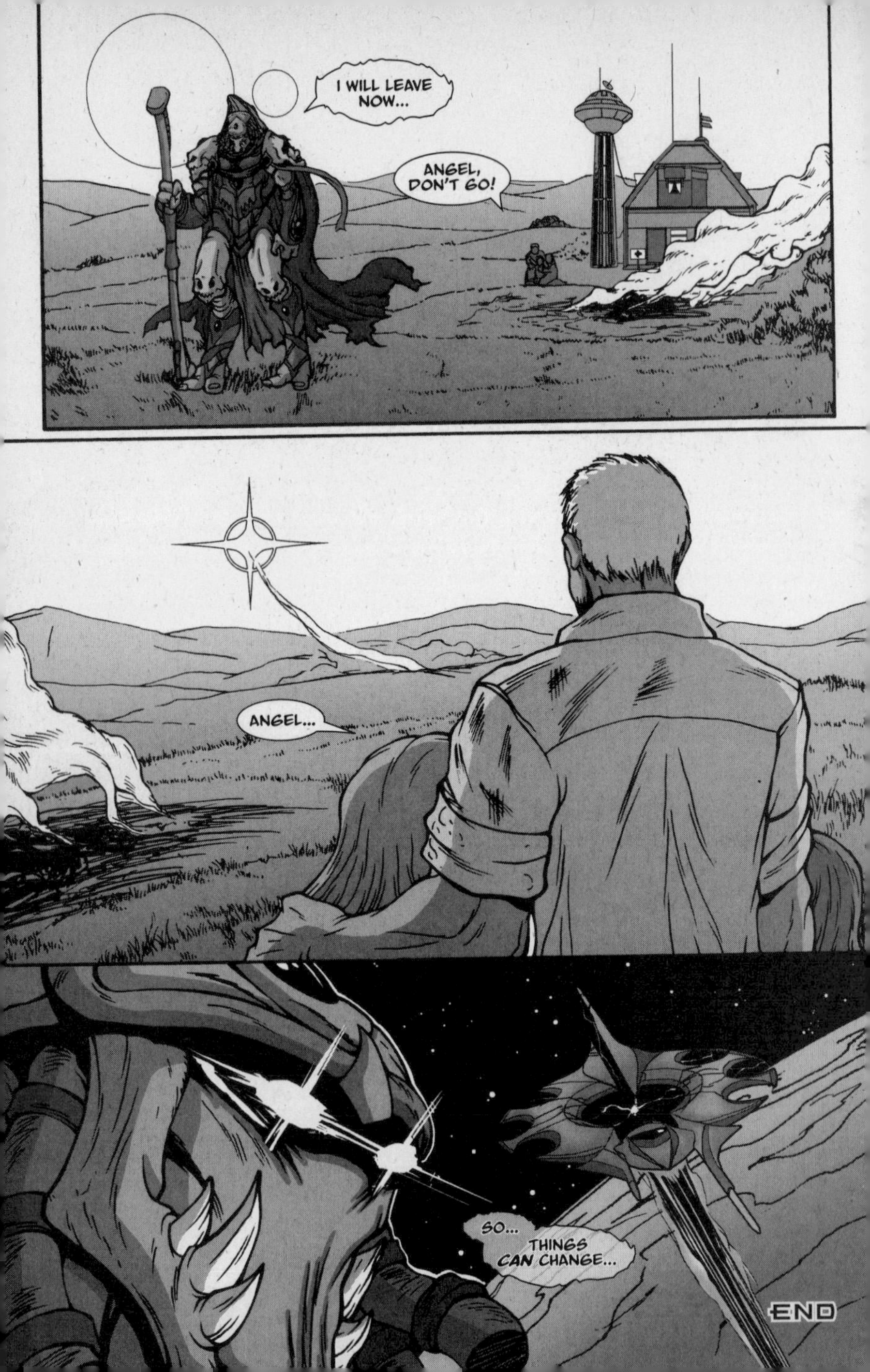
I WILL LEAVE NOW...
ANGEL, DON'T GO!
ANGEL...
SO...
THINGS *CAN* CHANGE...
END

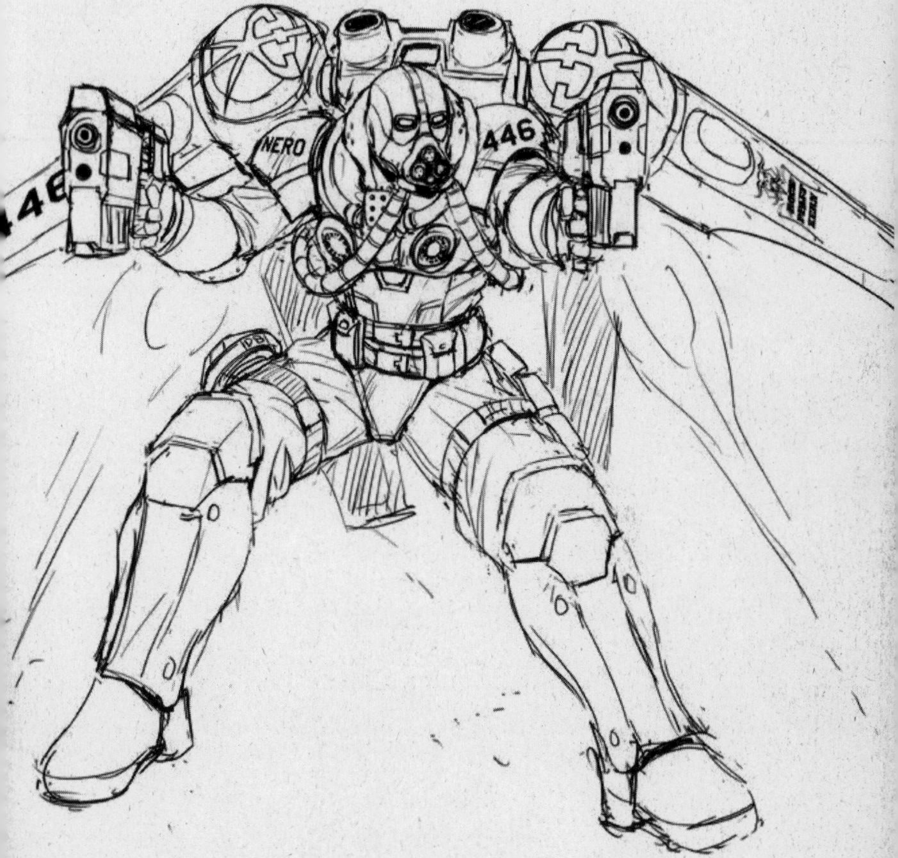
446
NERO
446

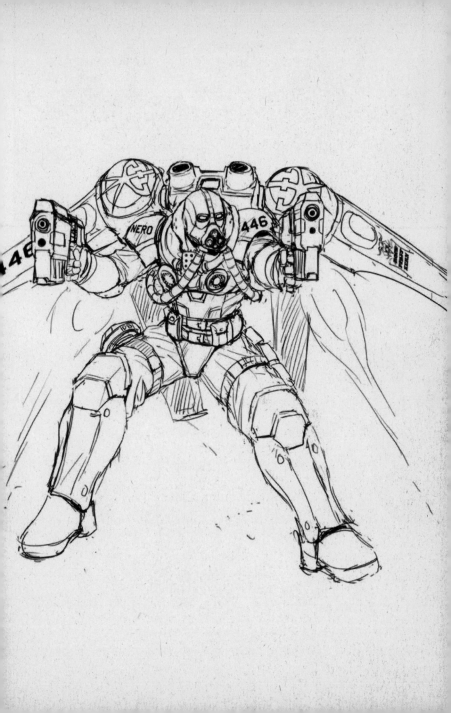

# STARCRAFT

## FRONTLINE
### VOLUME 4

# VOICE IN THE
# DARKNESS

Written by Josh Elder

Pencils by Ramanda Kamarga
Inks by Faisal, Junaidi and Ijur of Caravan Studio,
and Ryo Kawakami
Tones by Erfian Asafat of Caravan Studio, Beatusvir,
Lincy Chan, and Jake Myler

Letterer: Michael Paolilli

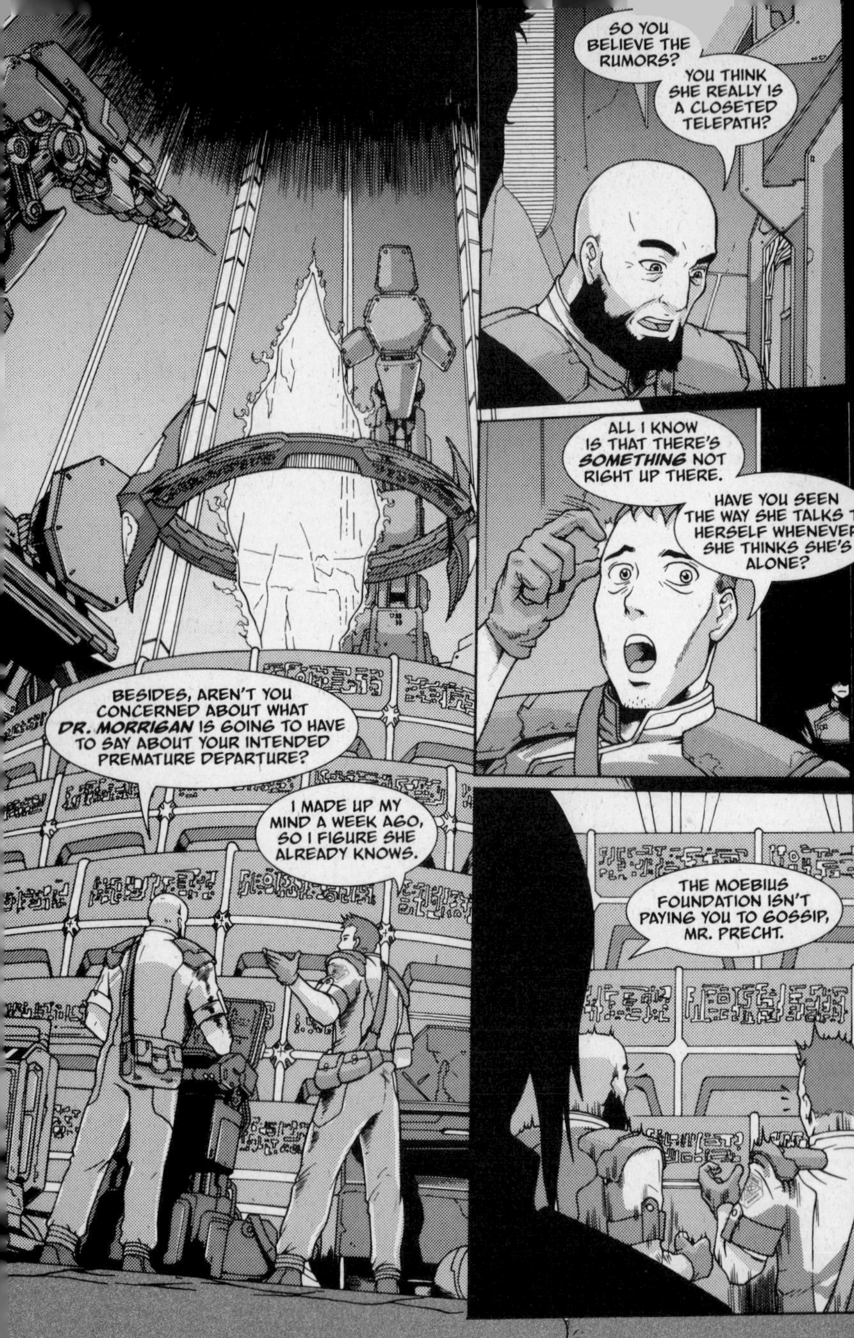
BESIDES, AREN'T YOU CONCERNED ABOUT WHAT *DR. MORRIGAN* IS GOING TO HAVE TO SAY ABOUT YOUR INTENDED PREMATURE DEPARTURE?
I MADE UP MY MIND A WEEK AGO, SO I FIGURE SHE ALREADY KNOWS.
SO YOU BELIEVE THE RUMORS?
YOU THINK SHE REALLY IS A CLOSETED TELEPATH?
ALL I KNOW IS THAT THERE'S *SOMETHING* NOT RIGHT UP THERE.
HAVE YOU SEEN THE WAY SHE TALKS TO HERSELF WHENEVER SHE THINKS SHE'S ALONE?
THE MOEBIUS FOUNDATION ISN'T PAYING YOU TO GOSSIP, MR. PRECHT.

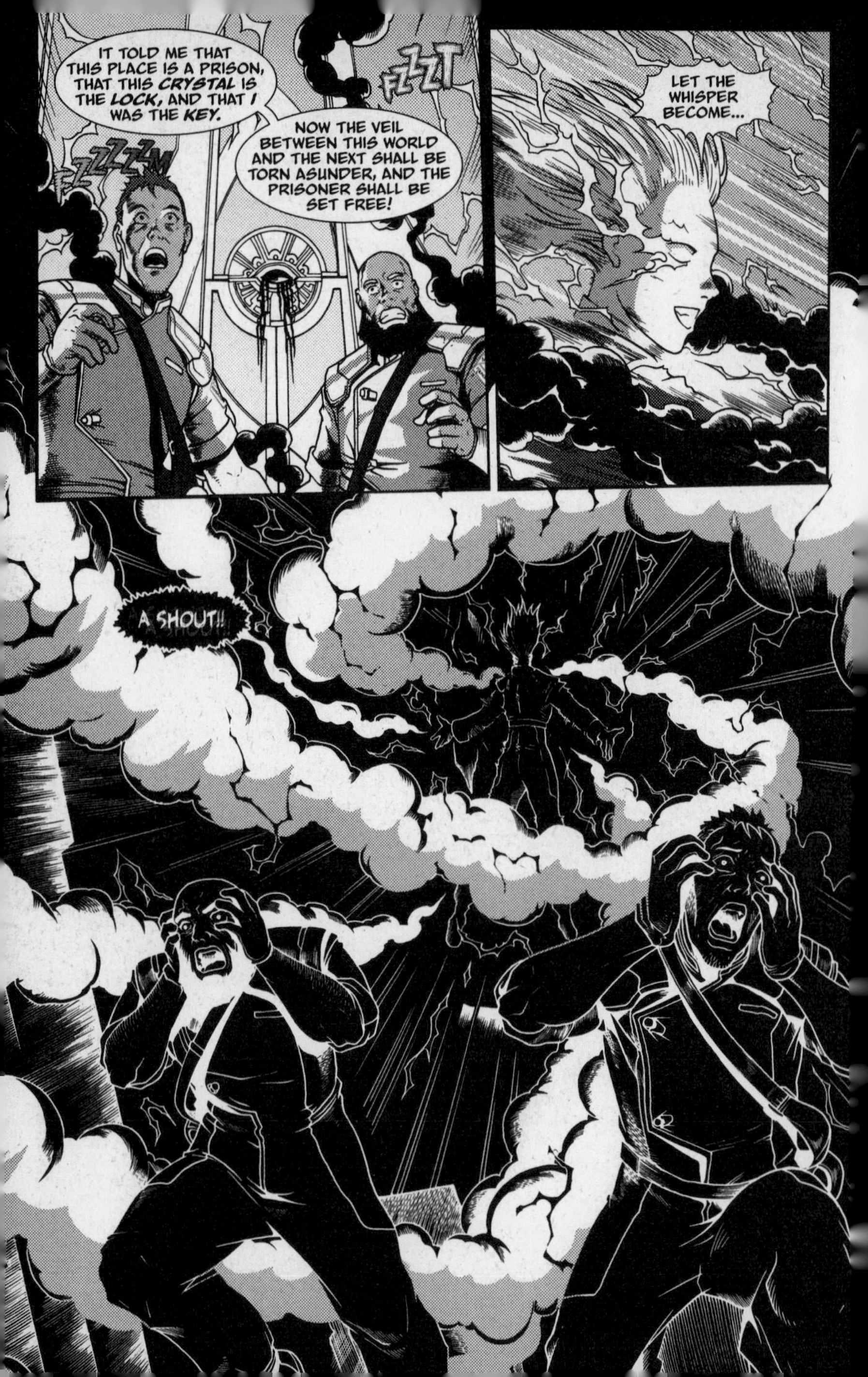
IT TOLD ME THAT THIS PLACE IS A PRISON, THAT THIS CRYSTAL IS THE LOCK, AND THAT I WAS THE KEY.
FZZZZZM
FZZZT
NOW THE VEIL BETWEEN THIS WORLD AND THE NEXT SHALL BE TORN ASUNDER, AND THE PRISONER SHALL BE SET FREE!
LET THE WHISPER BECOME...
A SHOUT!!

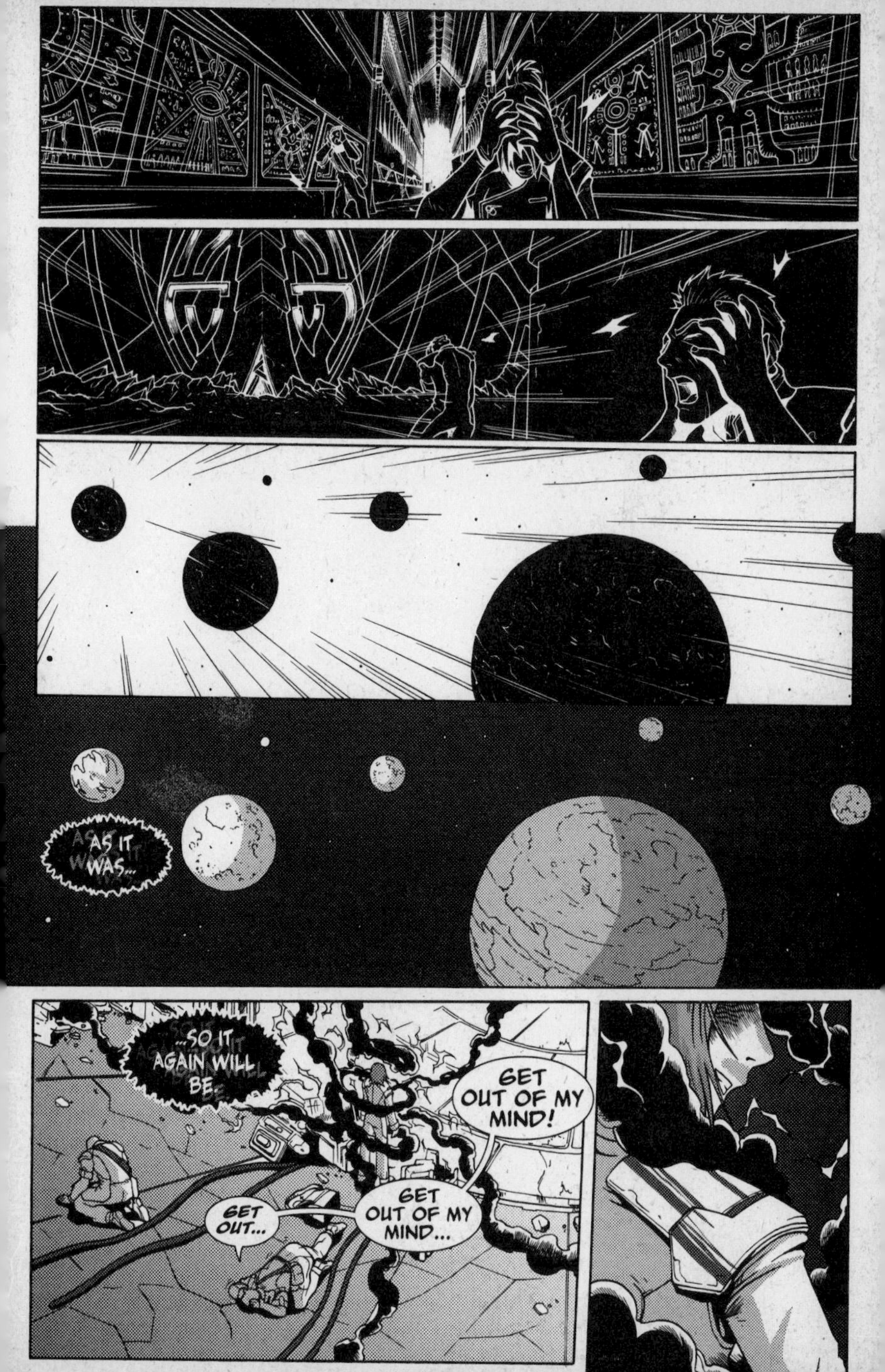
AS IT WAS...
...SO IT AGAIN WILL BE.
GET OUT OF MY MIND!
GET OUT...
GET OUT OF MY MIND...

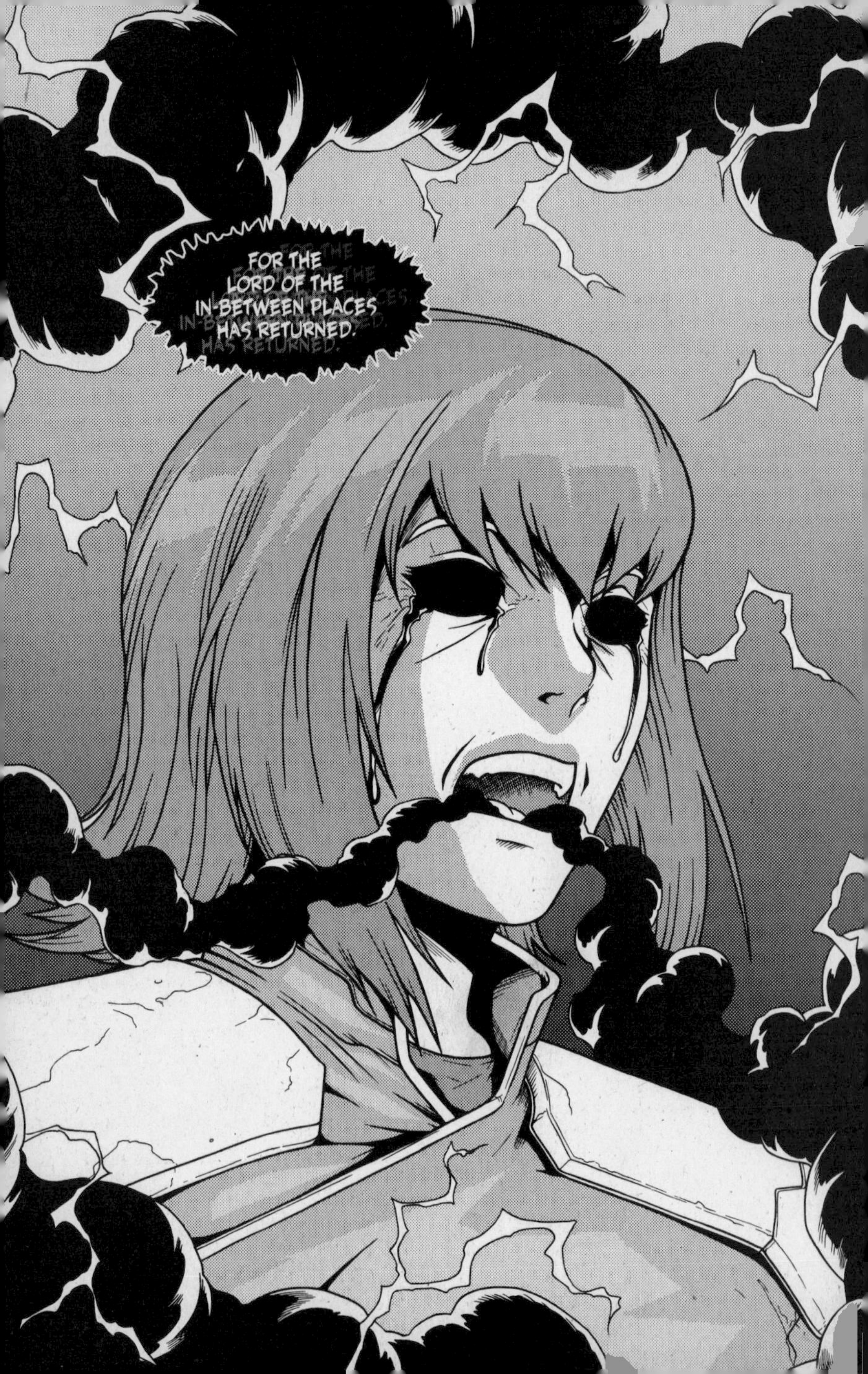
FOR THE LORD OF THE IN-BETWEEN PLACES HAS RETURNED.

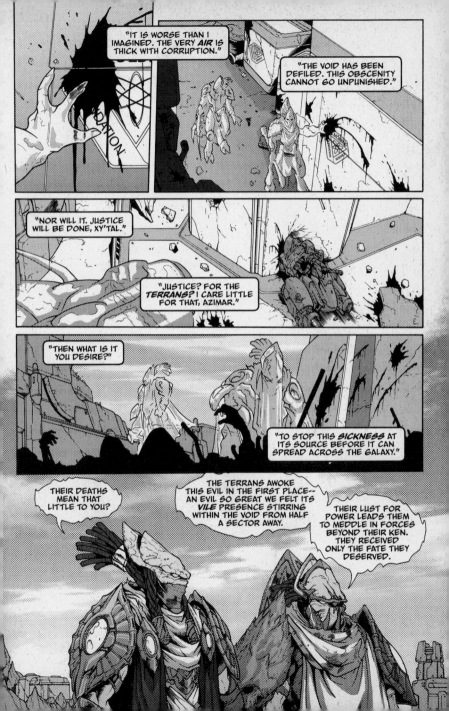

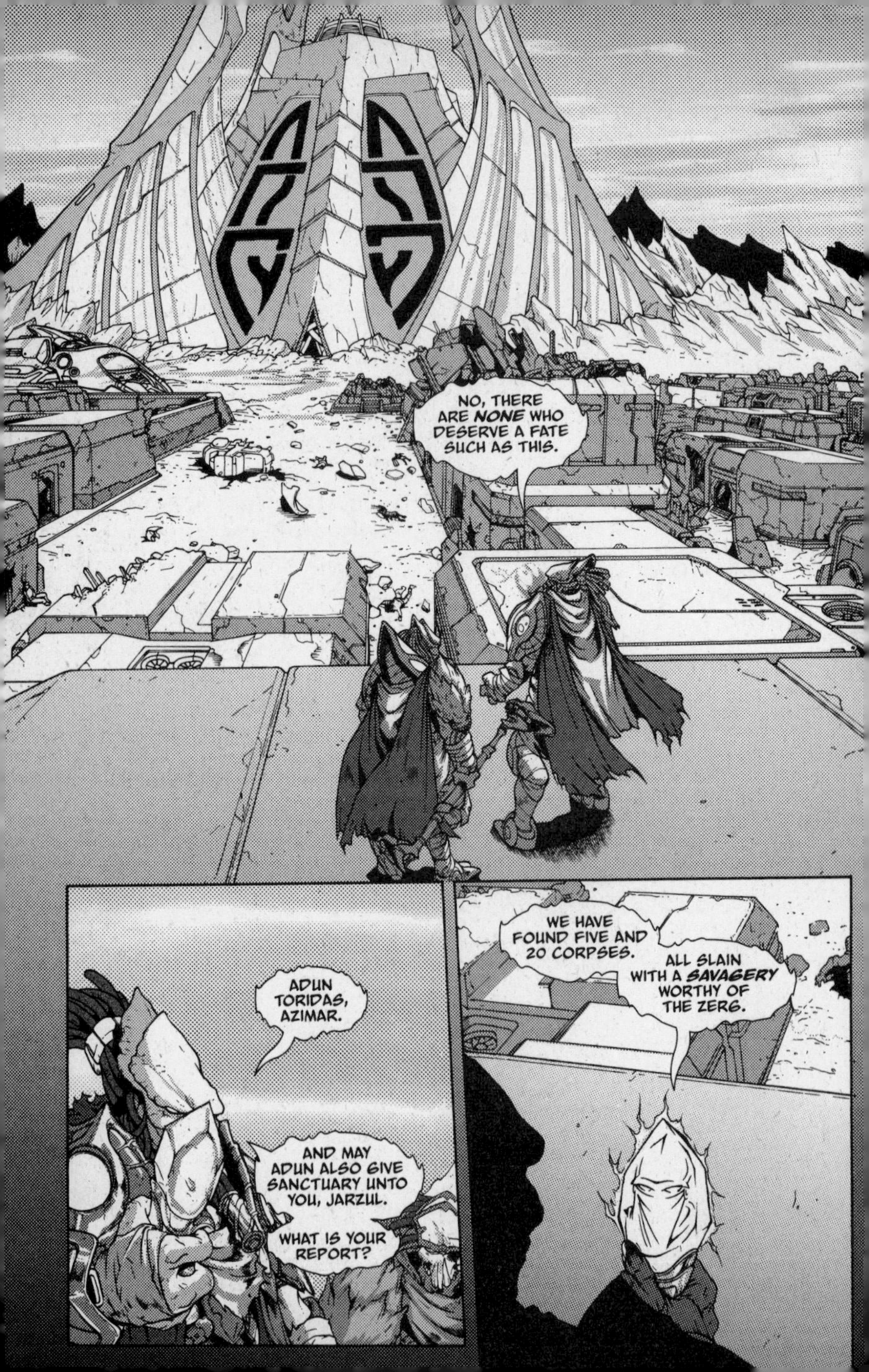
NO, THERE ARE NONE WHO DESERVE A FATE SUCH AS THIS.
ADUN TORIDAS, AZIMAR.
AND MAY ADUN ALSO GIVE SANCTUARY UNTO YOU, JARZUL.
WHAT IS YOUR REPORT?
WE HAVE FOUND FIVE AND 20 CORPSES.
ALL SLAIN WITH A SAVAGERY WORTHY OF THE ZERG.

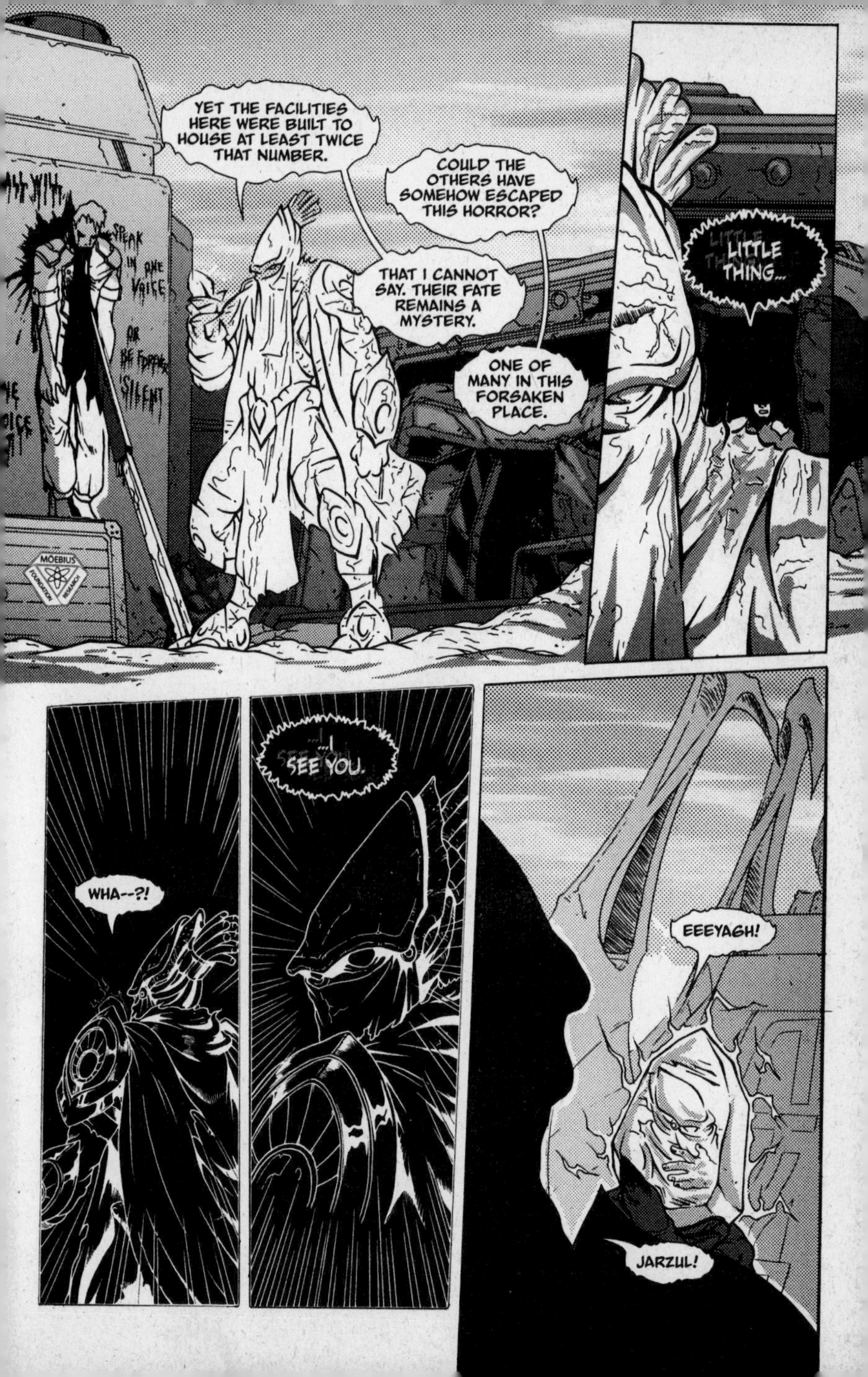
SPEAK IN ONE VOICE OR BE FOREVER SILENT
YET THE FACILITIES HERE WERE BUILT TO HOUSE AT LEAST TWICE THAT NUMBER.
COULD THE OTHERS HAVE SOMEHOW ESCAPED THIS HORROR?
THAT I CANNOT SAY. THEIR FATE REMAINS A MYSTERY.
ONE OF MANY IN THIS FORSAKEN PLACE.
LITTLE THING...
WHA--?!
...I SEE YOU.
EEEYAGH!
JARZUL!

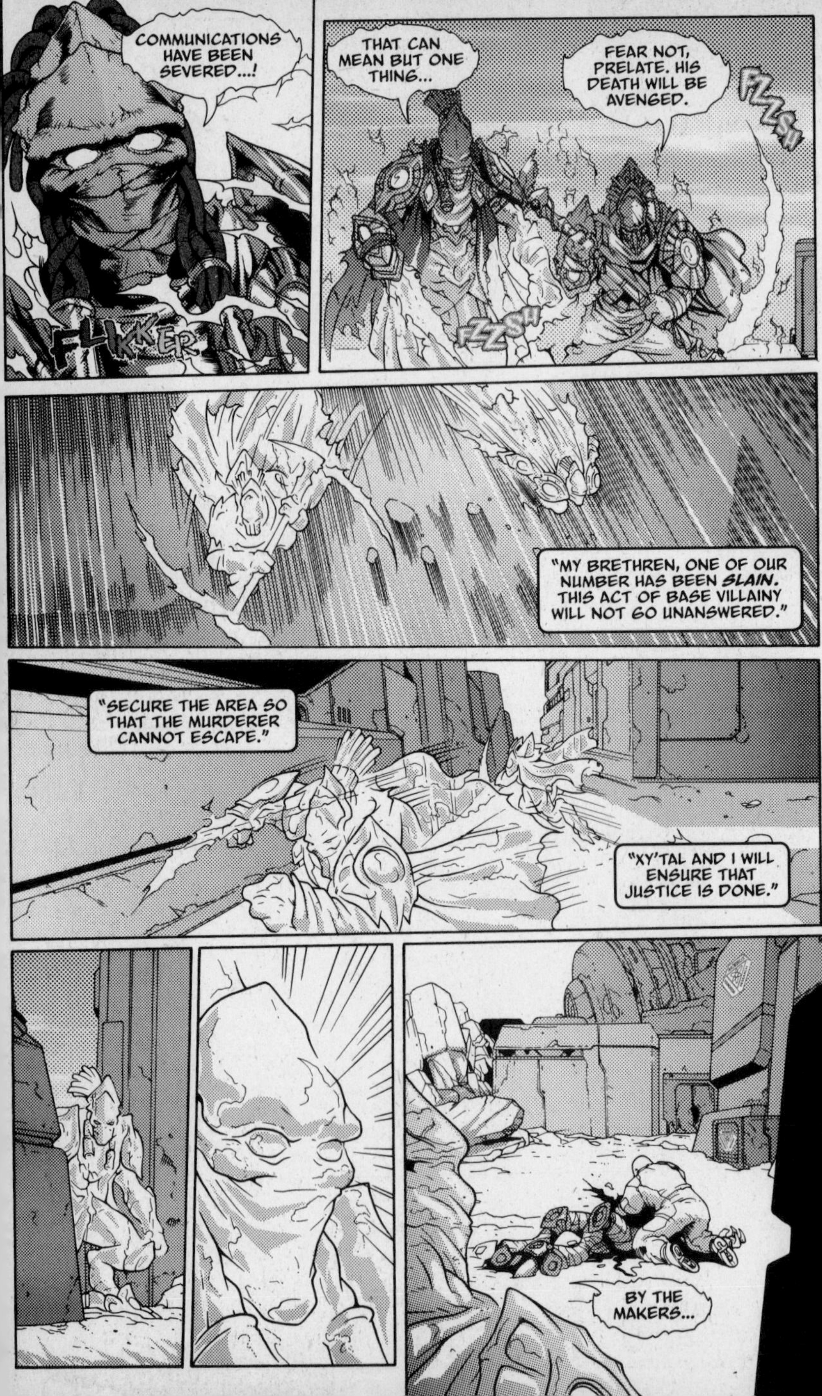
COMMUNICATIONS HAVE BEEN SEVERED...!
FLIKKER
THAT CAN MEAN BUT ONE THING...
FEAR NOT, PRELATE. HIS DEATH WILL BE AVENGED.
FZZSH
FZZSH
"MY BRETHREN, ONE OF OUR NUMBER HAS BEEN *SLAIN.* THIS ACT OF BASE VILLAINY WILL NOT GO UNANSWERED."
"SECURE THE AREA SO THAT THE MURDERER CANNOT ESCAPE."
"XY'TAL AND I WILL ENSURE THAT JUSTICE IS DONE."
BY THE MAKERS...

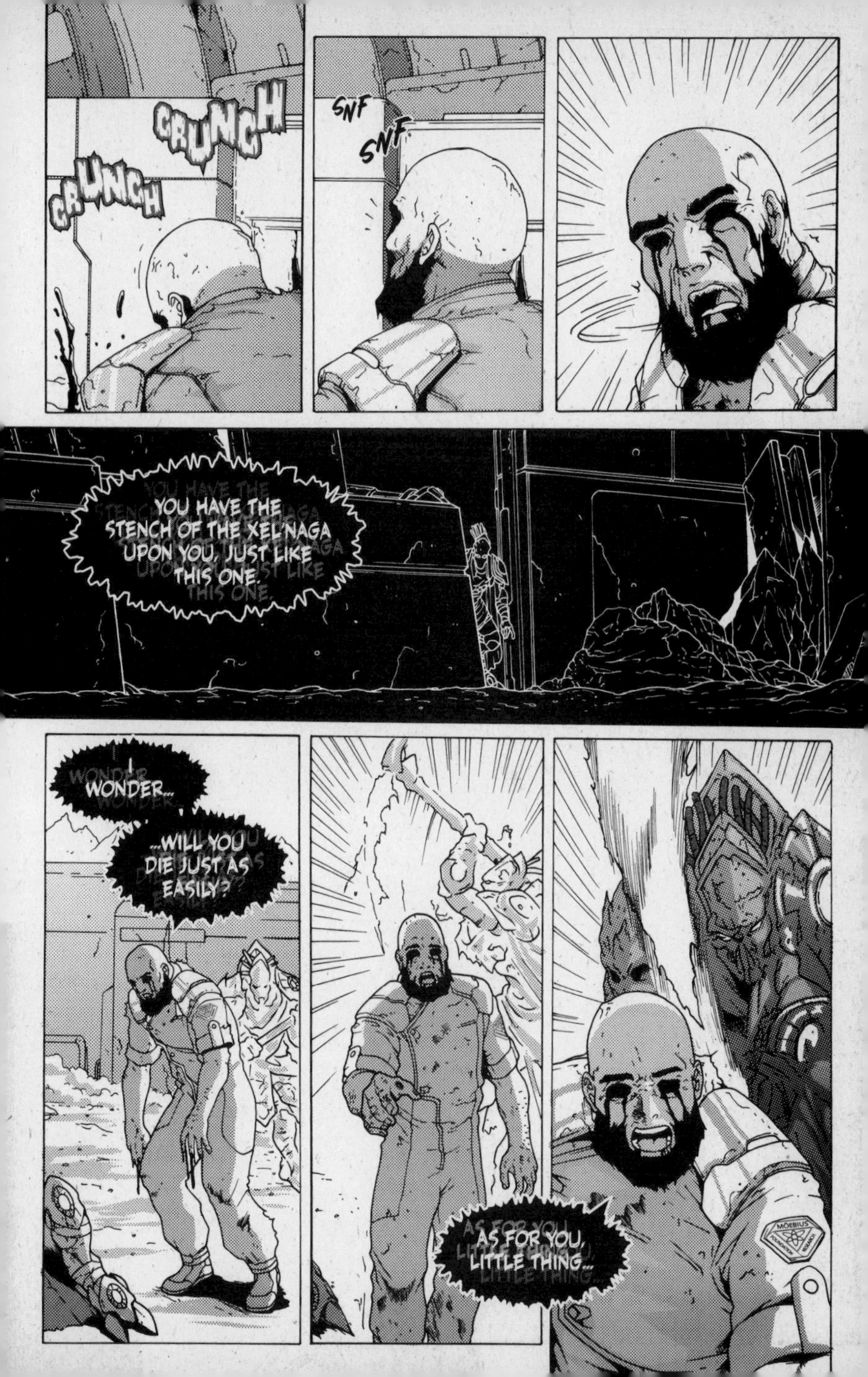
CRUNCH
CRUNCH
SNF
SNF
YOU HAVE THE STENCH OF THE XEL'NAGA UPON YOU, JUST LIKE THIS ONE.
I WONDER...
...WILL YOU DIE JUST AS EASILY?
AS FOR YOU, LITTLE THING...
MOEBIUS FOUNDATION RESEARCH

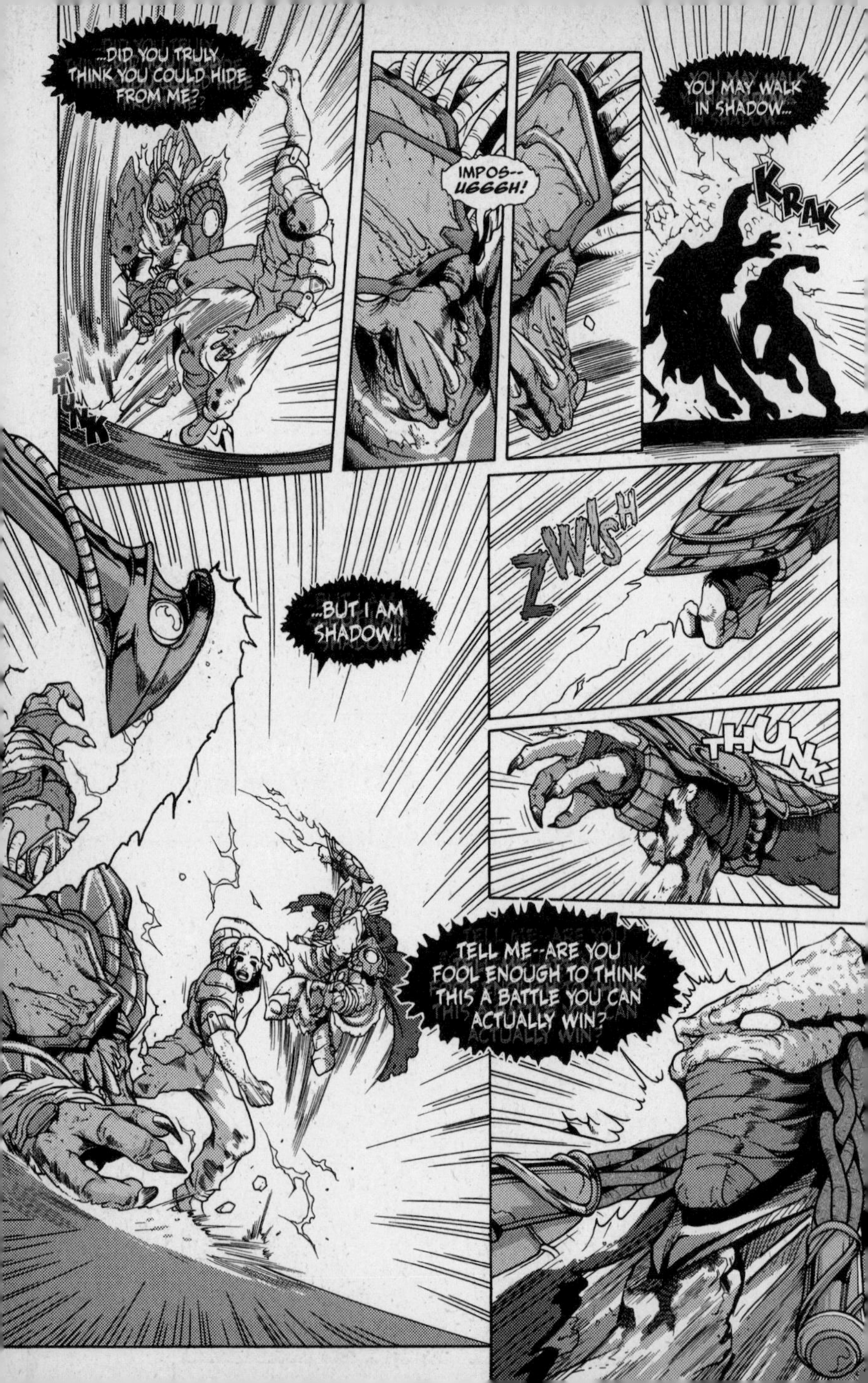
...DID YOU TRULY THINK YOU COULD HIDE FROM ME?
SHUNK
IMPOS-- UGGGH!
YOU MAY WALK IN SHADOW...
KRAK
...BUT I AM SHADOW!!
ZWISH
THUNK
TELL ME--ARE YOU FOOL ENOUGH TO THINK THIS A BATTLE YOU CAN ACTUALLY WIN?

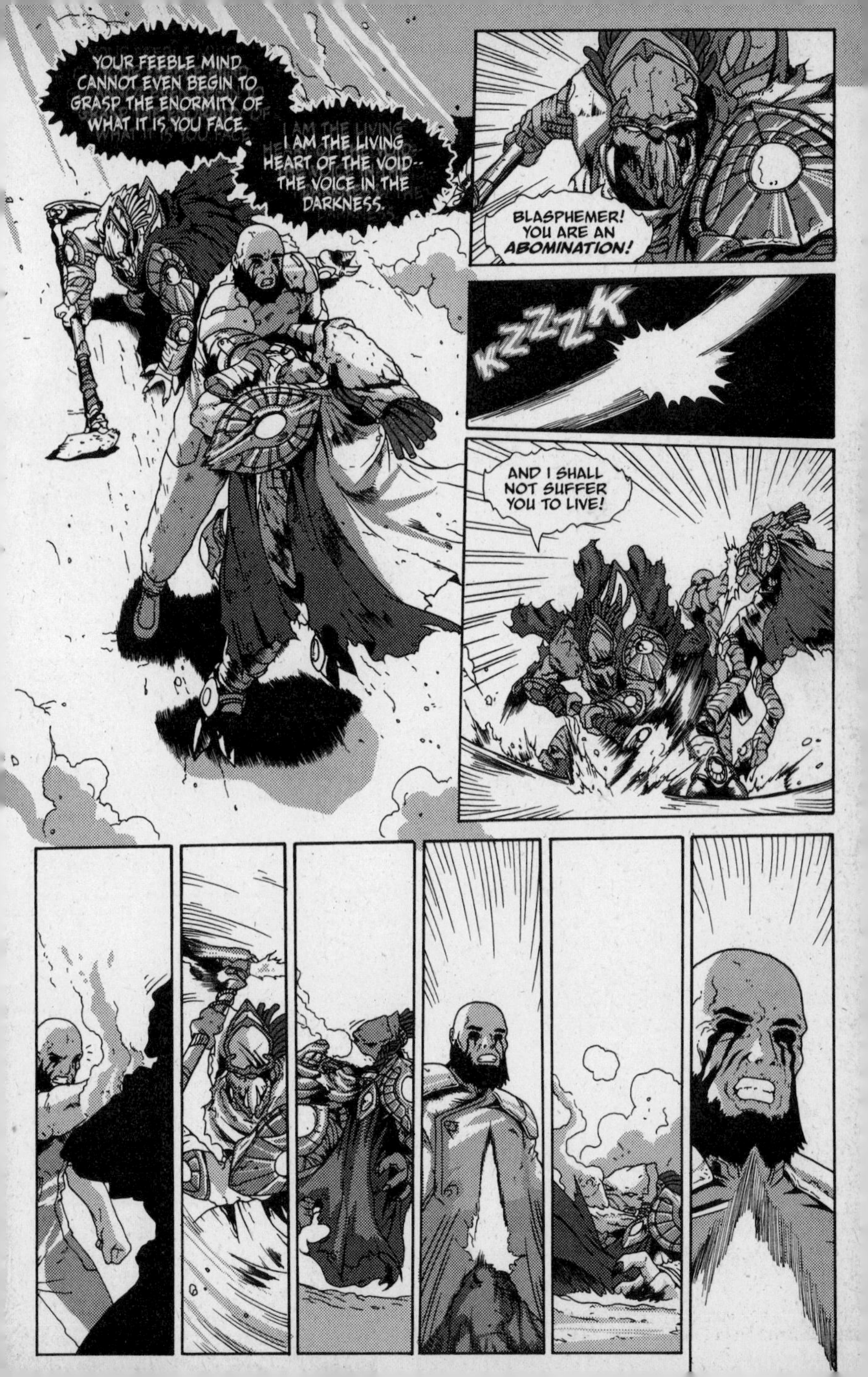
YOUR FEEBLE MIND CANNOT EVEN BEGIN TO GRASP THE ENORMITY OF WHAT IT IS YOU FACE.
I AM THE LIVING HEART OF THE VOID-- THE VOICE IN THE DARKNESS.
BLASPHEMER! YOU ARE AN ABOMINATION!
KZZZZK
AND I SHALL NOT SUFFER YOU TO LIVE!

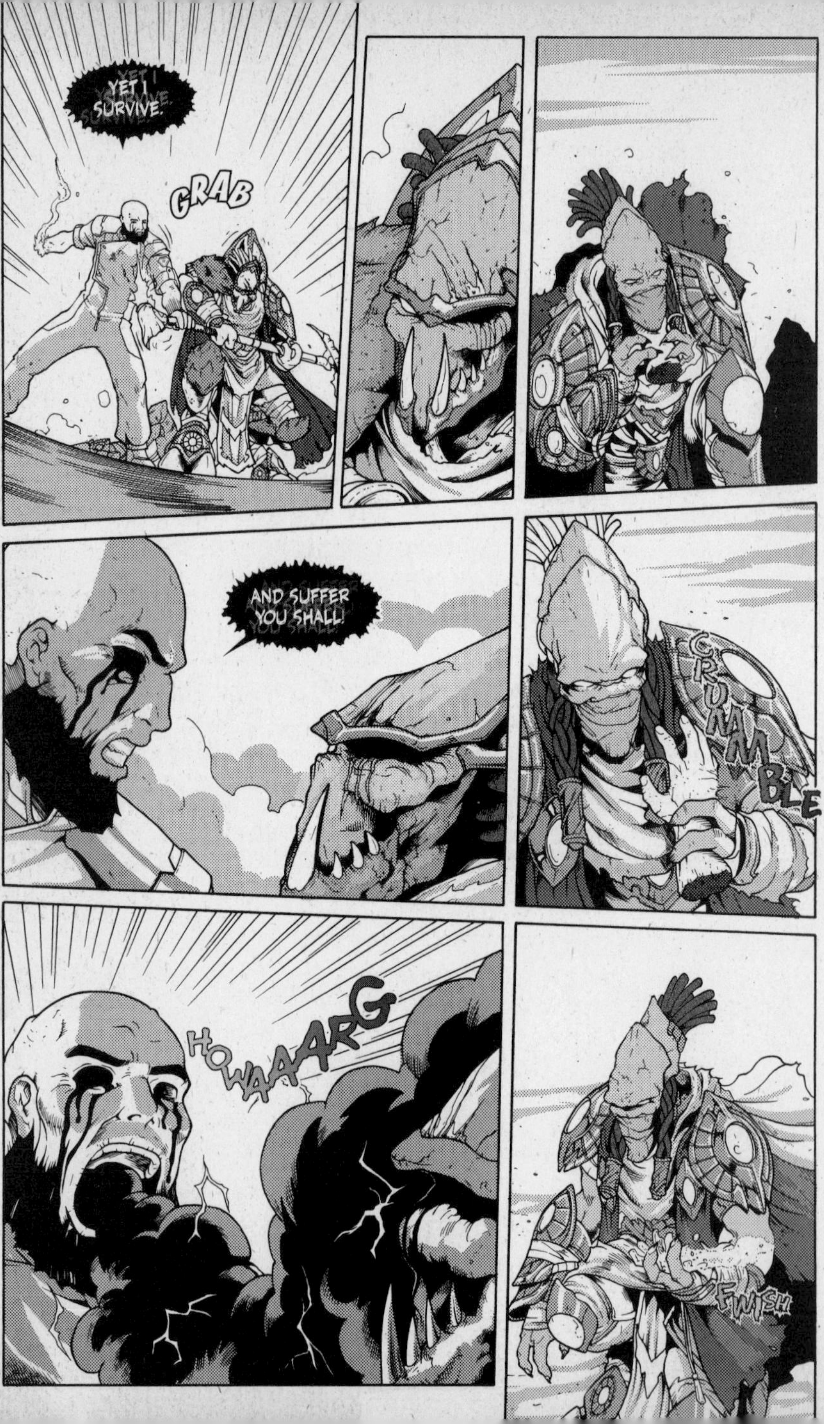
YET I SURVIVE.
GRAB
AND SUFFER YOU SHALL!
CRUMBLE
HOWAAARG
FWISH

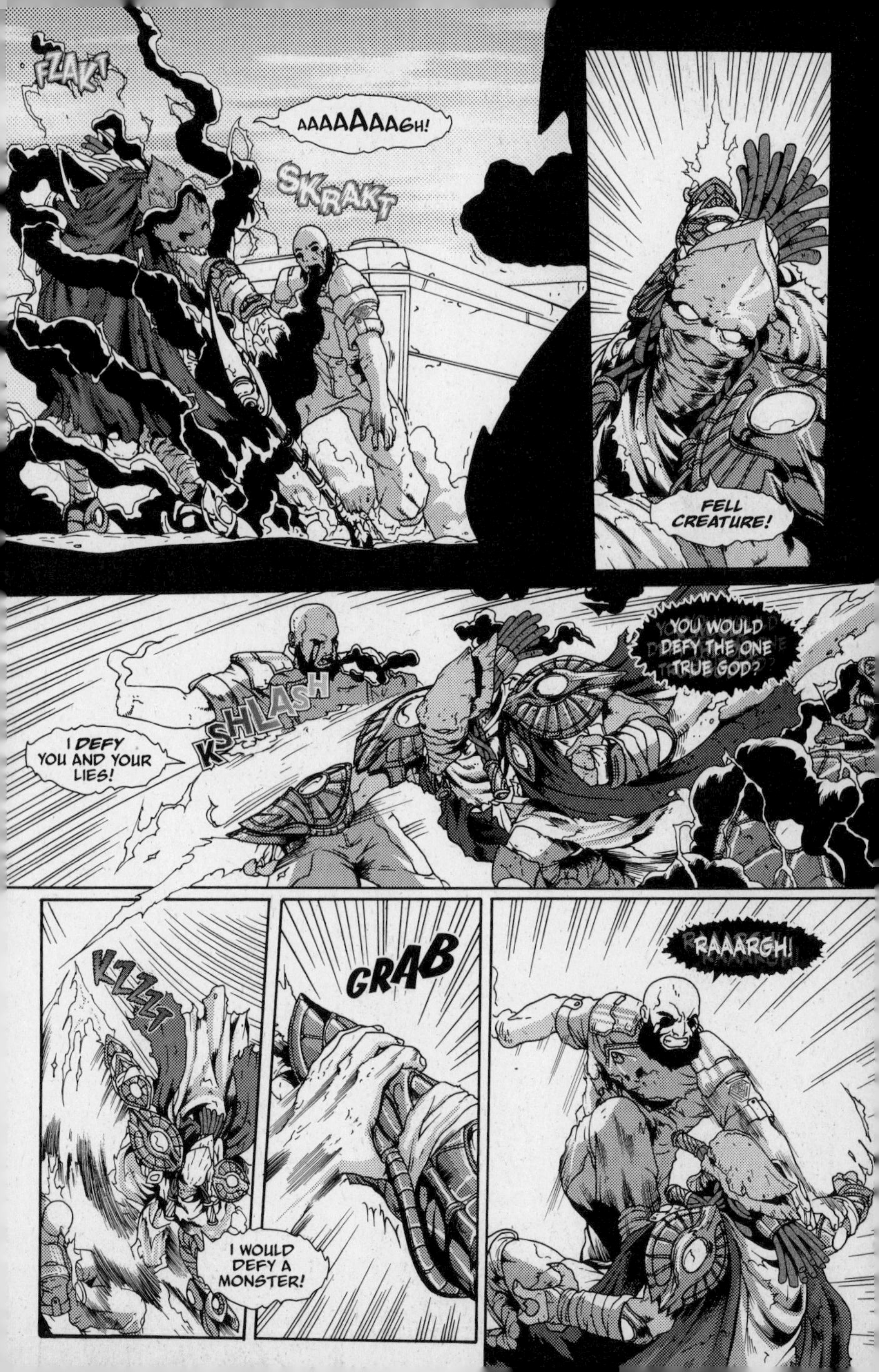
FZAKT
AAAAAAAGH!
SKRAKT
FELL CREATURE!
YOU WOULD DEFY THE ONE TRUE GOD?
KSHLASH
I DEFY YOU AND YOUR LIES!
KZZZT
I WOULD DEFY A MONSTER!
GRAB
RAAARGH!

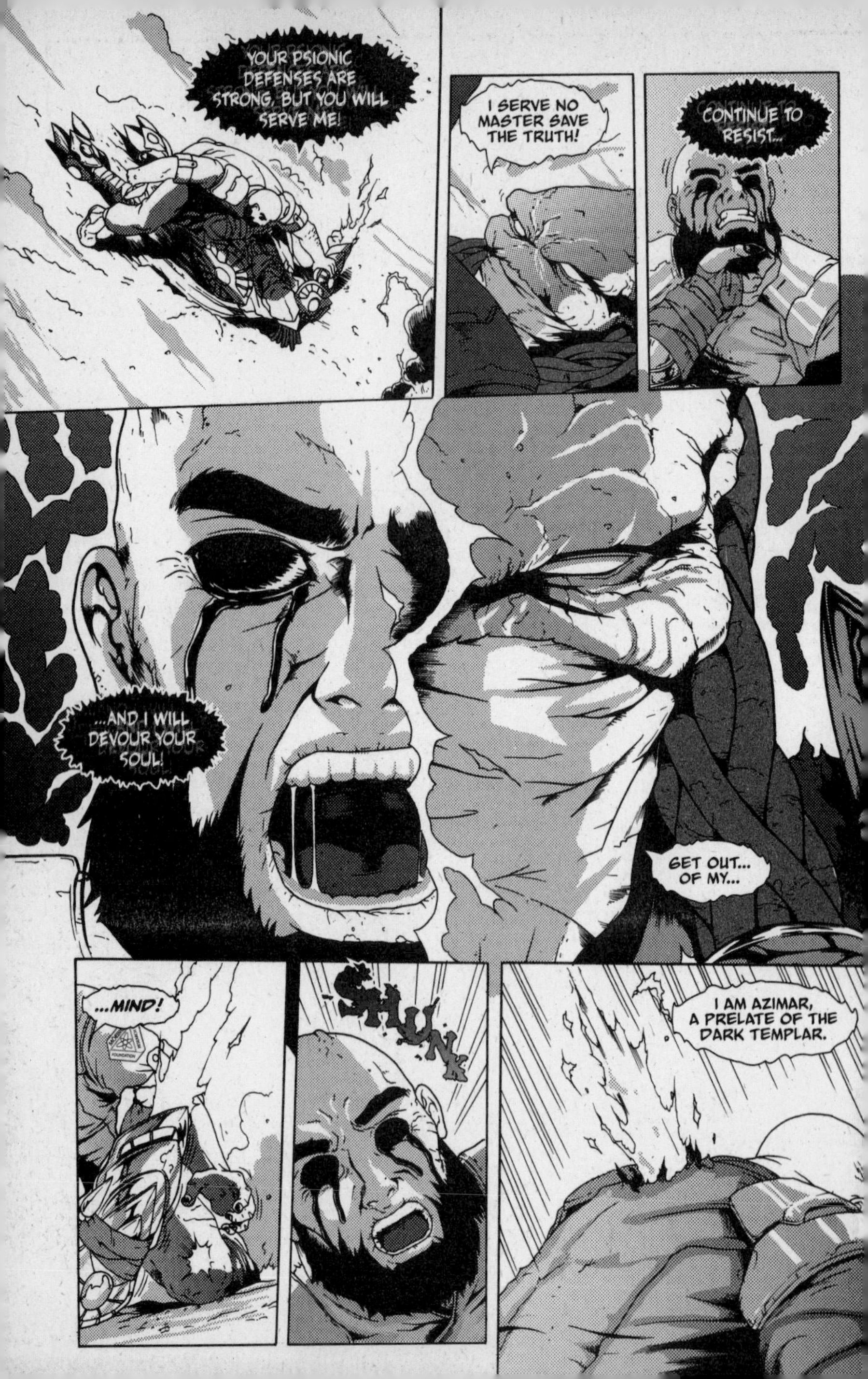
YOUR PSIONIC DEFENSES ARE STRONG, BUT YOU WILL SERVE ME!
I SERVE NO MASTER SAVE THE TRUTH!
CONTINUE TO RESIST...
...AND I WILL DEVOUR YOUR SOUL!
GET OUT... OF MY...
...MIND!
SHUNK
I AM AZIMAR, A PRELATE OF THE DARK TEMPLAR.

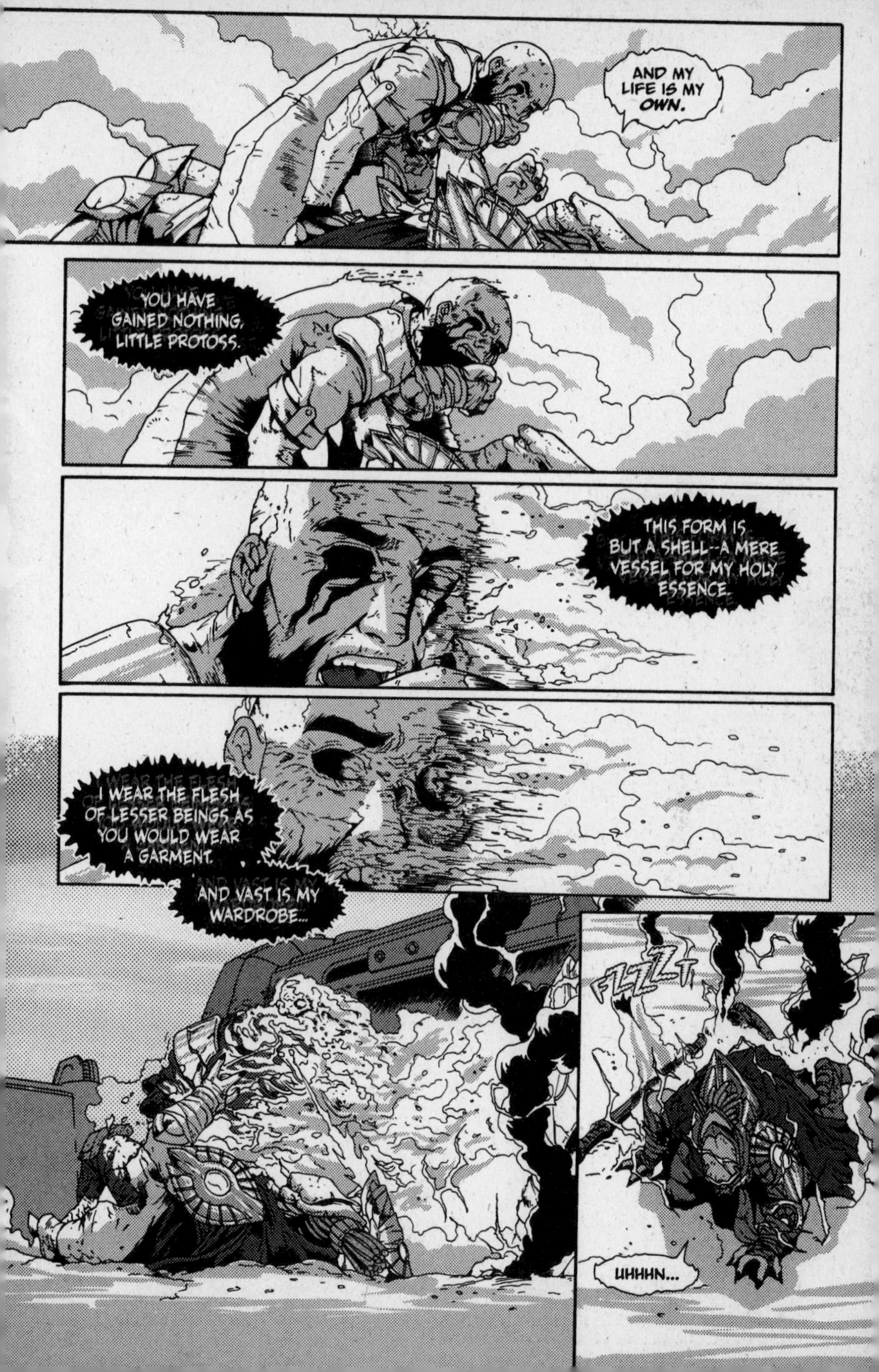
AND MY LIFE IS MY OWN.
YOU HAVE GAINED NOTHING, LITTLE PROTOSS.
THIS FORM IS BUT A SHELL--A MERE VESSEL FOR MY HOLY ESSENCE.
I WEAR THE FLESH OF LESSER BEINGS AS YOU WOULD WEAR A GARMENT.
AND VAST IS MY WARDROBE...
FZZZZT
UHHHN...

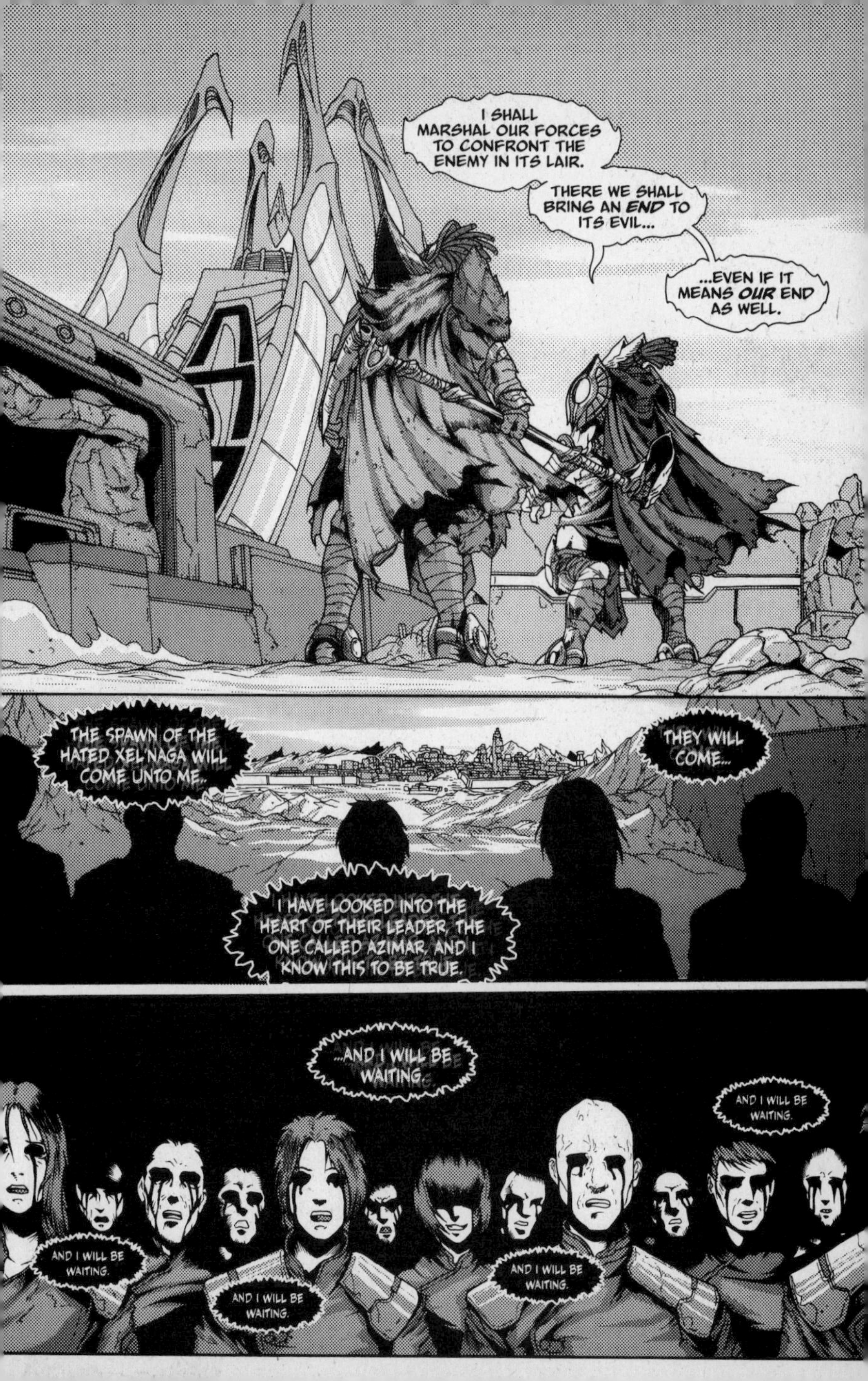
I SHALL MARSHAL OUR FORCES TO CONFRONT THE ENEMY IN ITS LAIR.
THERE WE SHALL BRING AN *END* TO ITS EVIL...
...EVEN IF IT MEANS *OUR* END AS WELL.
THE SPAWN OF THE HATED XEL'NAGA WILL COME UNTO ME.
THEY WILL COME...
I HAVE LOOKED INTO THE HEART OF THEIR LEADER, THE ONE CALLED AZIMAR, AND I KNOW THIS TO BE TRUE.
...AND I WILL BE WAITING.
AND I WILL BE WAITING.
AND I WILL BE WAITING.
AND I WILL BE WAITING.
AND I WILL BE WAITING.

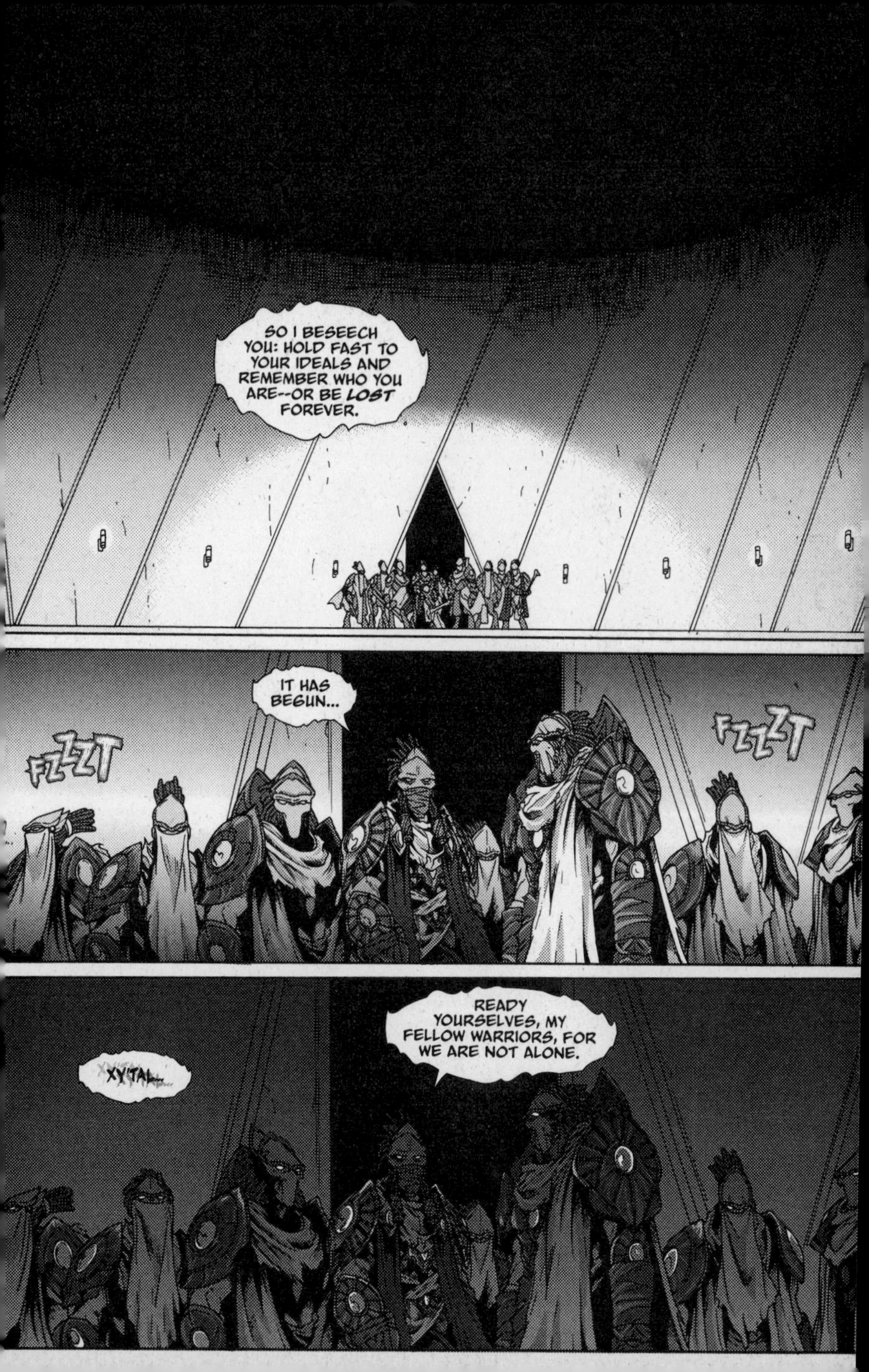
SO I BESEECH YOU: HOLD FAST TO YOUR IDEALS AND REMEMBER WHO YOU ARE--OR BE *LOST* FOREVER.
FZZZT
IT HAS BEGUN...
FZZZT
XY'TAL...
READY YOURSELVES, MY FELLOW WARRIORS, FOR WE ARE NOT ALONE.

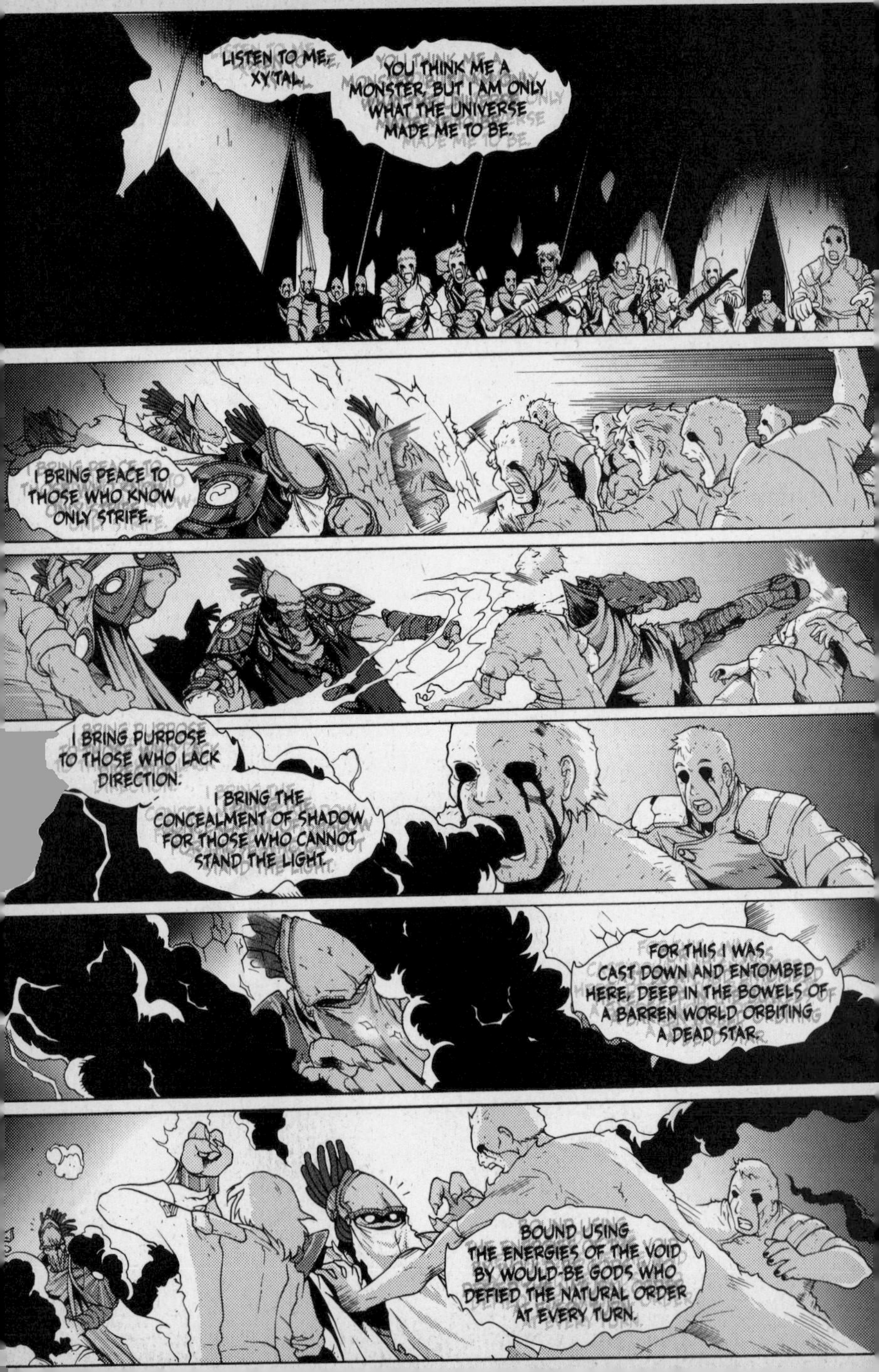
LISTEN TO ME, XYTAL.
YOU THINK ME A MONSTER, BUT I AM ONLY WHAT THE UNIVERSE MADE ME TO BE.
I BRING PEACE TO THOSE WHO KNOW ONLY STRIFE.
I BRING PURPOSE TO THOSE WHO LACK DIRECTION.
I BRING THE CONCEALMENT OF SHADOW FOR THOSE WHO CANNOT STAND THE LIGHT.
FOR THIS I WAS CAST DOWN AND ENTOMBED HERE, DEEP IN THE BOWELS OF A BARREN WORLD ORBITING A DEAD STAR.
BOUND USING THE ENERGIES OF THE VOID BY WOULD-BE GODS WHO DEFIED THE NATURAL ORDER AT EVERY TURN.

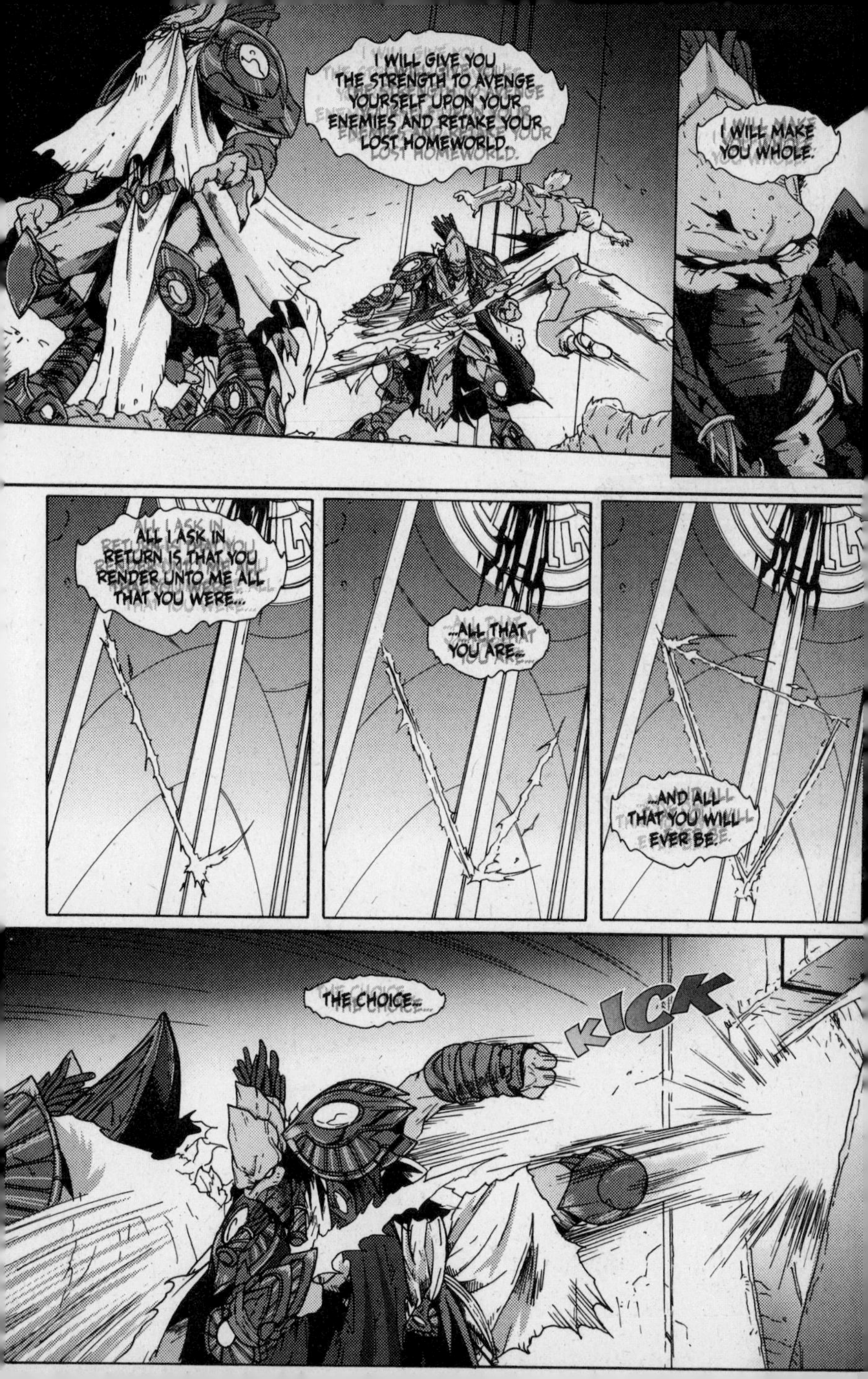
I WILL GIVE YOU THE STRENGTH TO AVENGE YOURSELF UPON YOUR ENEMIES AND RETAKE YOUR LOST HOMEWORLD.
I WILL MAKE YOU WHOLE.
ALL I ASK IN RETURN IS THAT YOU RENDER UNTO ME ALL THAT YOU WERE...
...ALL THAT YOU ARE...
...AND ALL THAT YOU WILL EVER BE.
THE CHOICE...
KICK

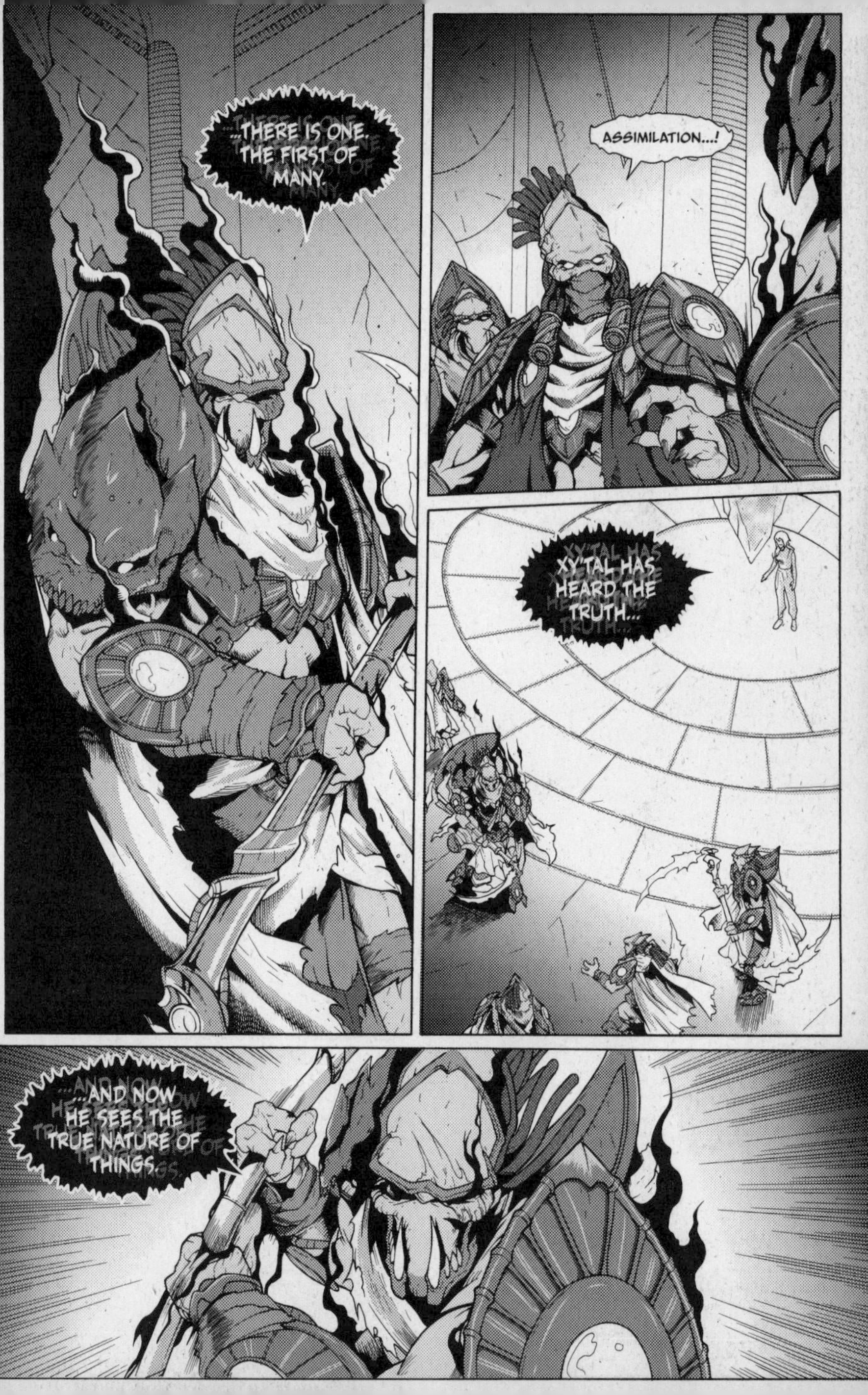

...THERE IS ONE. THE FIRST OF MANY.
ASSIMILATION...!
XY'TAL HAS HEARD THE TRUTH...
...AND NOW HE SEES THE TRUE NATURE OF THINGS.

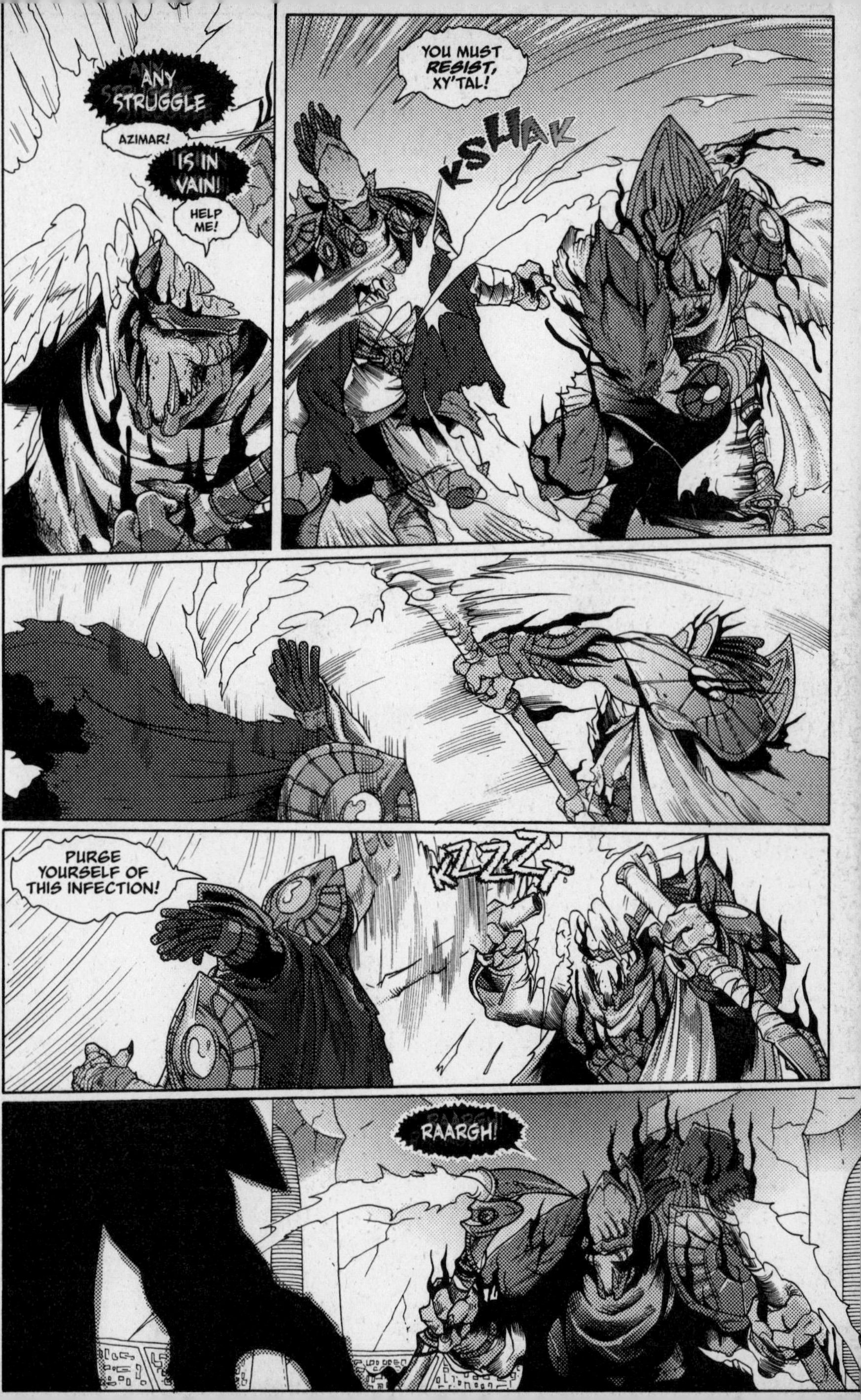
ANY STRUGGLE
AZIMAR!
IS IN VAIN!
HELP ME!
YOU MUST RESIST, XY'TAL!
KSHAK
PURGE YOURSELF OF THIS INFECTION!
KZZZT
RAARGH!

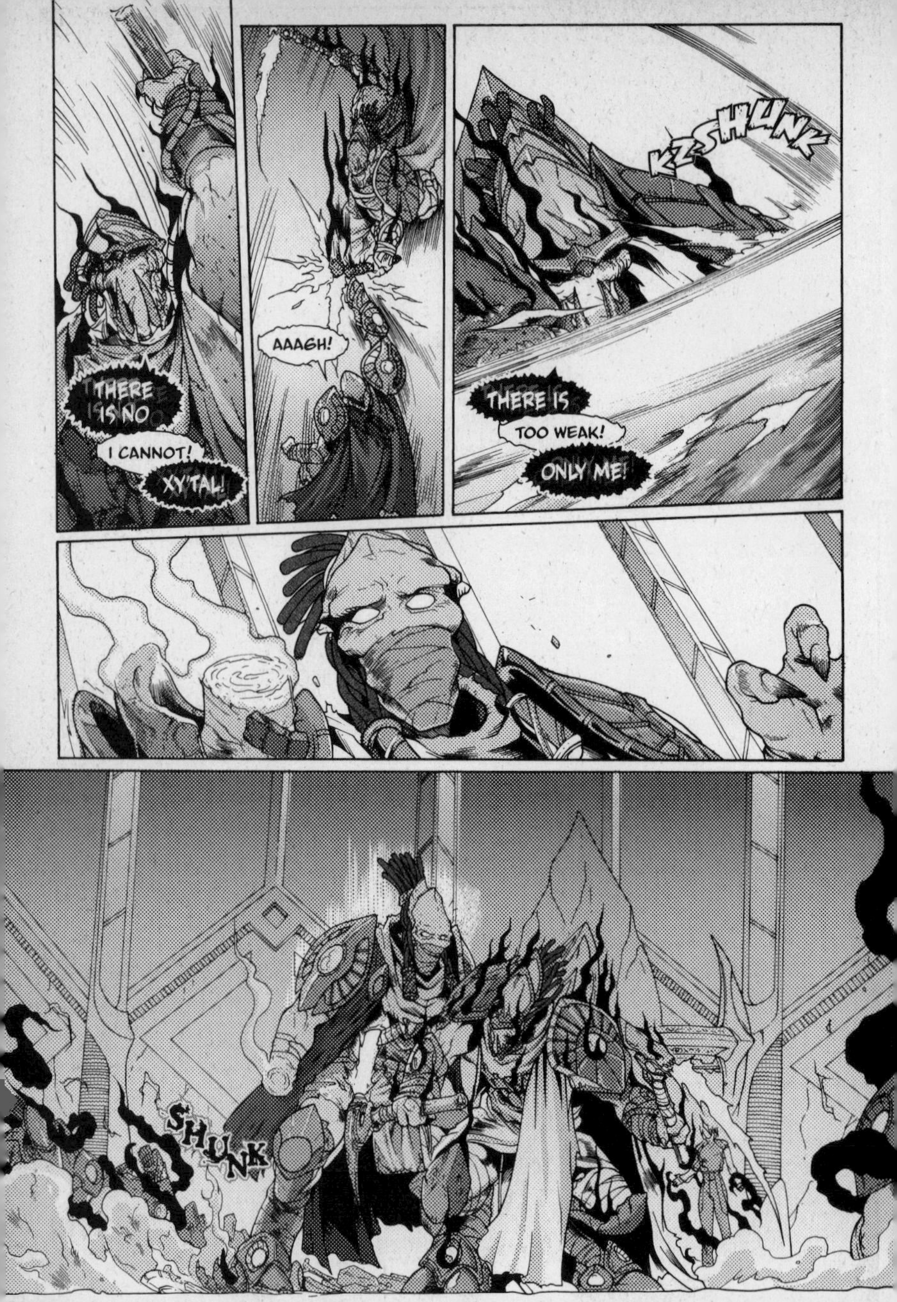
THERE IS NO
I CANNOT!
XY'TAL!
AAAGH!
KZSHUNK
THERE IS
TOO WEAK!
ONLY ME!
SHUNK

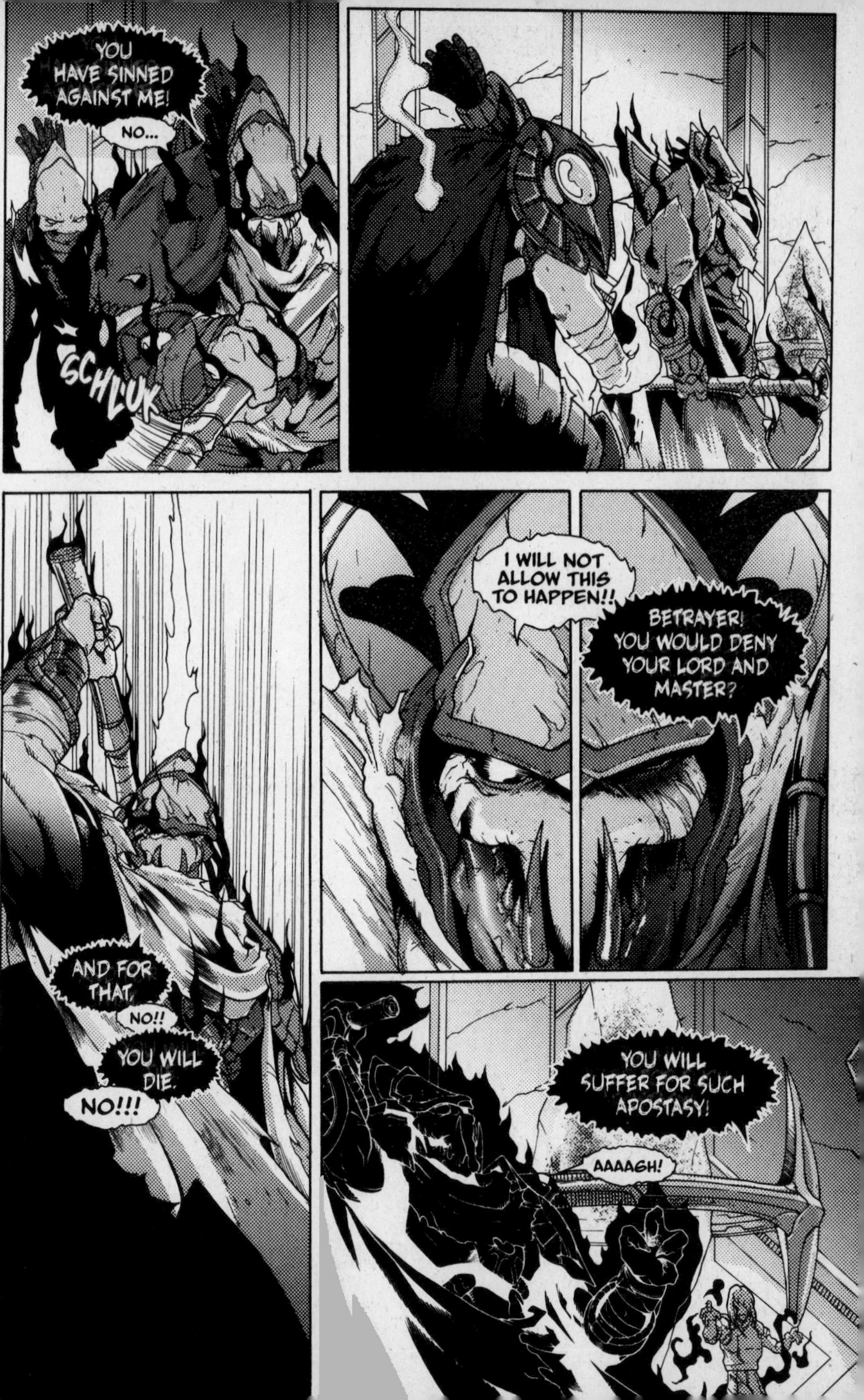
YOU HAVE SINNED AGAINST ME!
NO...
SCHLUK
I WILL NOT ALLOW THIS TO HAPPEN!!
BETRAYER! YOU WOULD DENY YOUR LORD AND MASTER?
AND FOR THAT
NO!!
YOU WILL DIE.
NO!!!
YOU WILL SUFFER FOR SUCH APOSTASY!
AAAAGH!

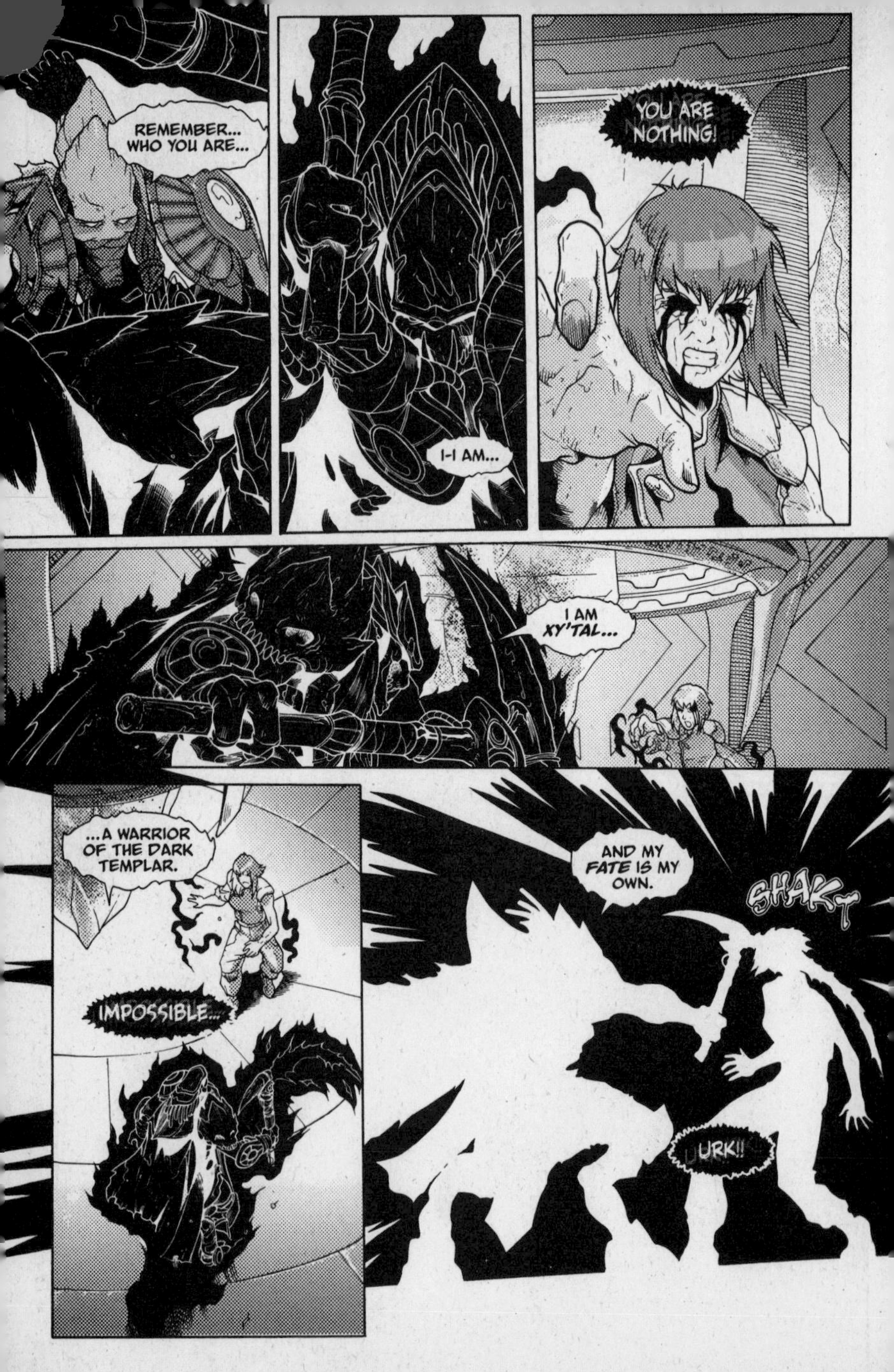
REMEMBER... WHO YOU ARE...
I-I AM...
YOU ARE NOTHING!
I AM XY'TAL...
...A WARRIOR OF THE DARK TEMPLAR.
IMPOSSIBLE...
AND MY FATE IS MY OWN.
SHAKT
URK!!

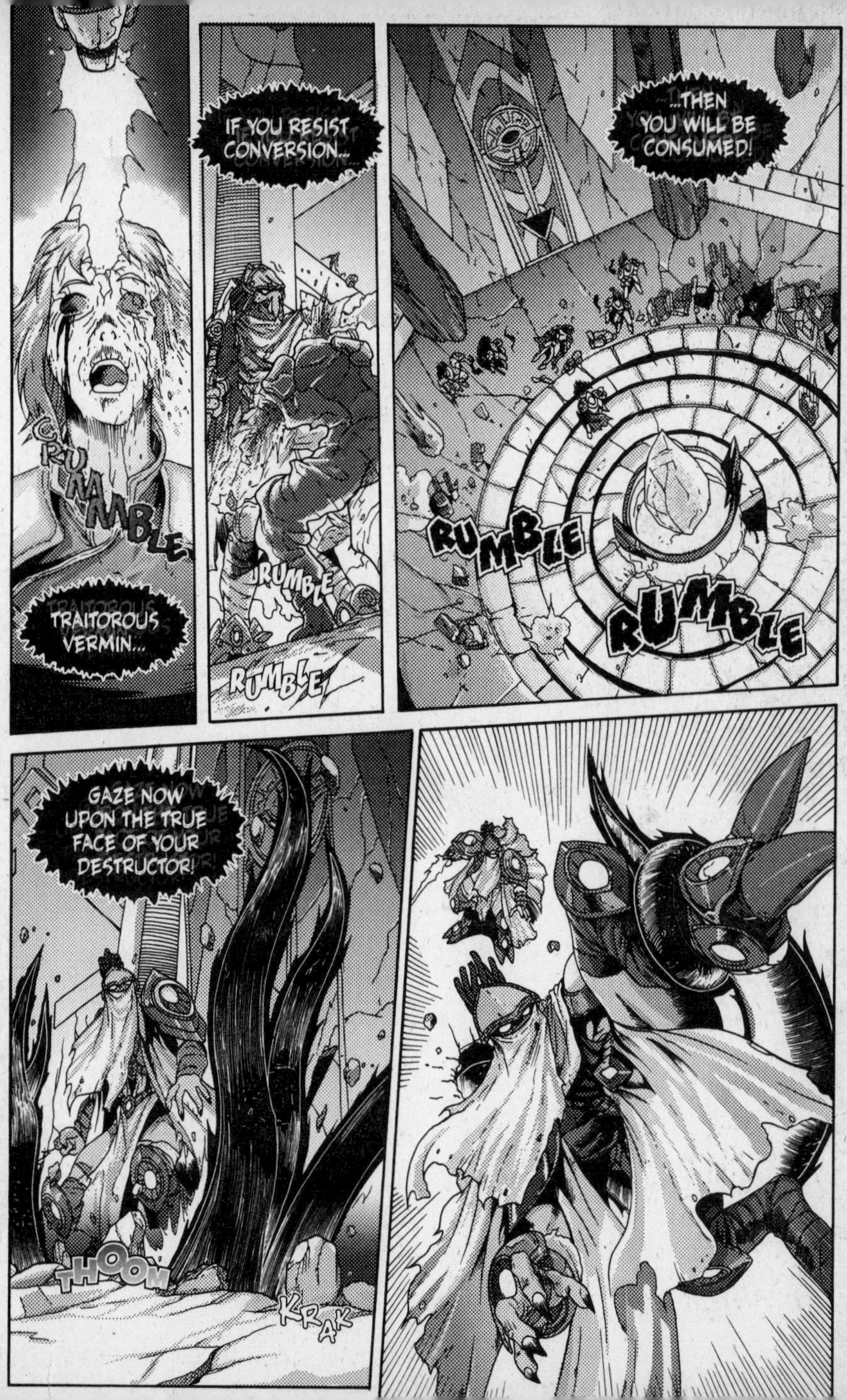
CRUMBLE
TRAITOROUS VERMIN...
IF YOU RESIST CONVERSION...
RUMBLE
RUMBLE
...THEN YOU WILL BE CONSUMED!
RUMBLE
RUMBLE
GAZE NOW UPON THE TRUE FACE OF YOUR DESTRUCTOR!
THOOM
KRAK

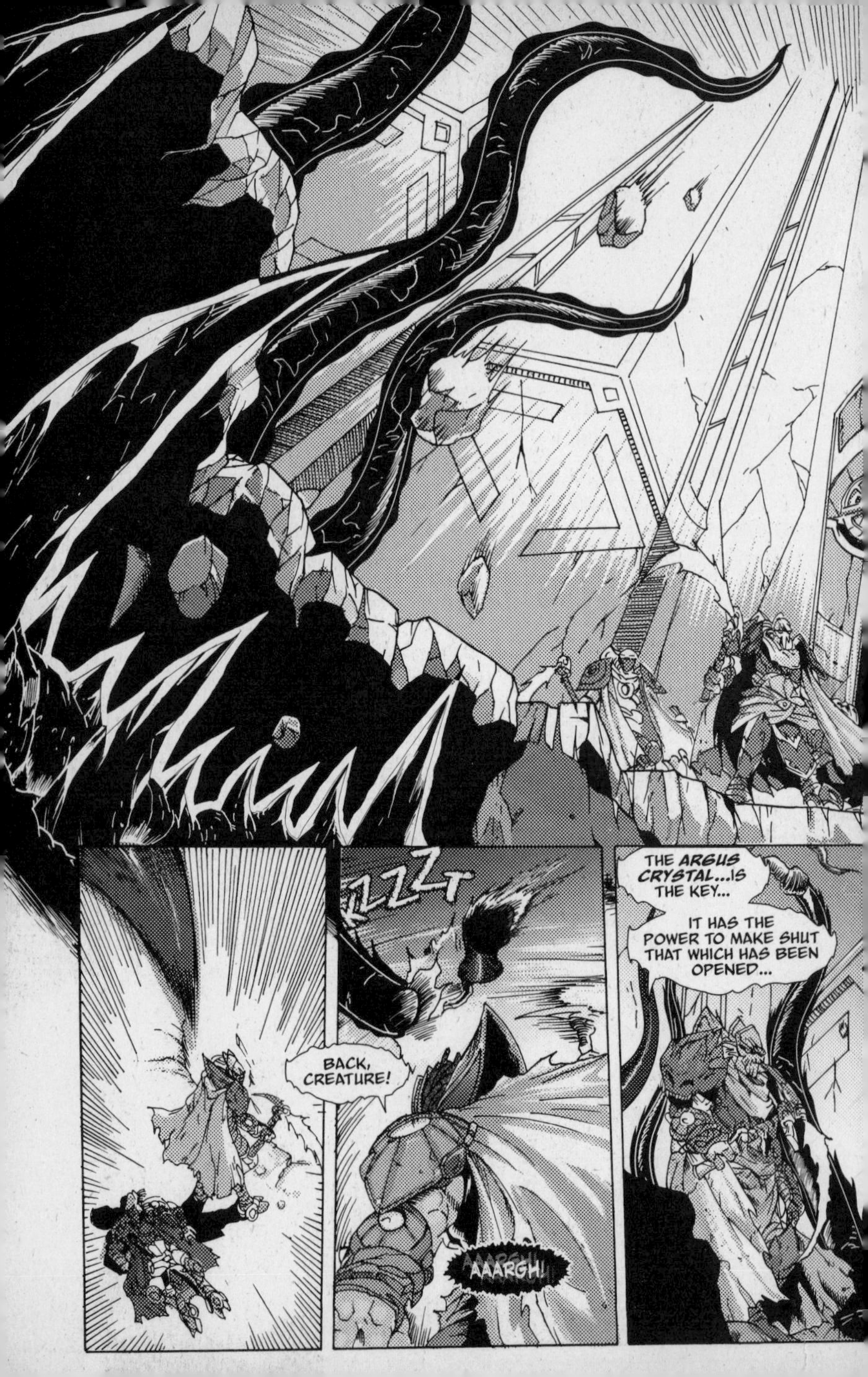
ZZZZT
BACK, CREATURE!
AAARGH!
THE ARGUS CRYSTAL...IS THE KEY...
IT HAS THE POWER TO MAKE SHUT THAT WHICH HAS BEEN OPENED...

YAAAAAAHHHH!!!
AZIMAR, I...
WHAT I HAVE DONE?
ENOUGH. THERE ARE MANY... WHO STUMBLE AND FALL...
...BUT FEW WHO FIND THE STRENGTH... TO *RISE* ONCE MORE.
GO...EARN YOUR REDEMPTION.
I WILL NOT FAIL.

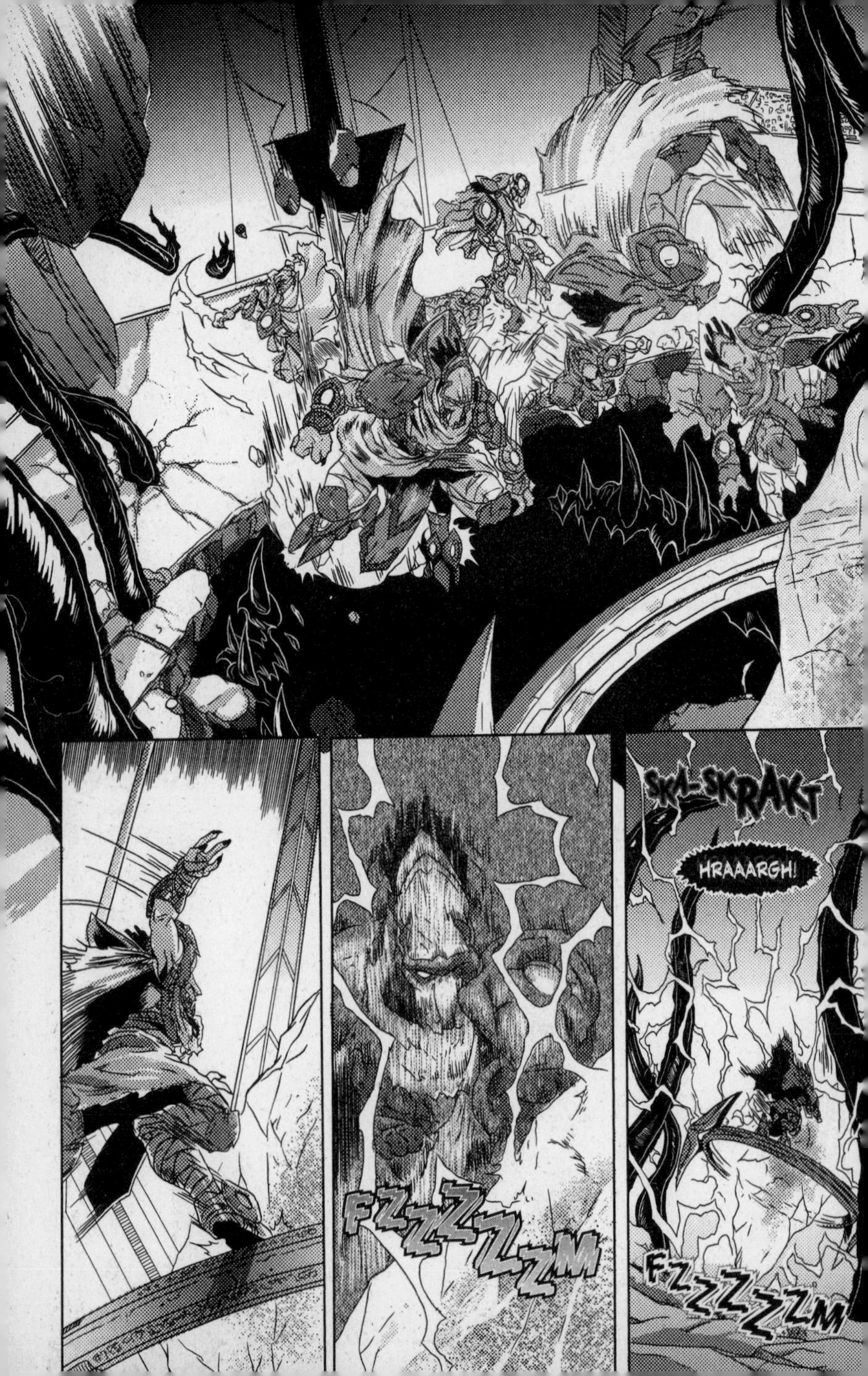
FZZZZZZZM
SKA-SKRAKT
HRAAARGH!
FZZZZZZZM

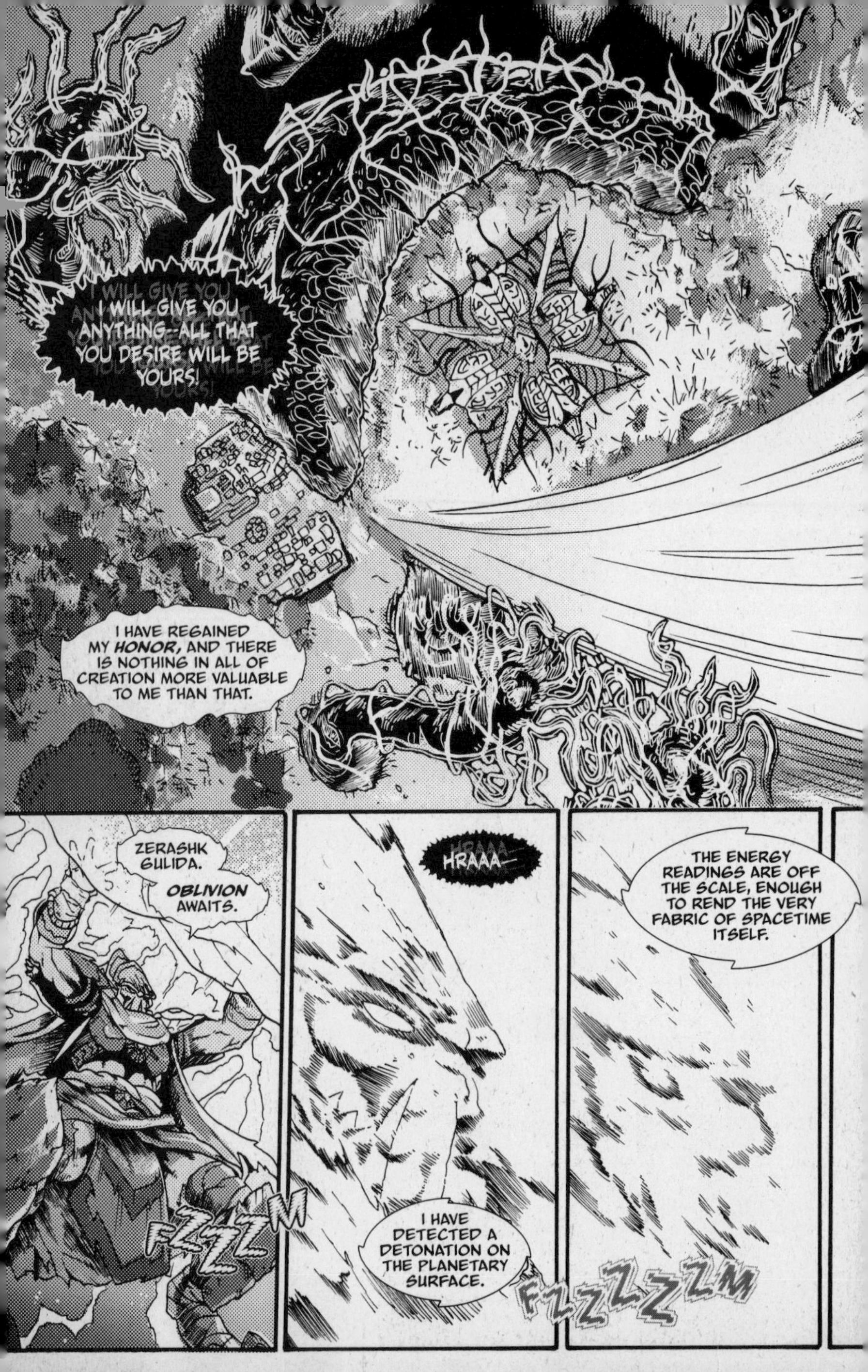
I WILL GIVE YOU ANYTHING--ALL THAT YOU DESIRE WILL BE YOURS!
I HAVE REGAINED MY **HONOR**, AND THERE IS NOTHING IN ALL OF CREATION MORE VALUABLE TO ME THAN THAT.
ZERASHK GULIDA.
**OBLIVION** AWAITS.
FZZZM
HRAAA--
I HAVE DETECTED A DETONATION ON THE PLANETARY SURFACE.
THE ENERGY READINGS ARE OFF THE SCALE, ENOUGH TO REND THE VERY FABRIC OF SPACETIME ITSELF.
FZZZZZM

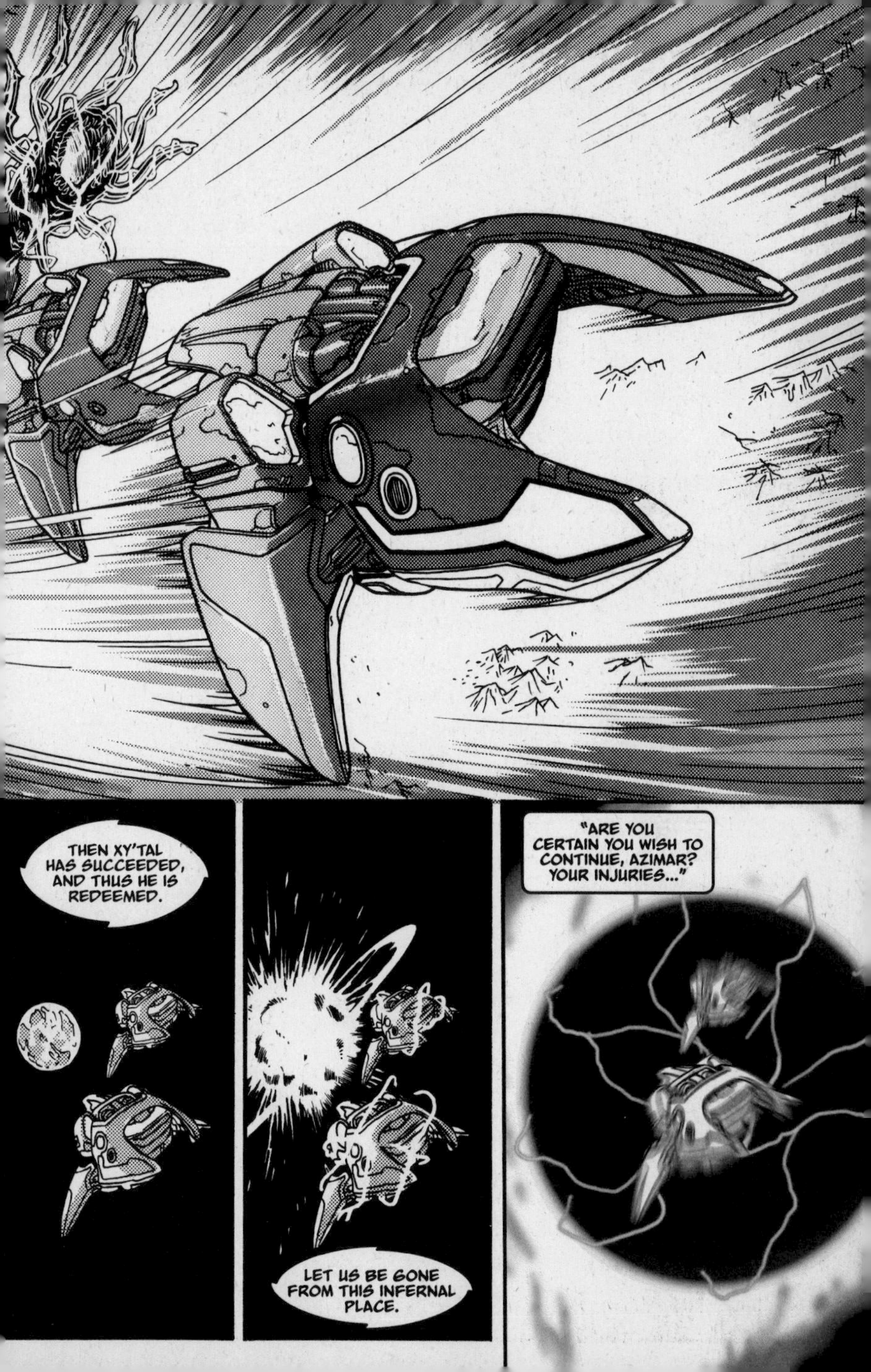
THEN XY'TAL HAS SUCCEEDED, AND THUS HE IS REDEEMED.
LET US BE GONE FROM THIS INFERNAL PLACE.
"ARE YOU CERTAIN YOU WISH TO CONTINUE, AZIMAR? YOUR INJURIES..."

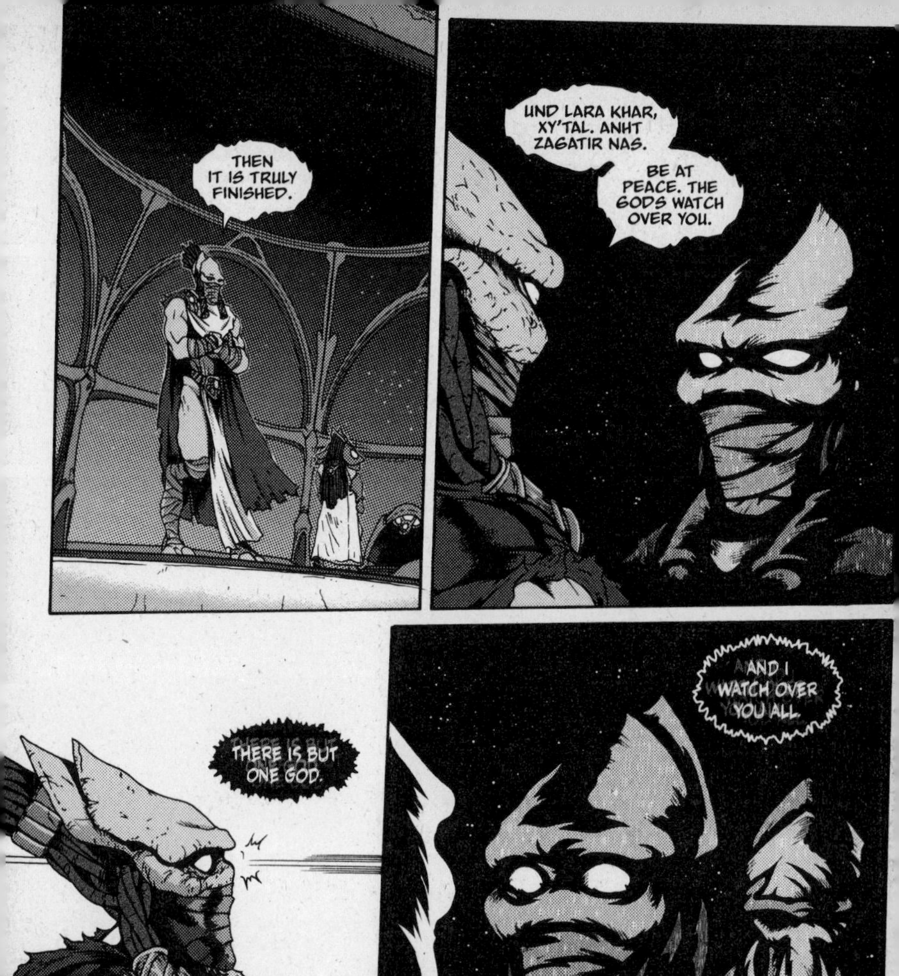
THEN IT IS TRULY FINISHED.
UND LARA KHAR, XY'TAL. ANHT ZAGATIR NAS.
BE AT PEACE. THE GODS WATCH OVER YOU.
THERE IS BUT ONE GOD.
AND I WATCH OVER YOU ALL.

# STARCRAFT

## FRONTLINE
### VOLUME 4

# ORIENTATION

Written by Paul Benjamin & Dave Shramek

Pencils by Mel joy San Juan
Inks by Noel Rodriguez, Jezreel Rojales, and Studio Sakka
Tones by Ryo Kawakami

Letterer: Michael Paolilli

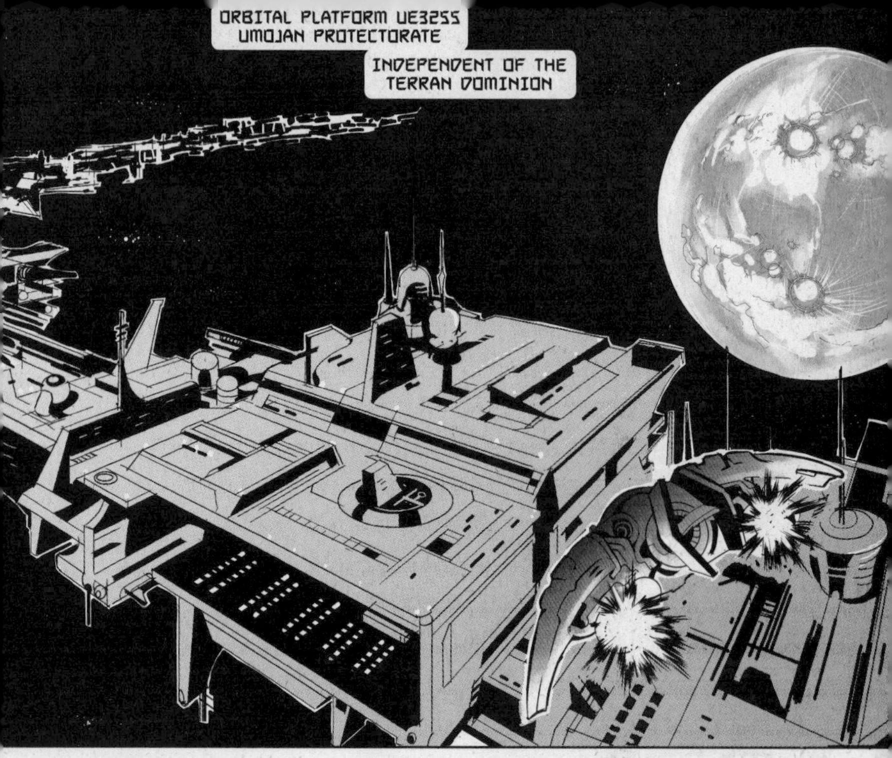
ORBITAL PLATFORM UE3255
UMOJAN PROTECTORATE
INDEPENDENT OF THE TERRAN DOMINION

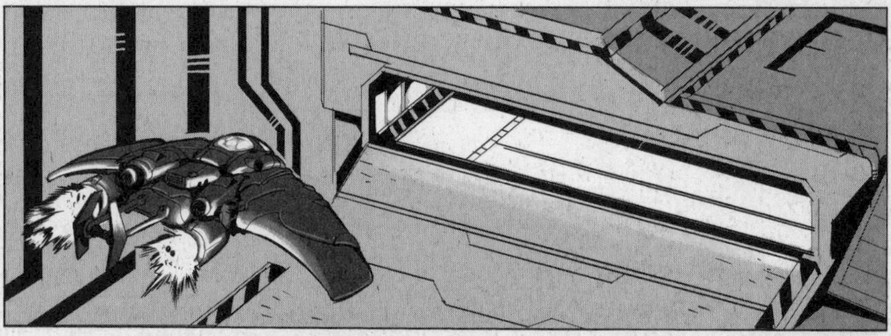

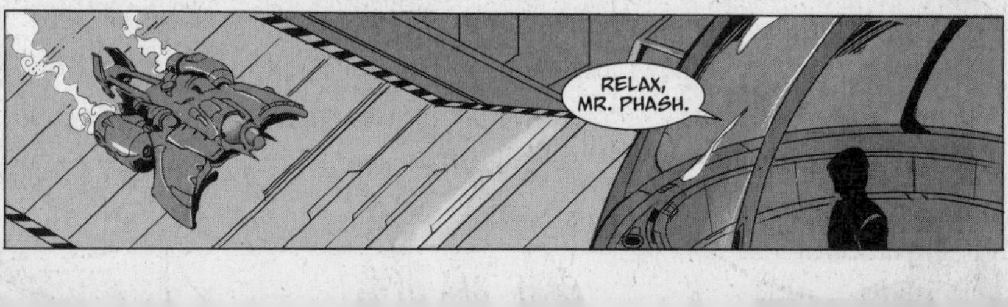
RELAX, MR. PHASH.

... SHIPPING LIVESTOCK IN CRATES?

VREENT

VERY OBSERVANT, MR. PHASH. THEY'RE PRESSURIZED IN CASE OF A HULL BREACH.

WE'VE HAD TO RESORT TO SMUGGLING FOOD TO OUR OWN PEOPLE.

BECAUSE OF MENGSK'S TARIFF INCREASES.

EXACTLY. RUNNING FOOD PAST PATROLS AND BLOCKADES HAS ALLOWED US TO WITHSTAND THE DOMINION'S ECONOMIC SANCTIONS.

GRANTING ME ASYLUM WILL CERTAINLY GET MENGSK'S ATTENTION FOR YOUR NEGOTIATIONS.

LOOK AT THAT! SCVs HAVE CERTAINLY IMPROVED THEIR MOTIVATORS.

A LOT SMOOTHER RIDE THAN THE ONES I DROVE IN MY OLD PROSPECTING DAYS.

I HAD NO IDEA YOU'D BEEN A LABORER, MR. PHASH...

I'M FULL OF SURPRISES.

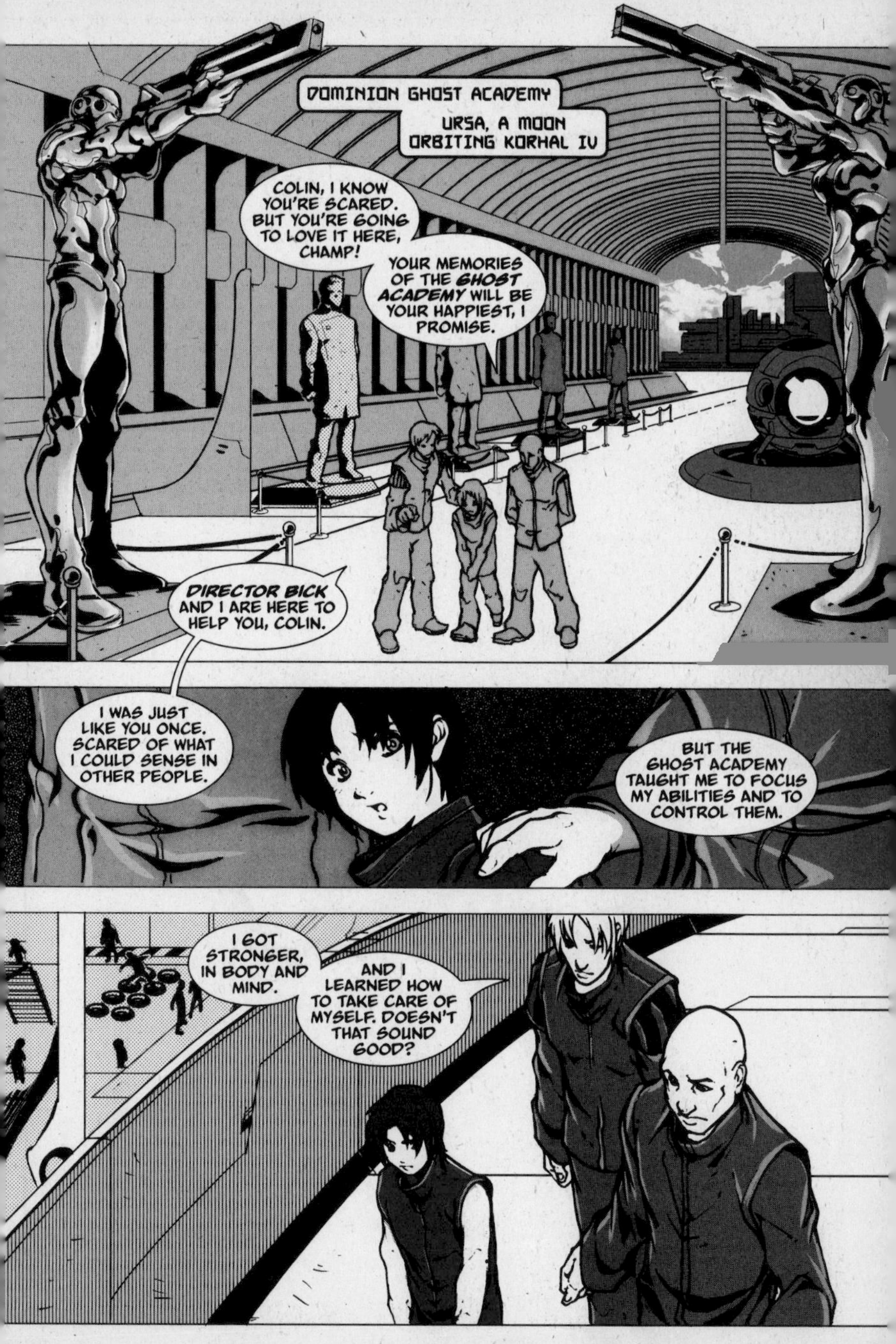
DOMINION GHOST ACADEMY
URSA, A MOON ORBITING KORHAL IV
COLIN, I KNOW YOU'RE SCARED. BUT YOU'RE GOING TO LOVE IT HERE, CHAMP!
YOUR MEMORIES OF THE *GHOST ACADEMY* WILL BE YOUR HAPPIEST, I PROMISE.
*DIRECTOR BICK* AND I ARE HERE TO HELP YOU, COLIN.
I WAS JUST LIKE YOU ONCE. SCARED OF WHAT I COULD SENSE IN OTHER PEOPLE.
BUT THE GHOST ACADEMY TAUGHT ME TO FOCUS MY ABILITIES AND TO CONTROL THEM.
I GOT STRONGER, IN BODY AND MIND.
AND I LEARNED HOW TO TAKE CARE OF MYSELF. DOESN'T THAT SOUND GOOD?

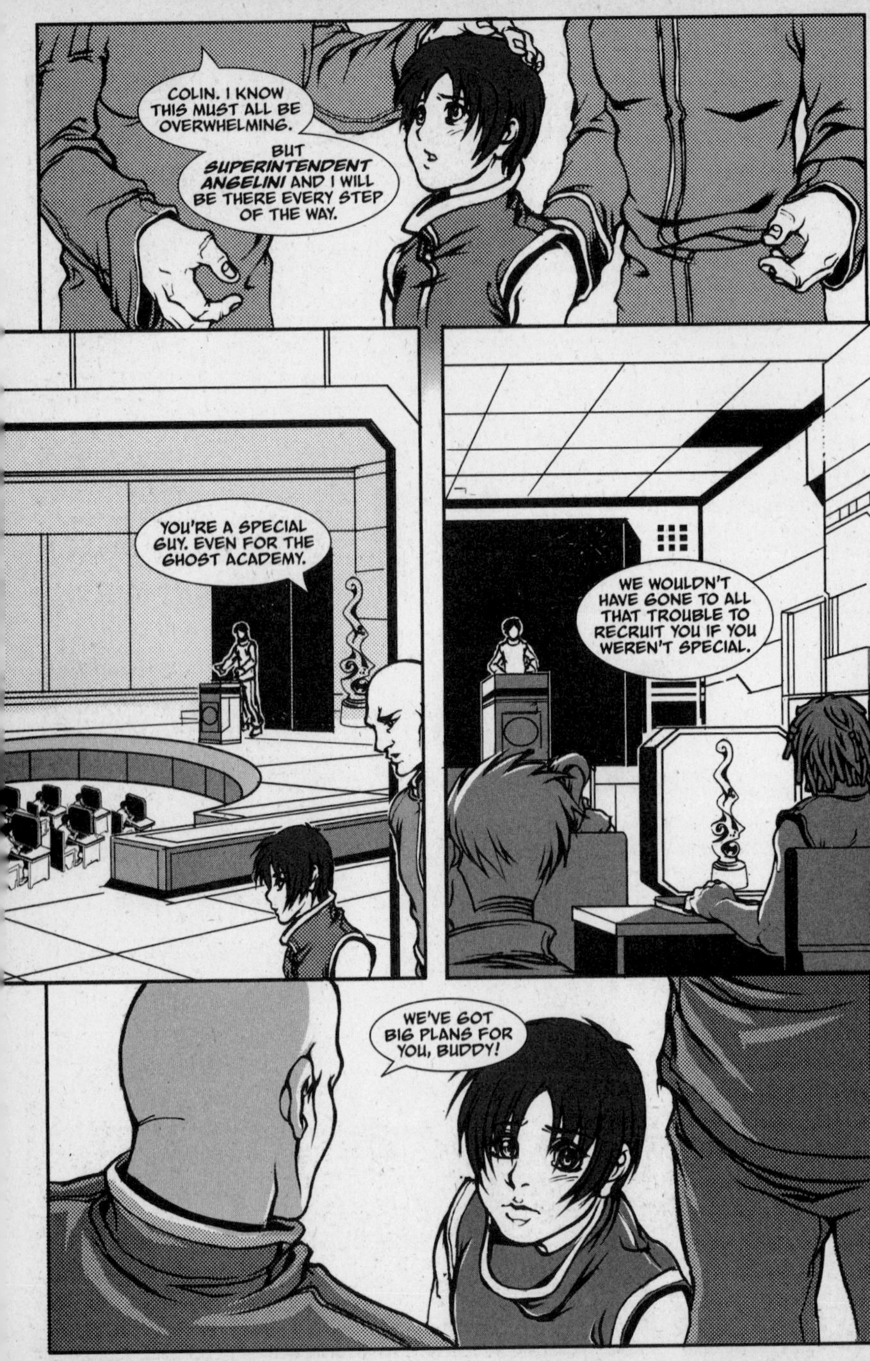
COLIN. I KNOW THIS MUST ALL BE OVERWHELMING.
BUT *SUPERINTENDENT ANGELINI* AND I WILL BE THERE EVERY STEP OF THE WAY.
YOU'RE A SPECIAL GUY. EVEN FOR THE GHOST ACADEMY.
WE WOULDN'T HAVE GONE TO ALL THAT TROUBLE TO RECRUIT YOU IF YOU WEREN'T SPECIAL.
WE'VE GOT BIG PLANS FOR YOU, BUDDY!

THIS WILL GIVE YOU A TASTE OF WHAT BEING A GHOST IS, COLIN.

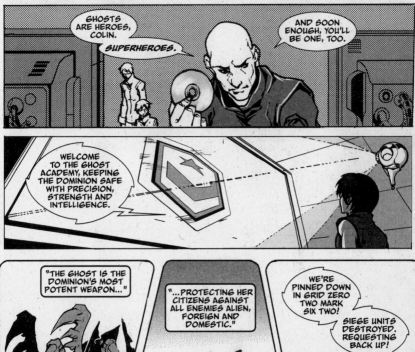

GHOSTS ARE HEROES, COLIN.

SUPERHEROES.

AND SOON ENOUGH, YOU'LL BE ONE, TOO.

WELCOME TO THE GHOST ACADEMY, KEEPING THE DOMINION SAFE WITH PRECISION, STRENGTH AND INTELLIGENCE.

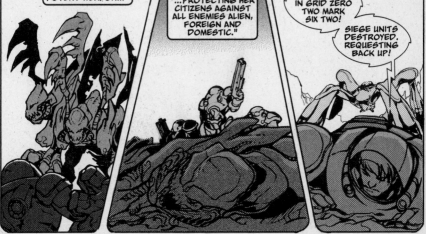

"THE GHOST IS THE DOMINION'S MOST POTENT WEAPON..."

"...PROTECTING HER CITIZENS AGAINST ALL ENEMIES ALIEN, FOREIGN AND DOMESTIC."

WE'RE PINNED DOWN IN GRID ZERO TWO MARK SIX TWO!

SIEGE UNITS DESTROYED. REQUESTING BACK UP!

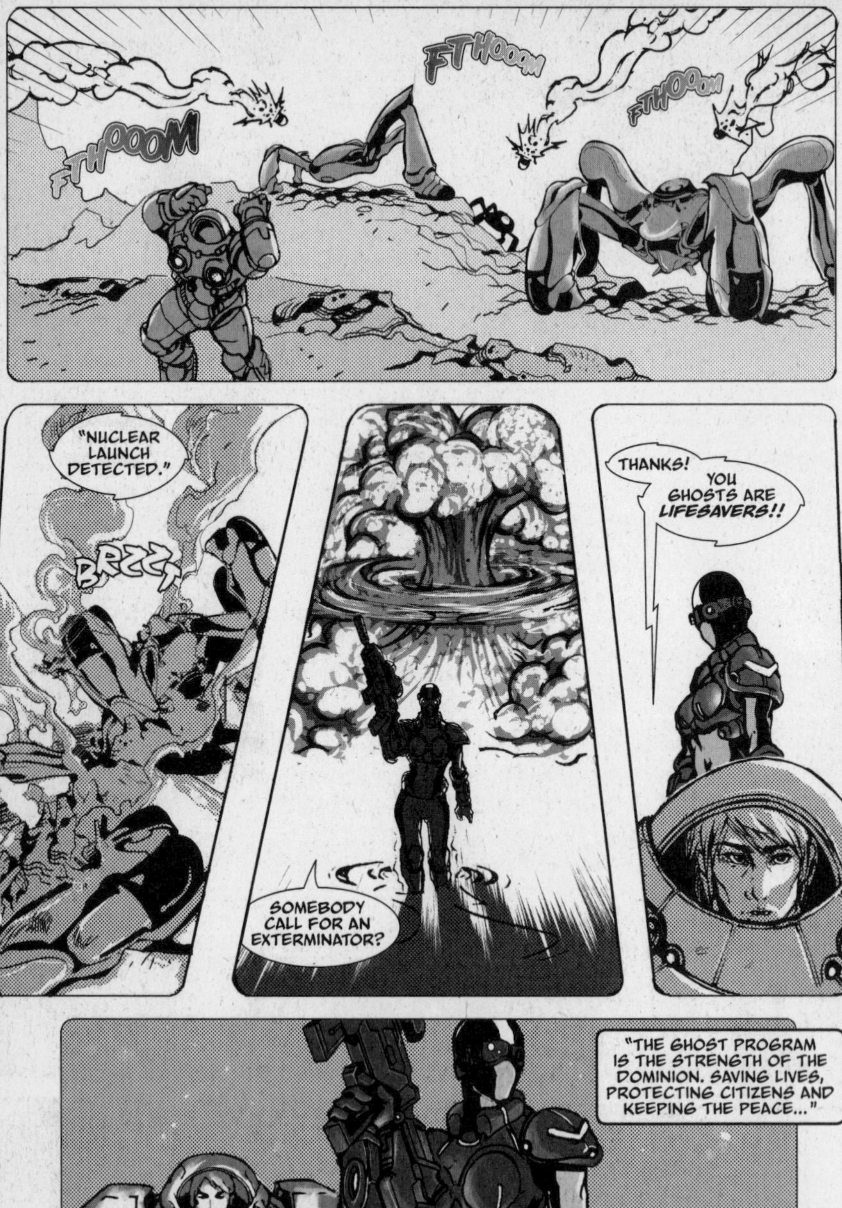
FTHOOOM
FTHOOOM
FTHOOOM
"NUCLEAR LAUNCH DETECTED."
BRZZT
SOMEBODY CALL FOR AN EXTERMINATOR?
THANKS!
YOU GHOSTS ARE *LIFESAVERS!!*
"THE GHOST PROGRAM IS THE STRENGTH OF THE DOMINION. SAVING LIVES, PROTECTING CITIZENS AND KEEPING THE PEACE..."

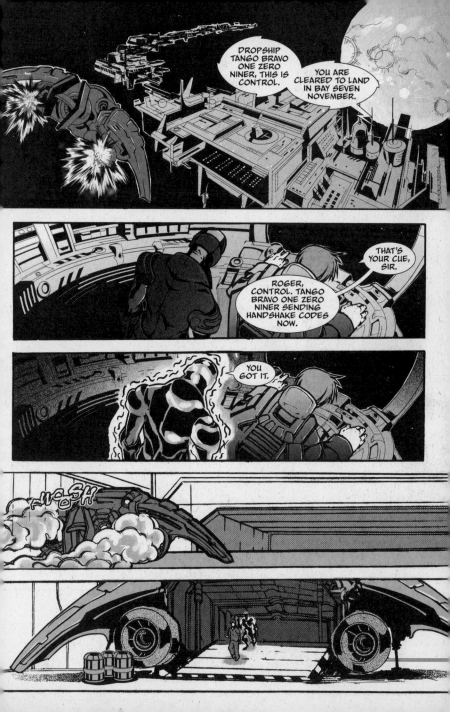

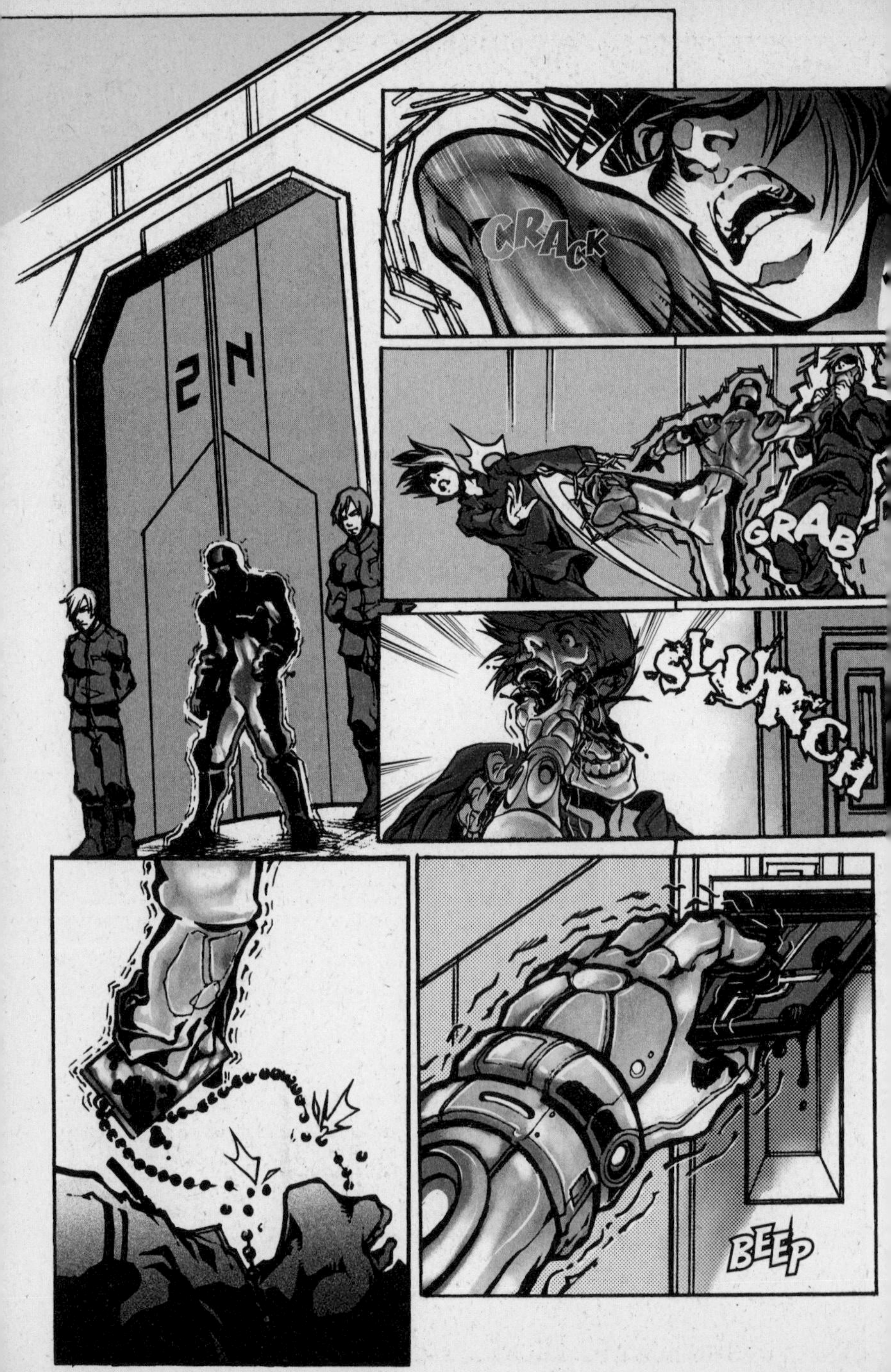
CRACK
GRAB
SLURCH
BEEP

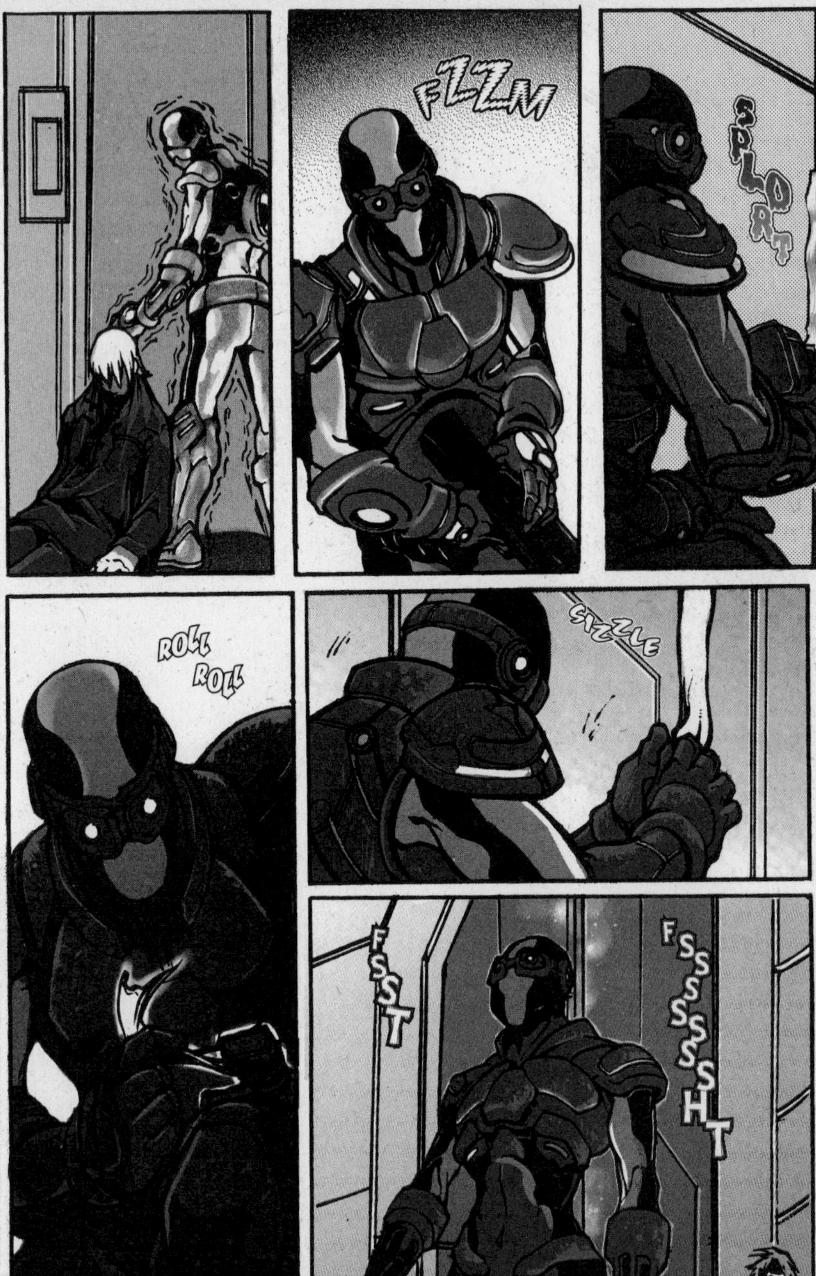
FZZM
SPLORT
ROLL ROLL
SIZZLE
FSST
FSSSSSSHT

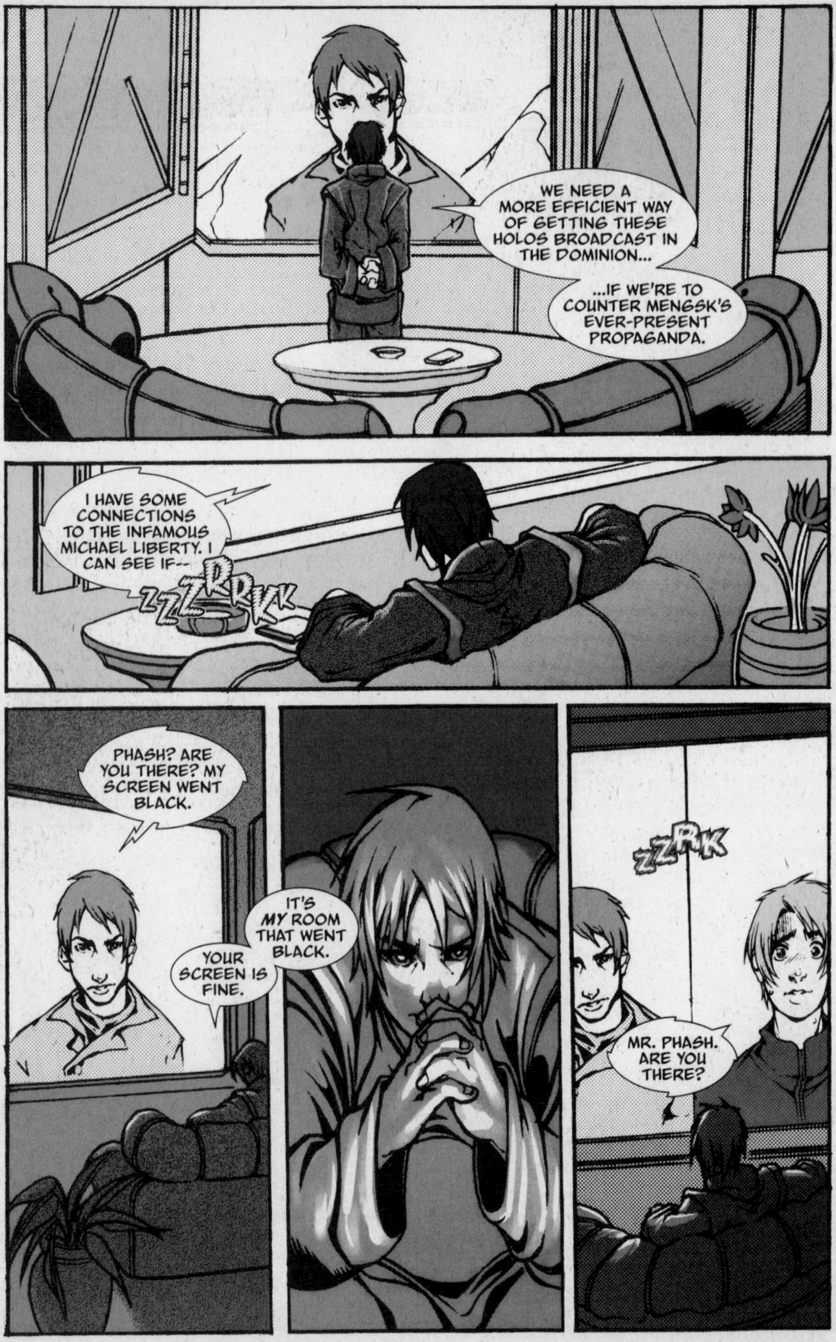
WE NEED A MORE EFFICIENT WAY OF GETTING THESE HOLOS BROADCAST IN THE DOMINION...
...IF WE'RE TO COUNTER MENGSK'S EVER-PRESENT PROPAGANDA.
I HAVE SOME CONNECTIONS TO THE INFAMOUS MICHAEL LIBERTY. I CAN SEE IF--
ZZZRRVK
PHASH? ARE YOU THERE? MY SCREEN WENT BLACK.
YOUR SCREEN IS FINE.
IT'S *MY* ROOM THAT WENT BLACK.
ZZRK
MR. PHASH. ARE YOU THERE?

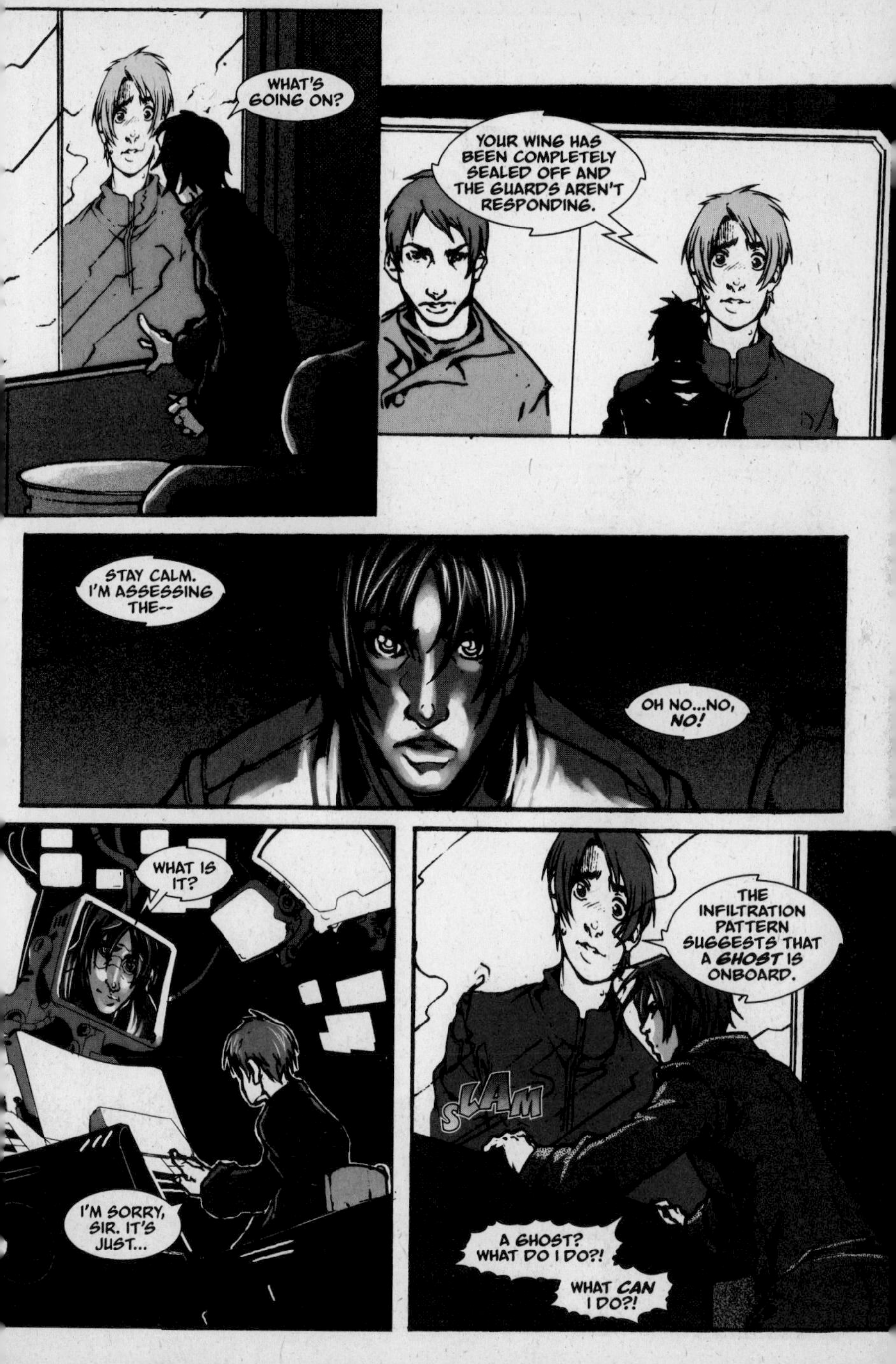
WHAT'S GOING ON?
YOUR WING HAS BEEN COMPLETELY SEALED OFF AND THE GUARDS AREN'T RESPONDING.
STAY CALM. I'M ASSESSING THE--
OH NO...NO, NO!
WHAT IS IT?
I'M SORRY, SIR. IT'S JUST...
THE INFILTRATION PATTERN SUGGESTS THAT A GHOST IS ONBOARD.
SLAM
A GHOST? WHAT DO I DO?!
WHAT CAN I DO?!

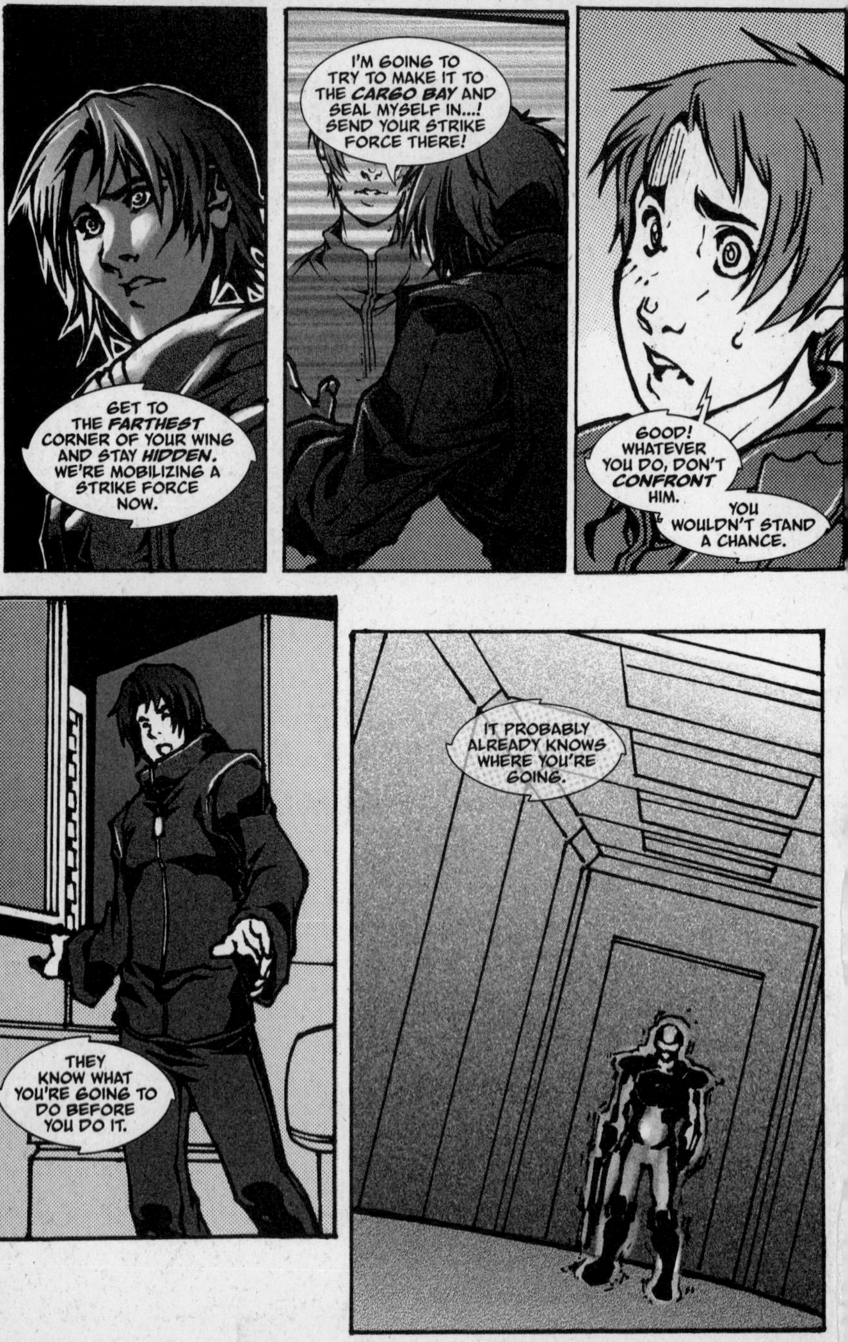
GET TO THE *FARTHEST* CORNER OF YOUR WING AND STAY *HIDDEN*. WE'RE MOBILIZING A STRIKE FORCE NOW.
I'M GOING TO TRY TO MAKE IT TO THE *CARGO BAY* AND SEAL MYSELF IN...! SEND YOUR STRIKE FORCE THERE!
GOOD! WHATEVER YOU DO, DON'T *CONFRONT* HIM.
YOU WOULDN'T STAND A CHANCE.
THEY KNOW WHAT YOU'RE GOING TO DO BEFORE YOU DO IT.
IT PROBABLY ALREADY KNOWS WHERE YOU'RE GOING.

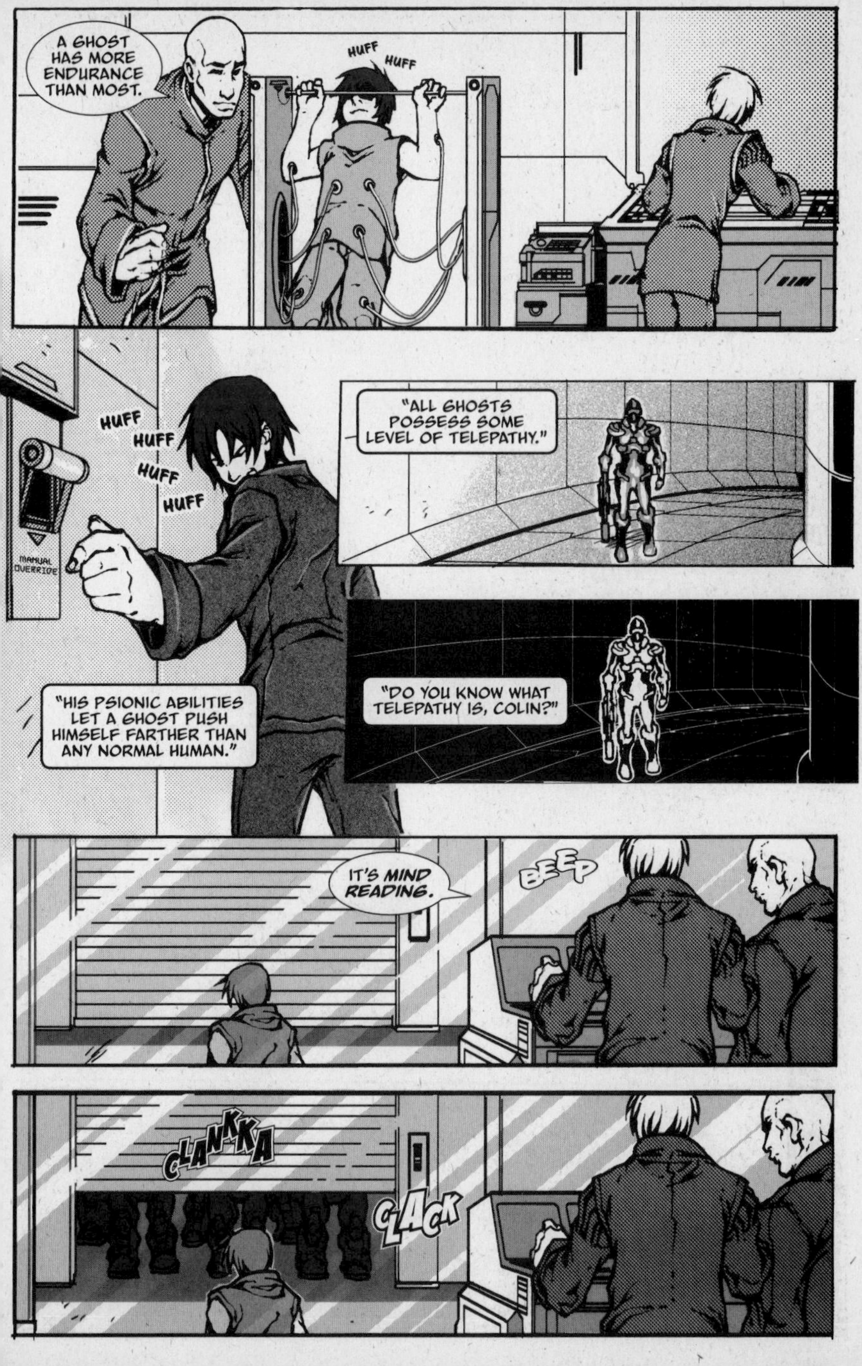
A GHOST HAS MORE ENDURANCE THAN MOST.
HUFF
HUFF
HUFF
HUFF
HUFF
HUFF
MANUAL OVERRIDE
"HIS PSIONIC ABILITIES LET A GHOST PUSH HIMSELF FARTHER THAN ANY NORMAL HUMAN."
"ALL GHOSTS POSSESS SOME LEVEL OF TELEPATHY."
"DO YOU KNOW WHAT TELEPATHY IS, COLIN?"
IT'S MIND READING.
BEEP
CLANKKA
CLACK

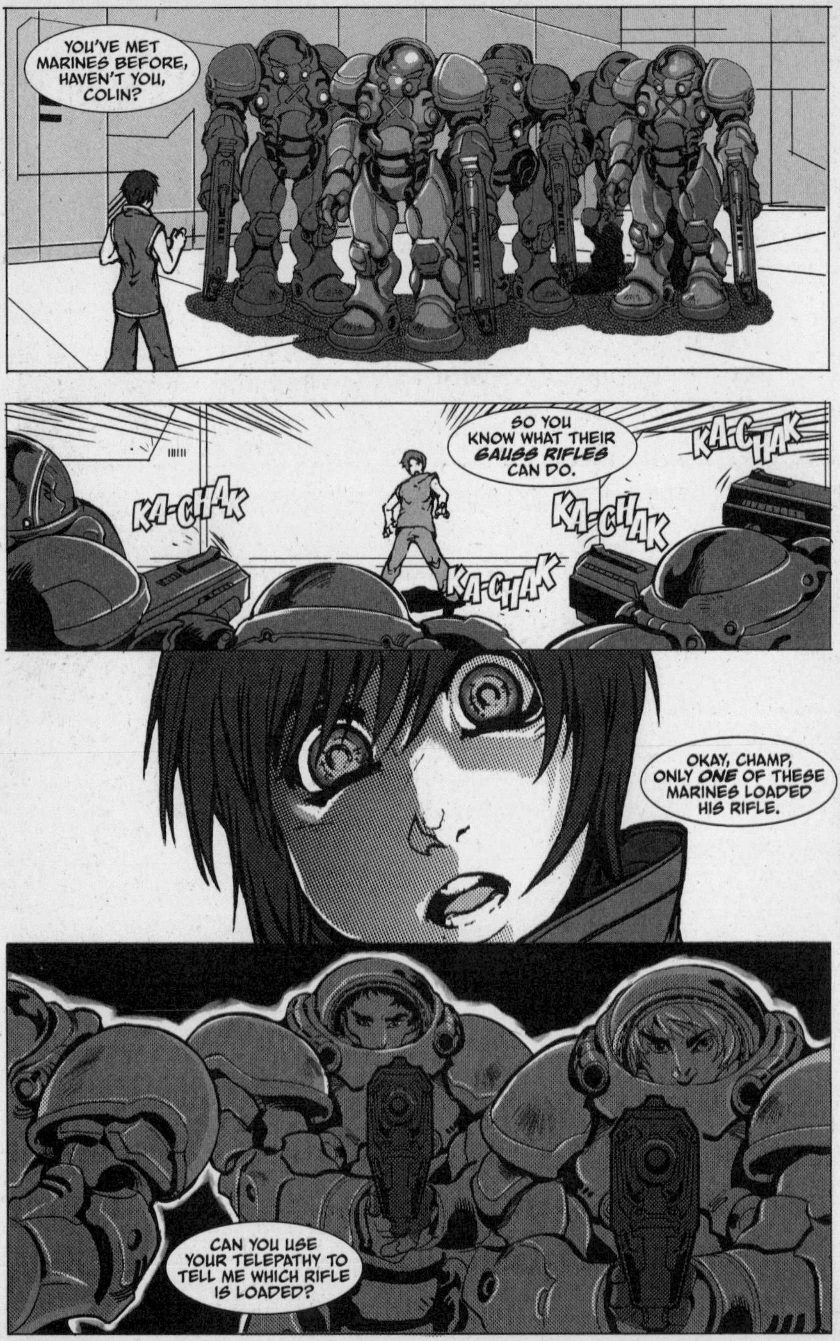
YOU'VE MET MARINES BEFORE, HAVEN'T YOU, COLIN?
SO YOU KNOW WHAT THEIR *GAUSS RIFLES* CAN DO.
KA-CHAK
KA-CHAK
KA-CHAK
KA-CHAK
OKAY, CHAMP, ONLY *ONE* OF THESE MARINES LOADED HIS RIFLE.
CAN YOU USE YOUR TELEPATHY TO TELL ME WHICH RIFLE IS LOADED?

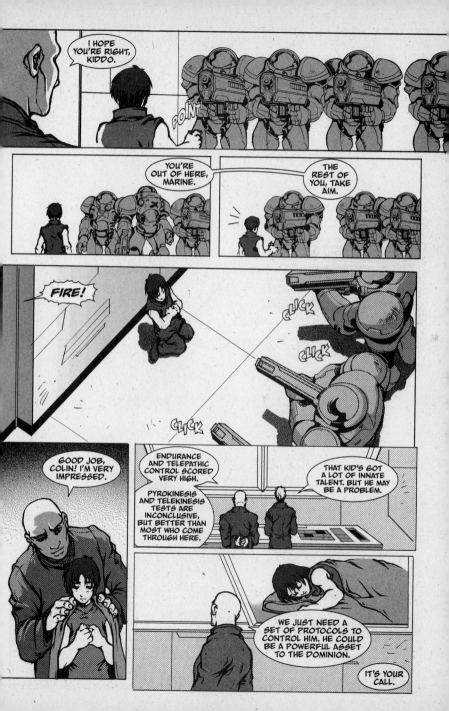

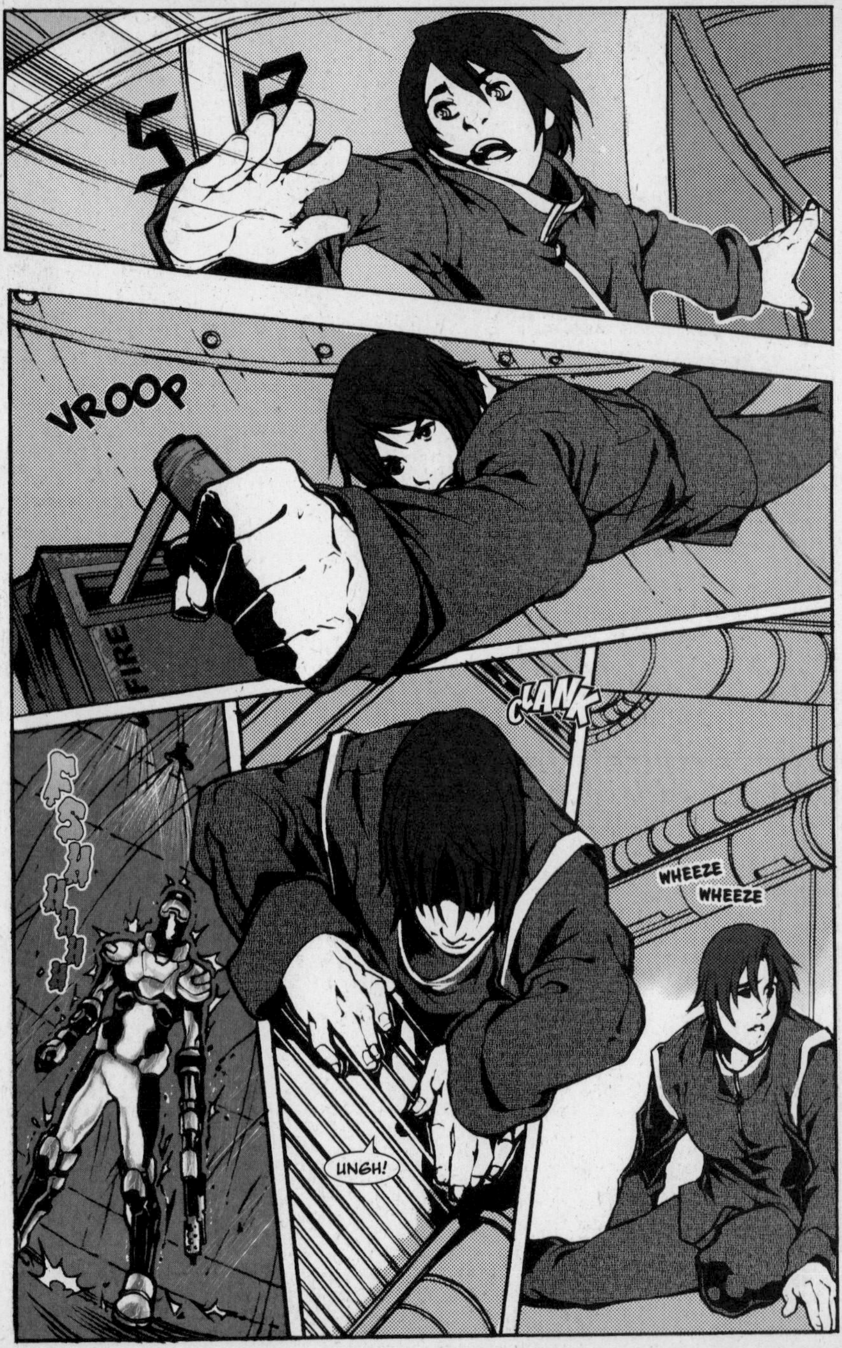
VROOP
FIRE
CLANK
WHEEZE
WHEEZE
UNGH!

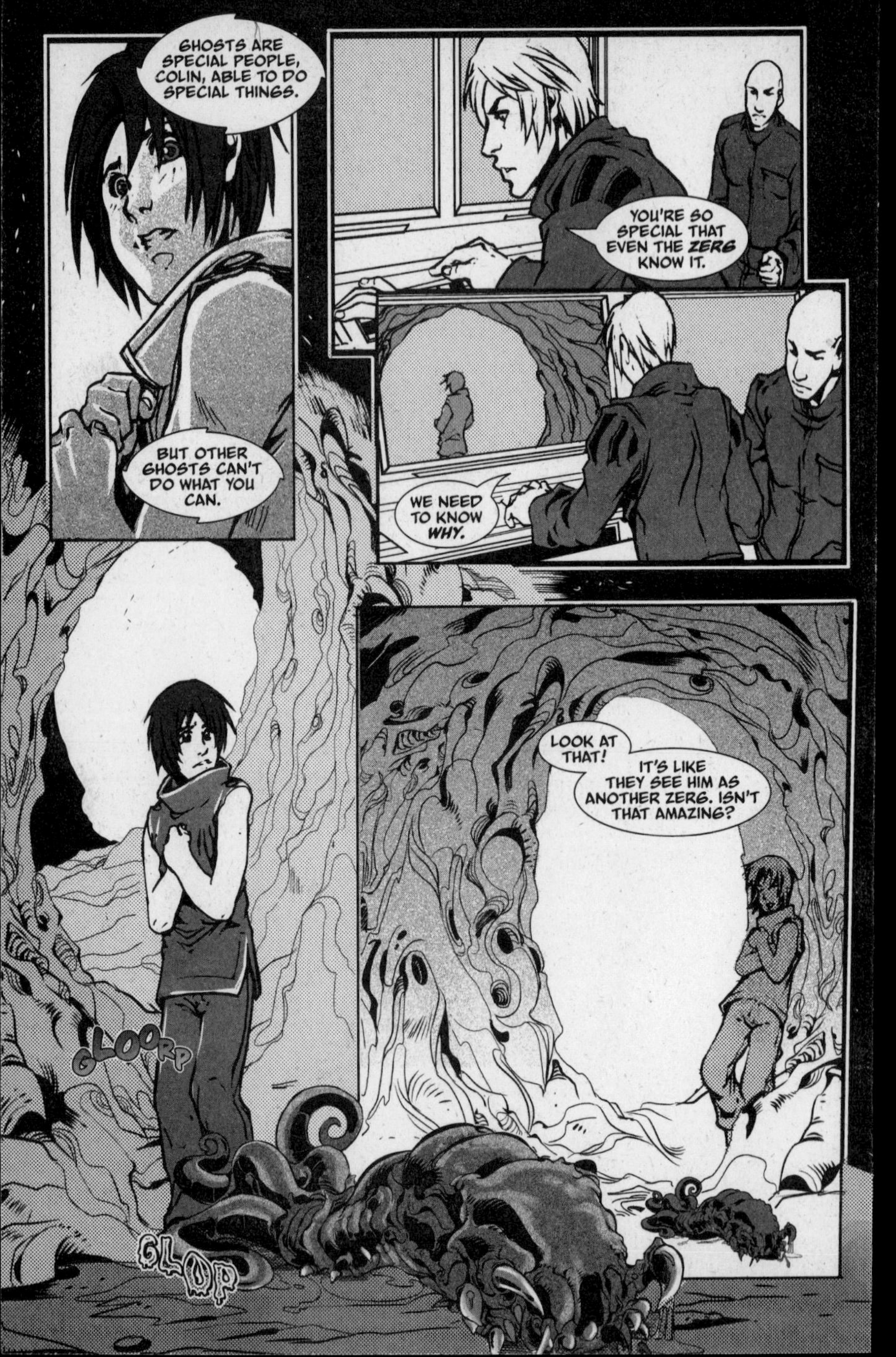
GHOSTS ARE SPECIAL PEOPLE, COLIN, ABLE TO DO SPECIAL THINGS.
BUT OTHER GHOSTS CAN'T DO WHAT YOU CAN.
YOU'RE SO SPECIAL THAT EVEN THE *ZERG* KNOW IT.
WE NEED TO KNOW *WHY.*
GLOORP
GLOP
LOOK AT THAT!
IT'S LIKE THEY SEE HIM AS ANOTHER ZERG. ISN'T THAT AMAZING?

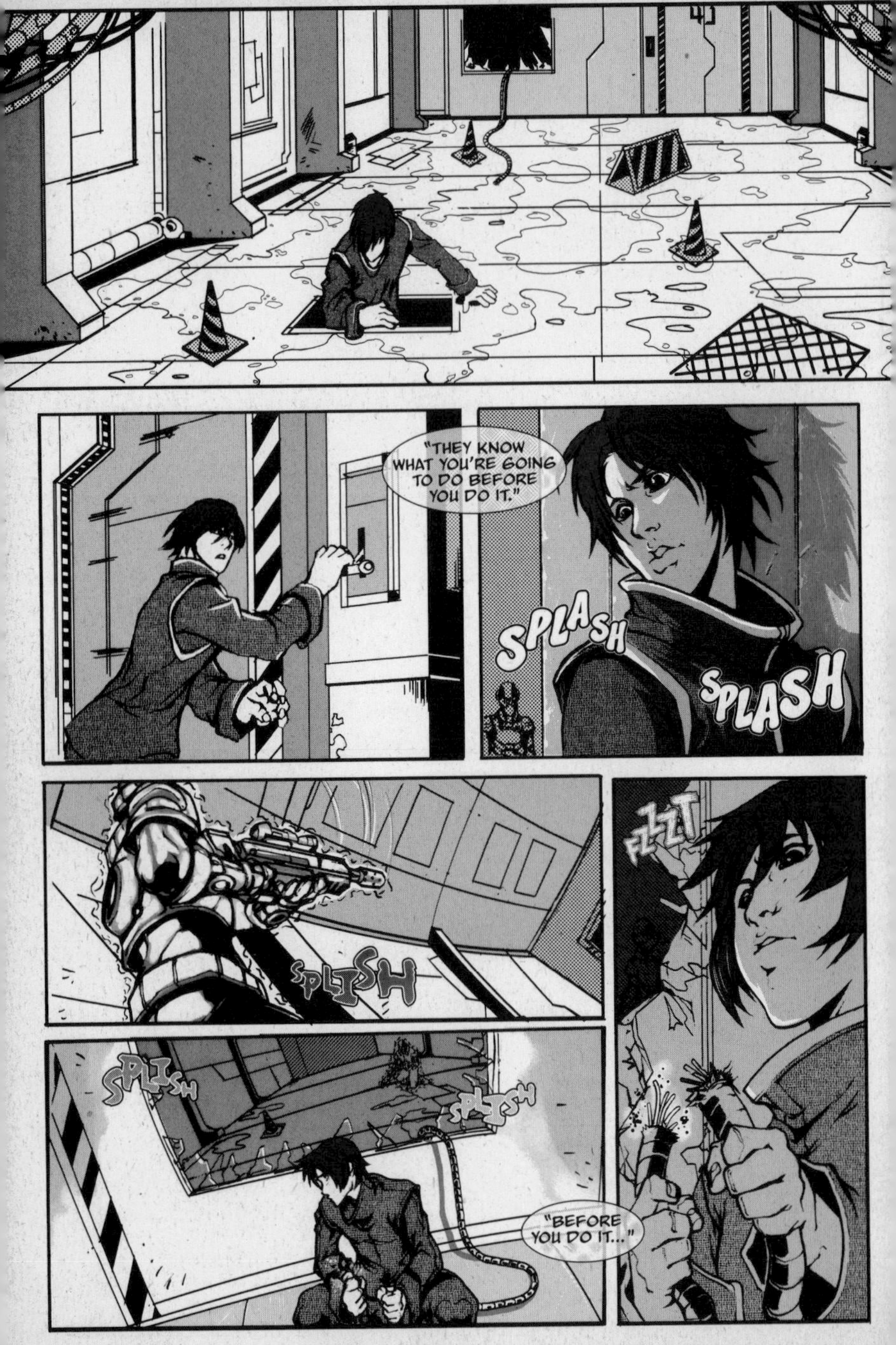
"THEY KNOW WHAT YOU'RE GOING TO DO BEFORE YOU DO IT."
SPLASH
SPLASH
SPLISH
FZZZT
SPLISH
SPLISH
"BEFORE YOU DO IT..."

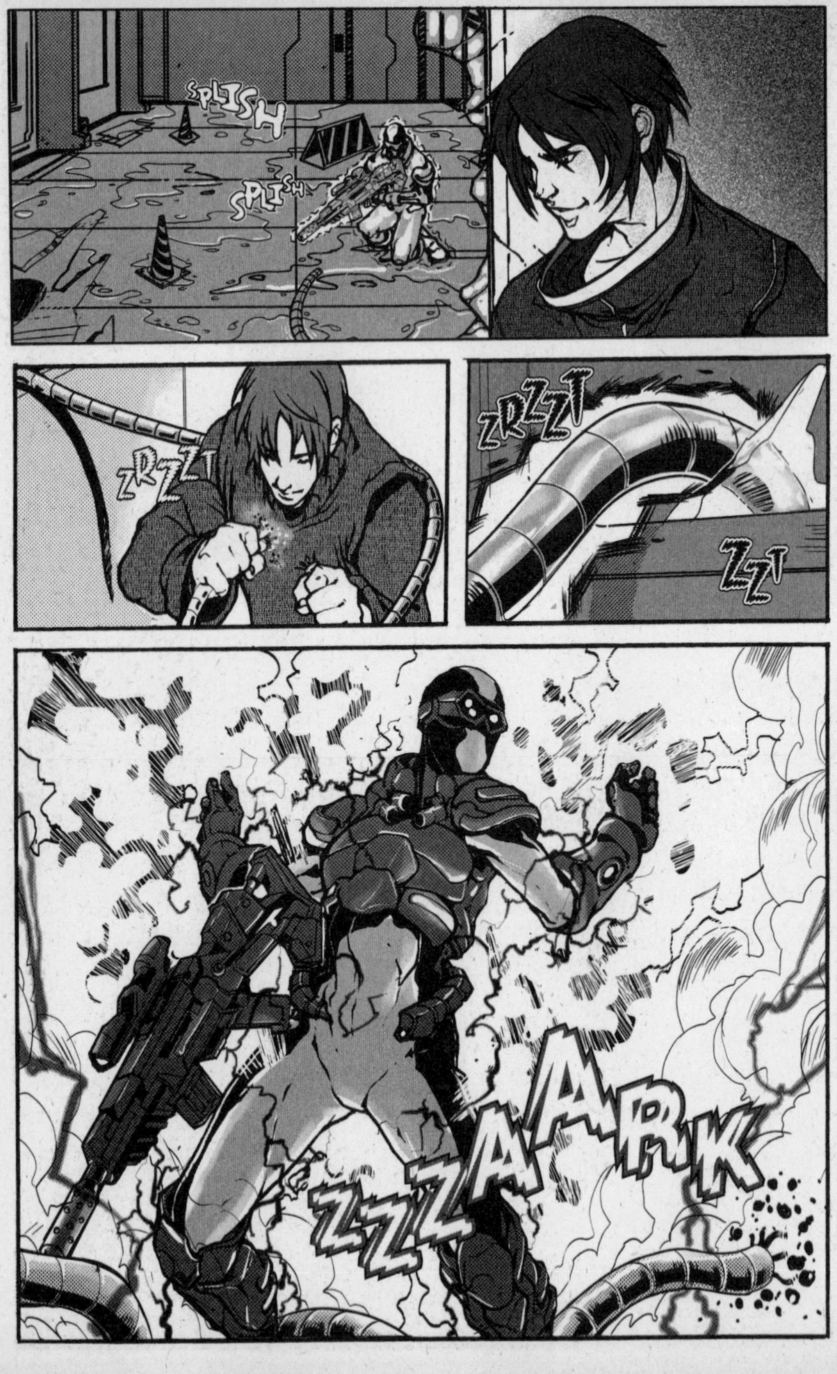
SPLISH
SPLISH
ZRZZT
ZZT
ZRZZT
ZZZAARK

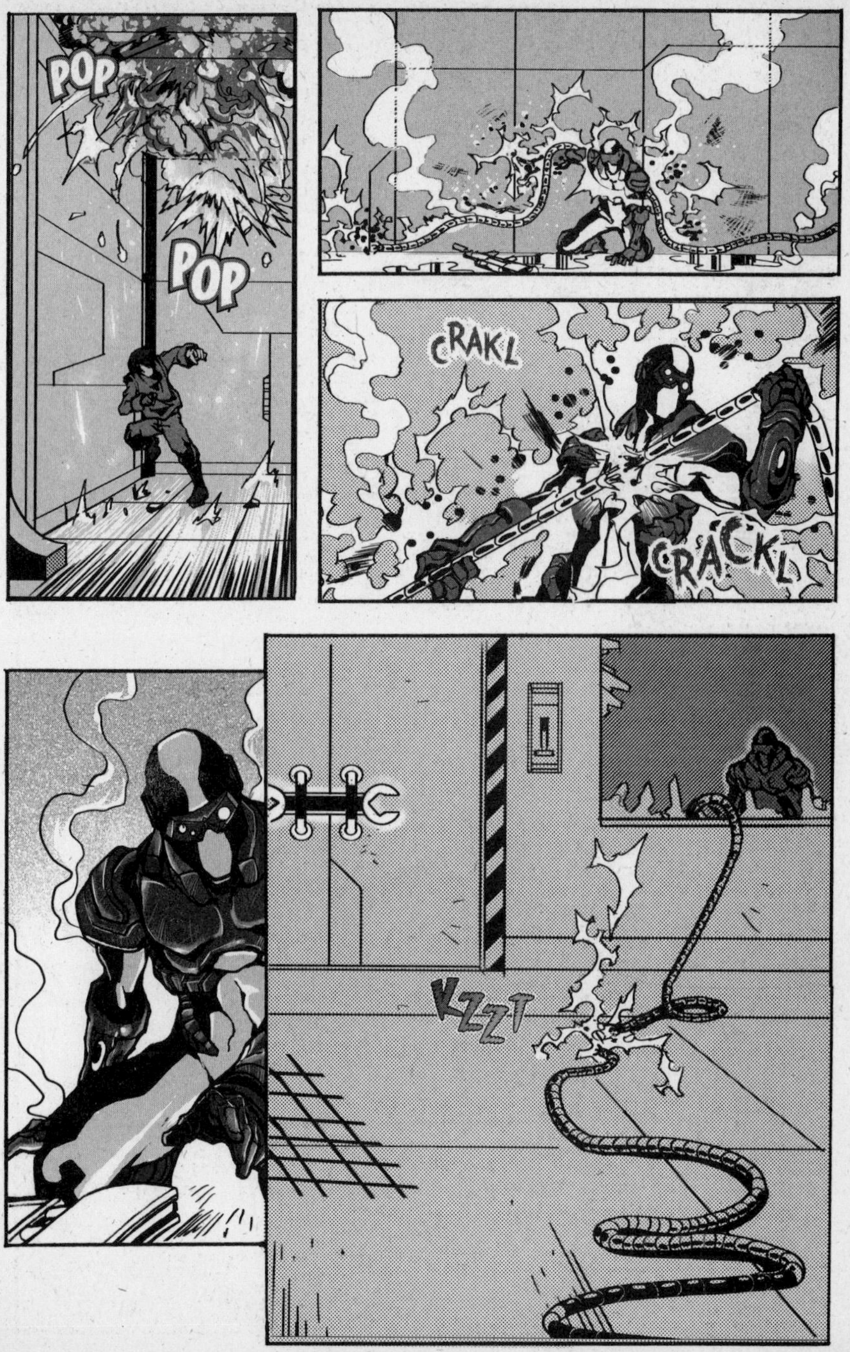
POP
POP
CRAKL
CRACKL
KZZT

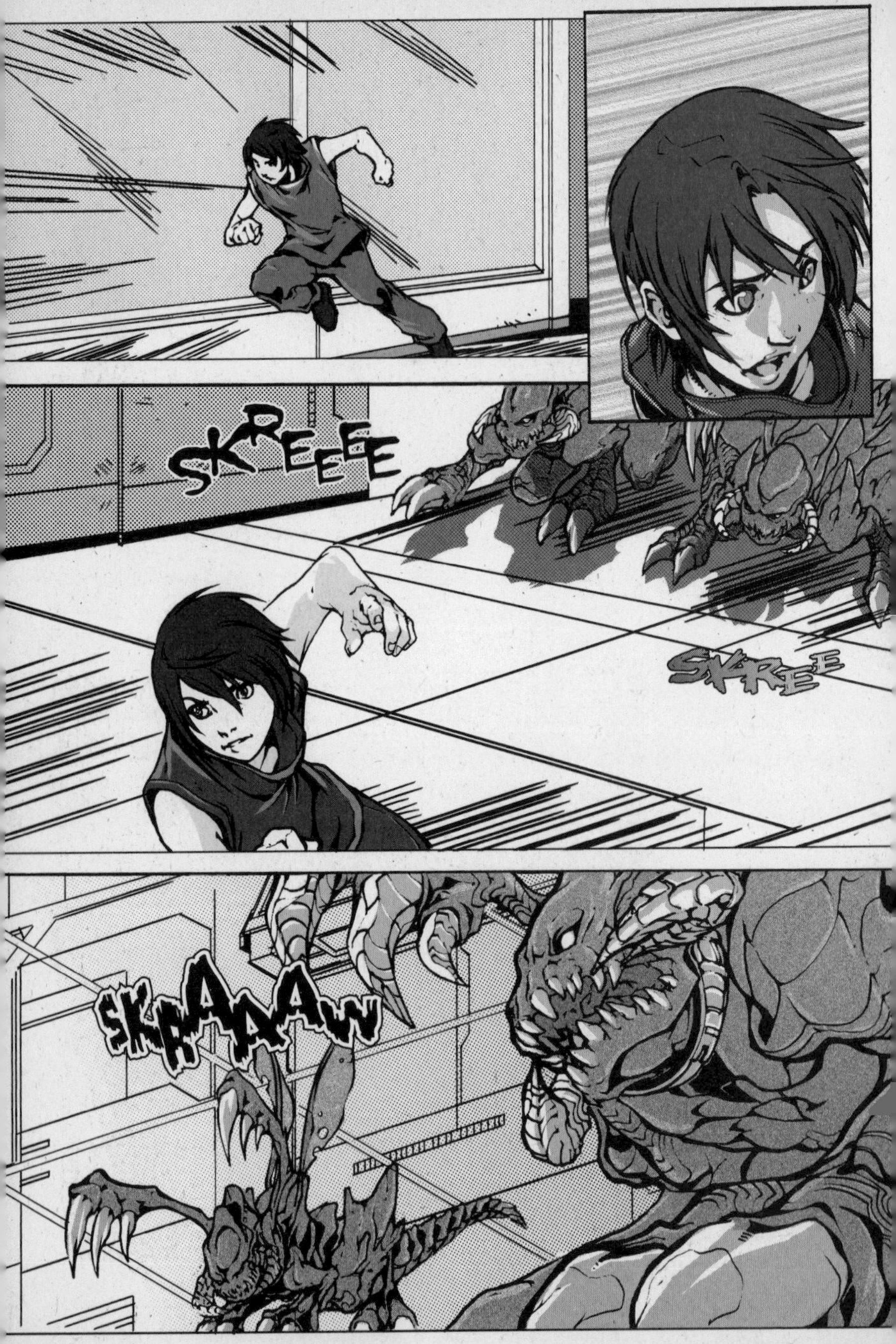
SKREEEE
SKREE
SKRAAAW

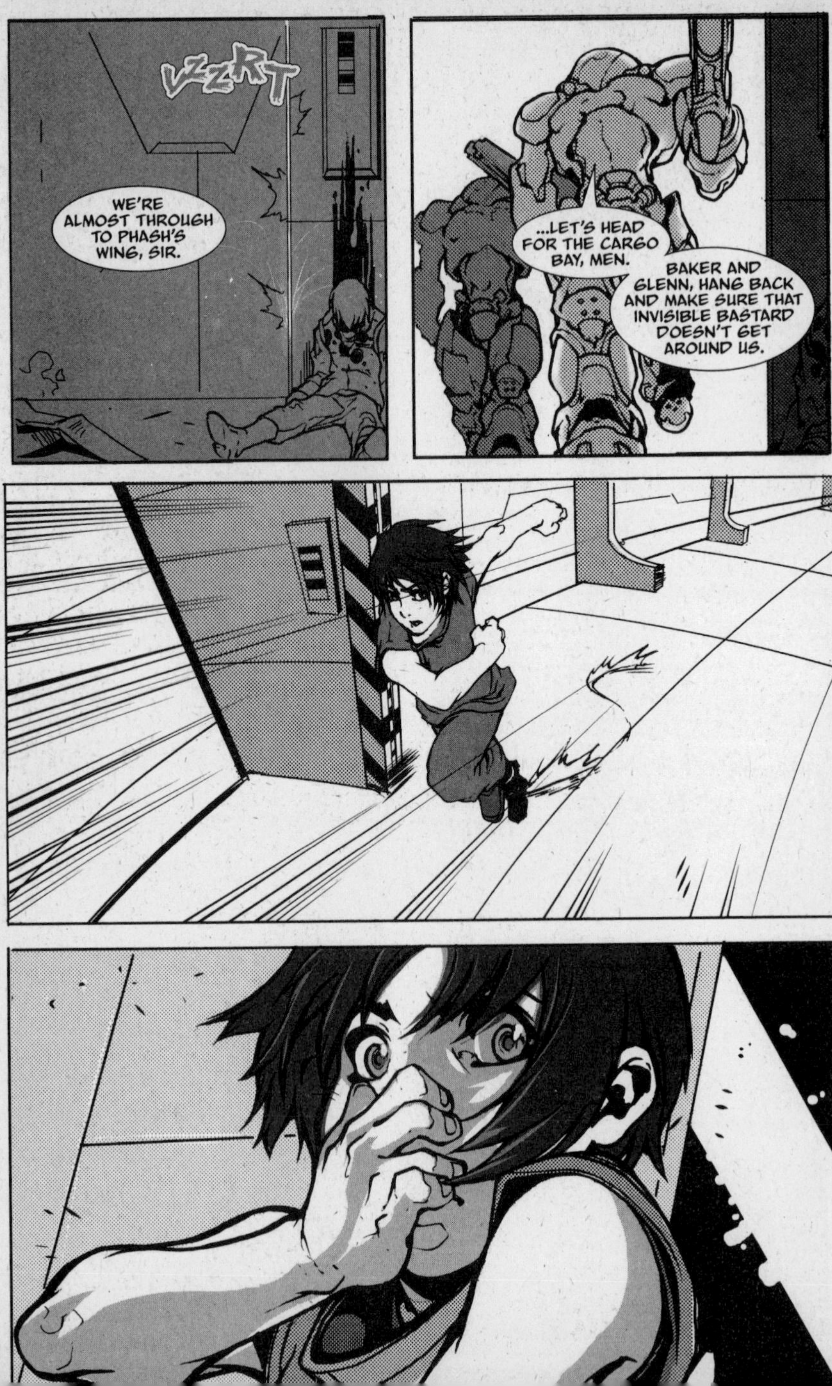
VZZRT
WE'RE ALMOST THROUGH TO PHASH'S WING, SIR.
...LET'S HEAD FOR THE CARGO BAY, MEN.
BAKER AND GLENN, HANG BACK AND MAKE SURE THAT INVISIBLE BASTARD DOESN'T GET AROUND US.

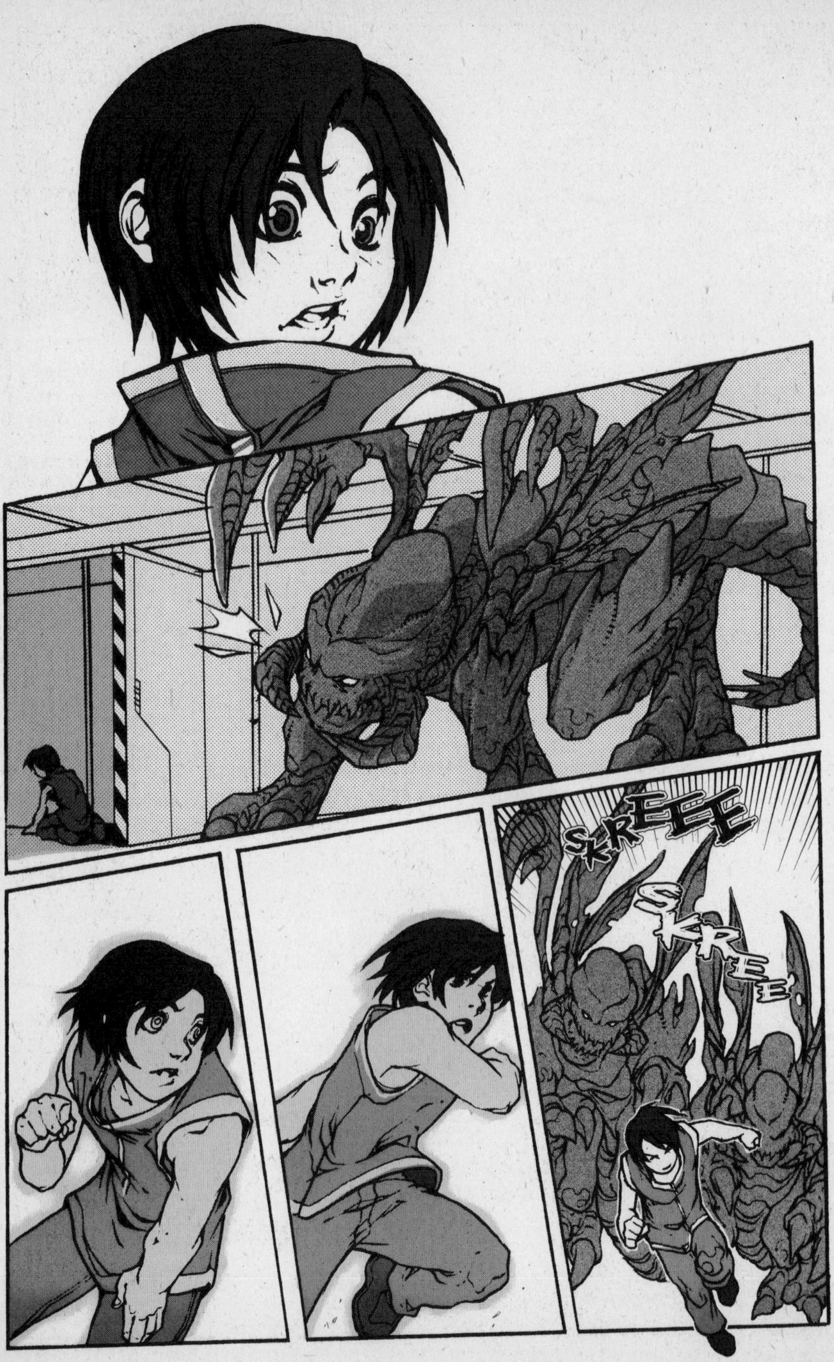
SKREEEE
SKREEE

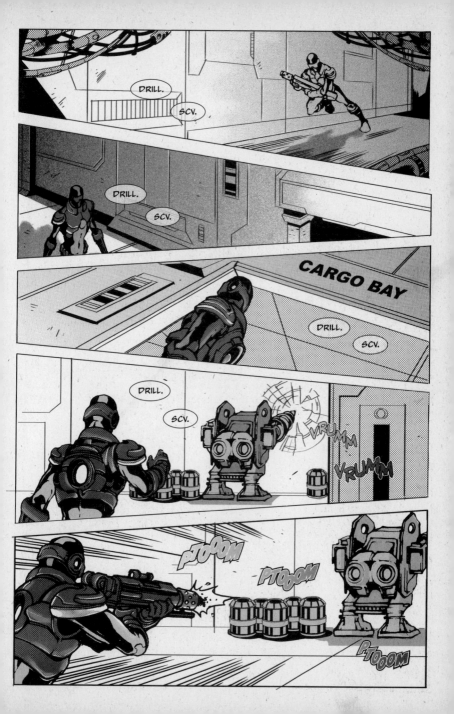

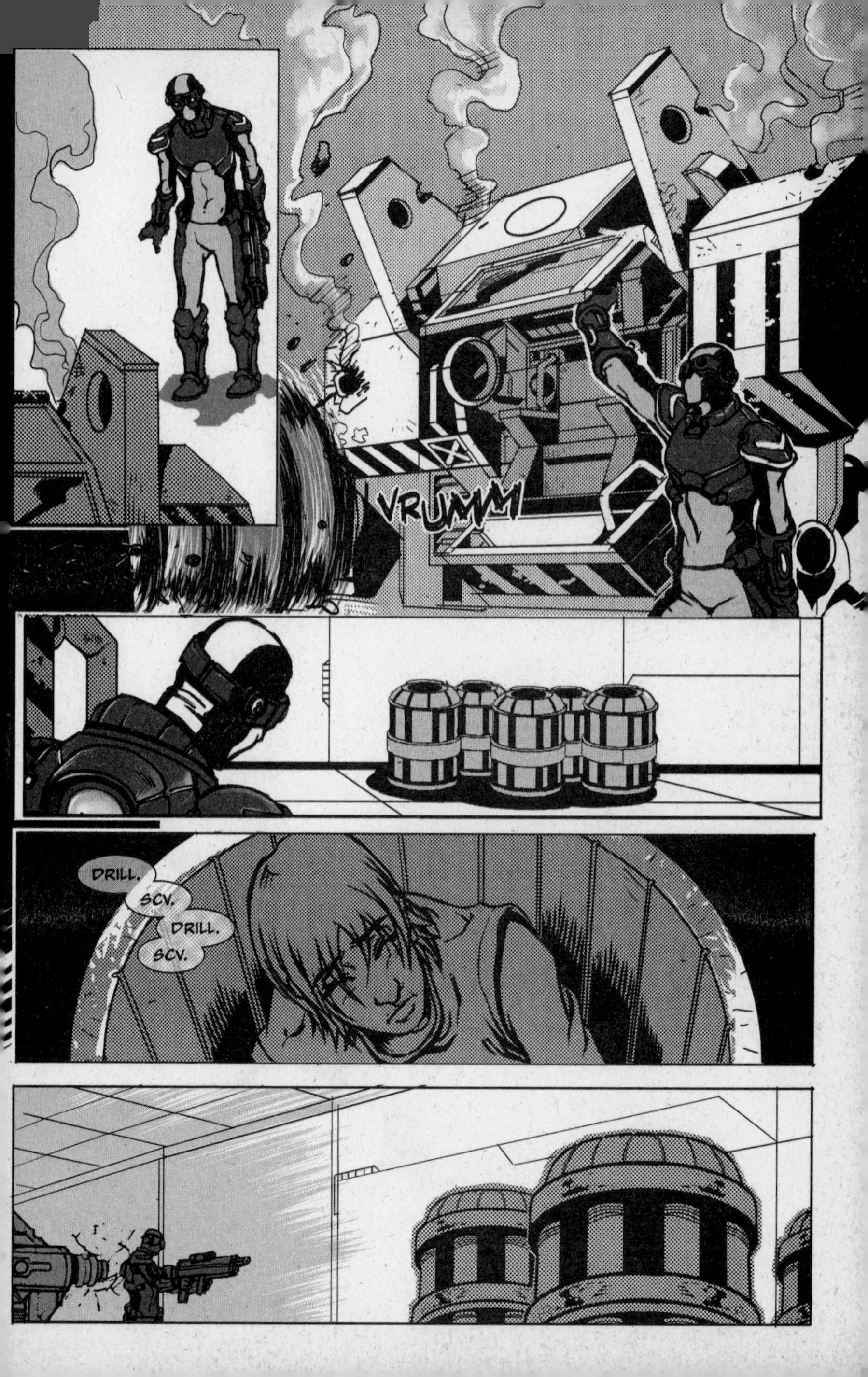
VRUMMM
DRILL.
SCV.
DRILL.
SCV.

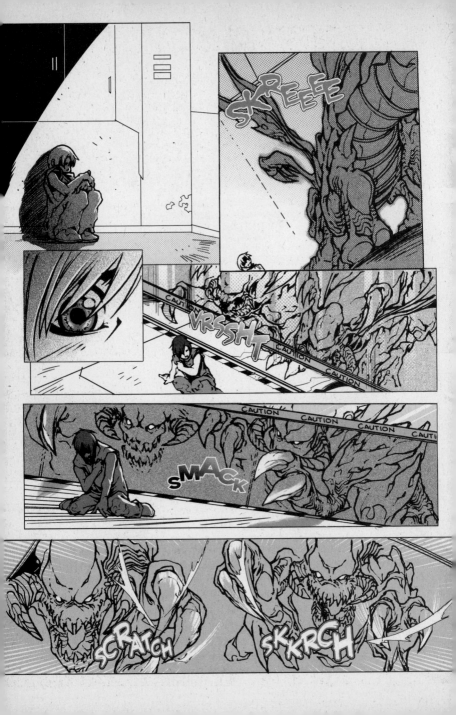

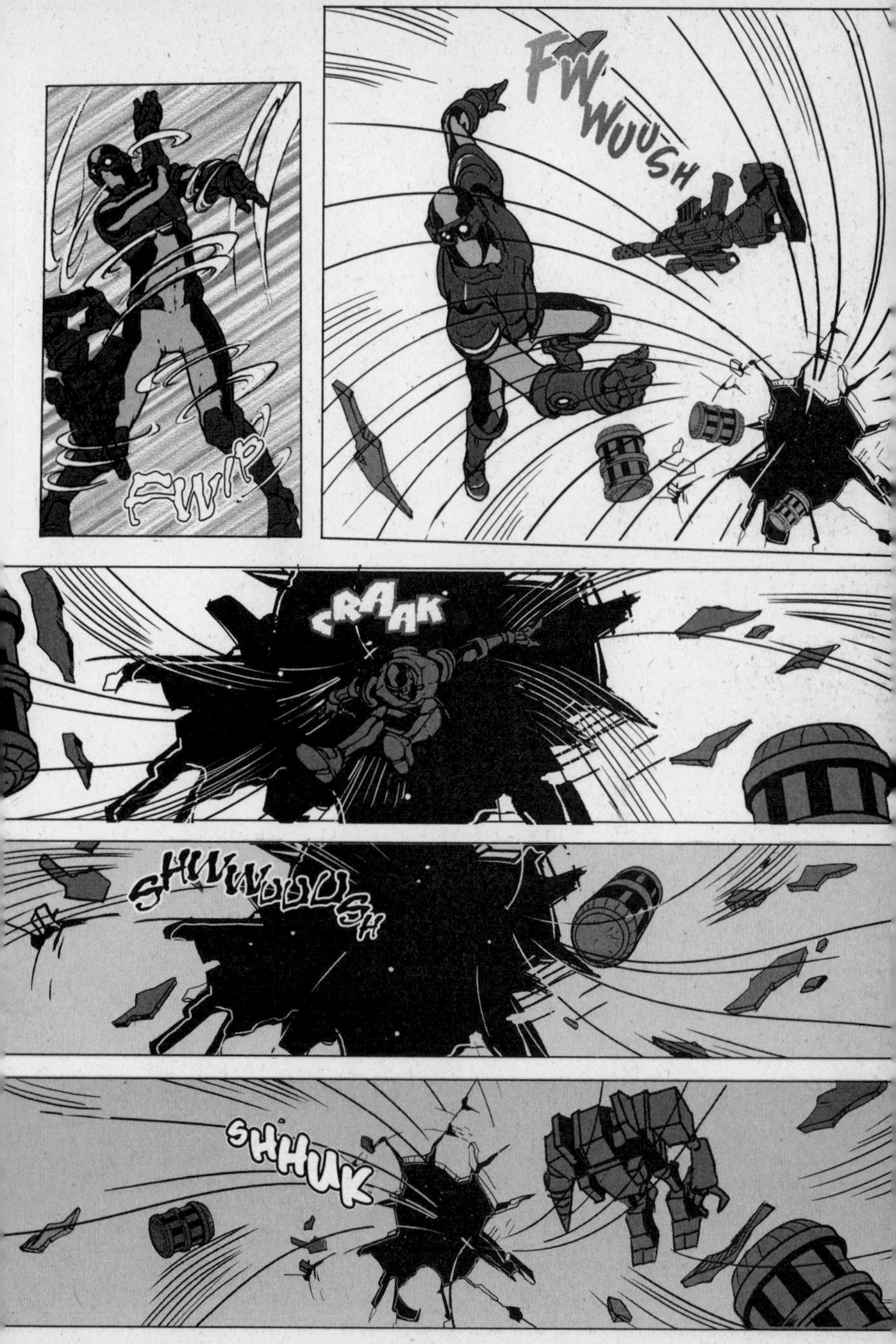
FWIP
FWWUUSH
CRAAK
SHWWUUUSH
SHHUK

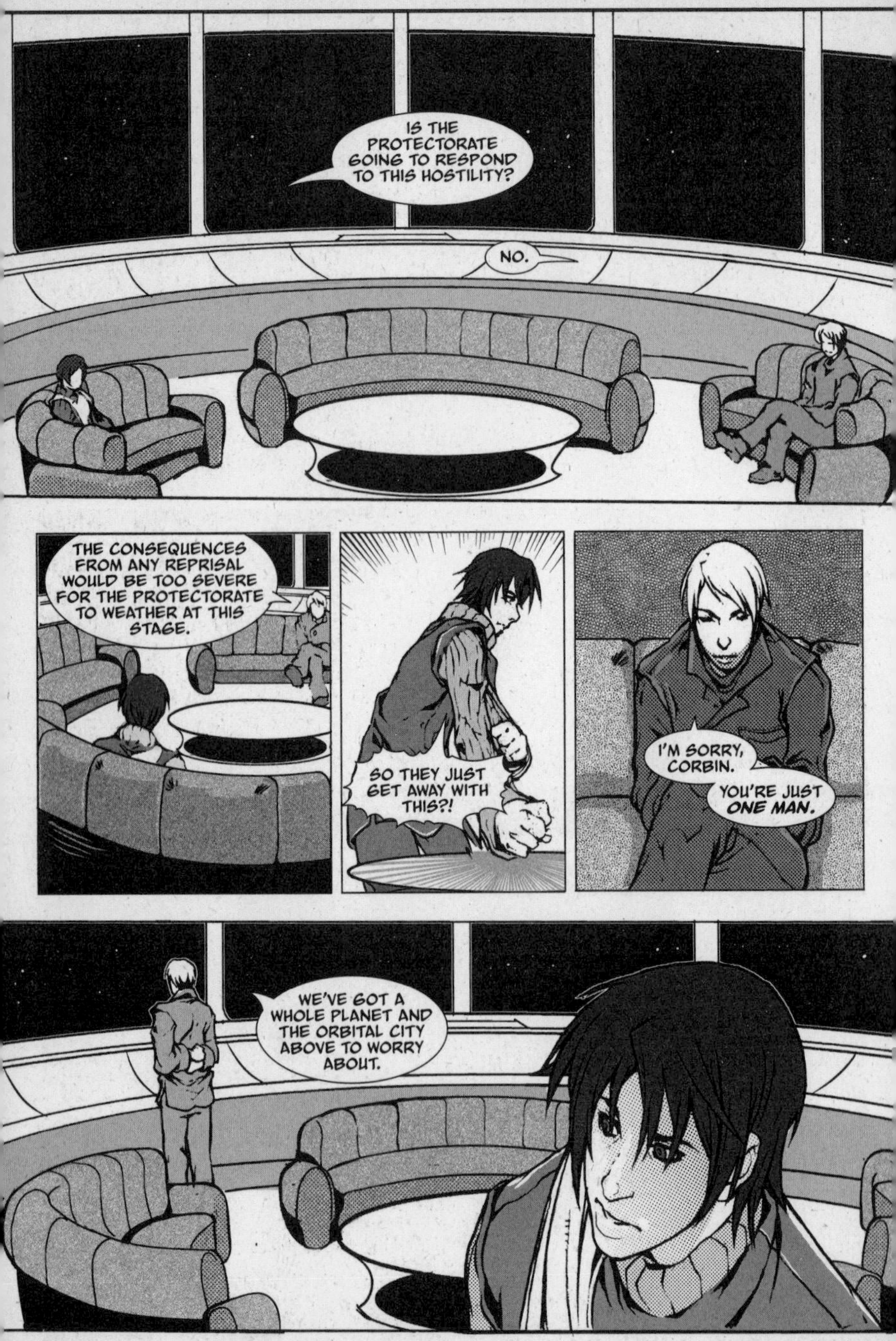
IS THE PROTECTORATE GOING TO RESPOND TO THIS HOSTILITY?
NO.
THE CONSEQUENCES FROM ANY REPRISAL WOULD BE TOO SEVERE FOR THE PROTECTORATE TO WEATHER AT THIS STAGE.
SO THEY JUST GET AWAY WITH THIS?!
I'M SORRY, CORBIN.
YOU'RE JUST *ONE MAN.*
WE'VE GOT A WHOLE PLANET AND THE ORBITAL CITY ABOVE TO WORRY ABOUT.

WELCOME TO THE GHOST ACADEMY, COLIN.

I THINK YOU'RE GOING TO BE QUITE VALUABLE TO US.

MEMORY REASSIGNMENT PROGRAM: INITIATE? Y/N

DON'T WORRY IF ANY OF THIS WAS UNCOMFORTABLE.

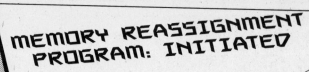

# MEMORY REASSIGNMENT PROGRAM: INITIATED

YOU WON'T REMEMBER A THING.

YAAARGH!

TO BE CONTINUED IN STARCRAFT: GHOST ACADEMY!

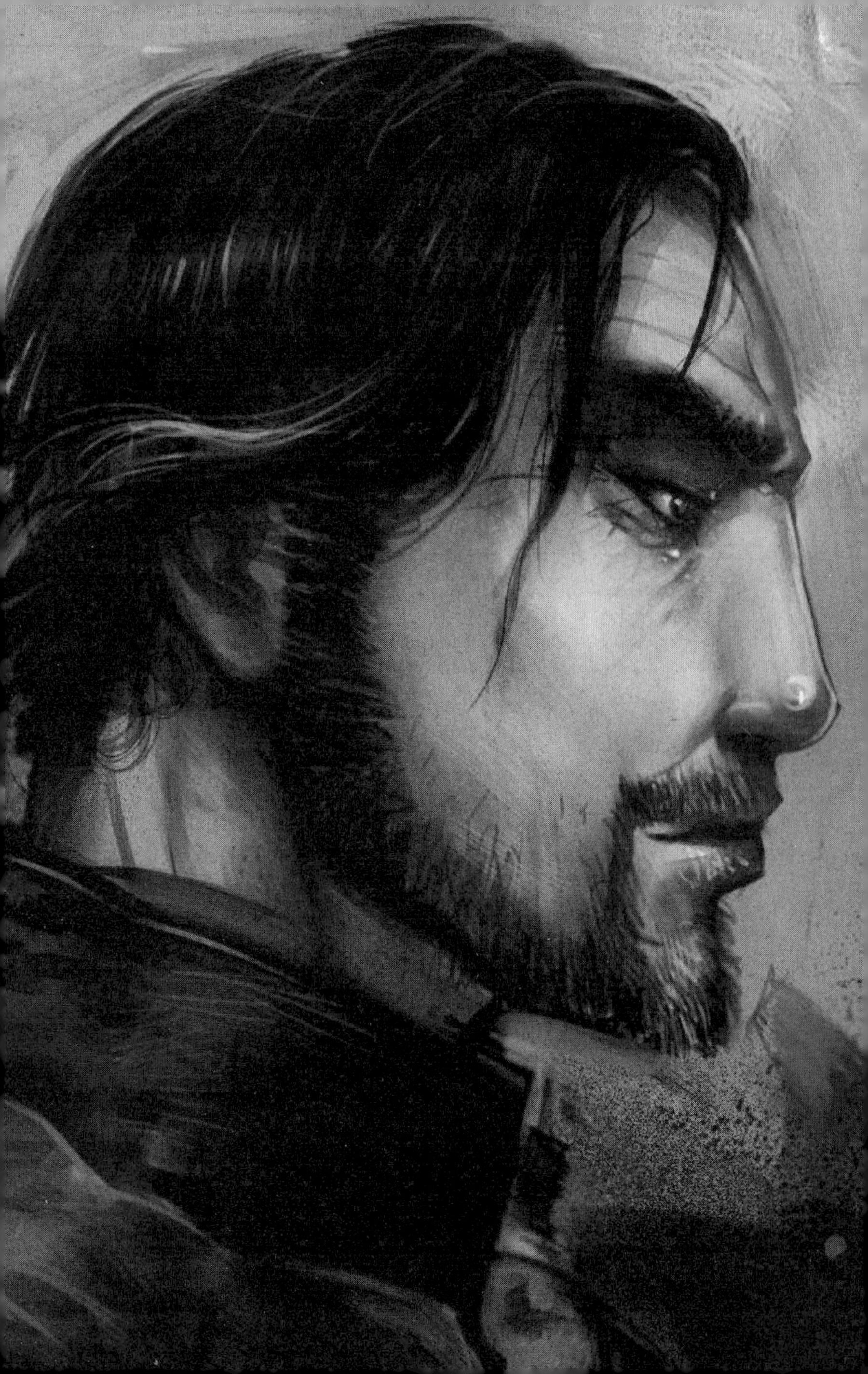

# CHRIS METZEN

Some people write stories; **Chris Metzen** helps build worlds. As Blizzard Entertainment, Inc.'s Senior Vice-President of Creative Development, Metzen oversees the creation of the memorable and immersive characters, places, events, and histories behind all Blizzard Entertainment® games. While the majority of his time is spent writing, Metzen also has a hand in game design, conceptual artwork, and the voice direction of Blizzard Entertainment's titles. When he is not playing or working on building games, the Southern California native can be found reading comics, enjoying music, or reciting the dialogue from his favorite movies.

# DAVID GERROLD

**David Gerrold** has been writing tales of wonder for more than forty years. His first script was "The Trouble With Tribbles" episode of *Star Trek*. He has written multiple episodes of *Twilight Zone, Land Of The Lost, Babylon 5, Tales From the Darkside,* and other hit TV series. His novels include *The Man Who Folded Himself, Jumping Off the Planet,* and *The War Against the Chtorr.* His autobiographical story of his son's adoption, *The Martian Child,* won the Hugo and the Nebula awards and was adapted into a movie starring John Cusack and Angela Peet. Gerrold is currently completing the fifth novel in his *Chtorr* series.

# JOSH ELDER

**Josh Elder** is the handsome and brilliant writer of *Mail Order Ninja*, which he's pretty sure has been acclaimed by some critic, somewhere. A graduate of Northwestern University with a degree in Film, Joshua currently resides in the quaint, little Midwestern town of Chicago, Illinois. A longtime *StarCraft* fanboy, Josh is still geekgasming over the fact that he gets to write for *Frontline*. But Josh also played football, so he isn't a total dork. But he also played Dungeons & Dragons. So yeah, he kind of is a total dork.

# PAUL BENJAMIN

**Paul Benjamin** is a writer, editor, supermodel and video game writer/producer based in Austin, Texas. His comic book and graphic novel work ranges from his original manga series *Pantheon High* to *Marvel Adventures Hulk* and *Marvel Adventures Spider-Man*. His stories have appeared in numerous other Marvel titles as well as TOKYOPOP's *Star Trek: the manga* and *StarCraft: Frontline* series. Paul's video game writing and producing credits include Sega's *The Incredible Hulk* and Activision's *Spider-Man: Web of Shadows* for the Nintendo DS as well as the upcoming *X-Men Origins: Wolverine* for Wii and PlayStation 2 and Electronic Arts' *G.I. JOE: The Rise of COBRA* for many platforms. And, of course, everyone is familiar with Paul's long list of credits as a supermodel. For more info, go to http://www.thepaulbenjamin.com.

# DAVE SHRAMEK

**Dave Shramek** is a game designer and writer in Austin, Texas. As is so often the case, he settled there after graduating from the University of Texas with a degree in Radio, Television and Film. Much to the delight of his parents, he was able to turn this normally unemployable degree into an actual profession with regular employment opportunities in the game development rich environment of Austin. He currently resides there with his ambitions of global dominance and an unhealthy addiction to Tex-Mex.

# ARTISTS:

## HECTOR SEVILLA

**Hector Sevilla** hails from Chihuahua, Mexico. He is a huge fan of *StarCraft*, and never imagined he would ever help create a part of the *StarCraft* universe. He thanks Kathy Schilling, Paul Morrissey and Blizzard for the wonderful opportunity—and Hope Donovan for her great patience. In addition, Hector has created *Lullaby,* and is working on *Leviticus Cross* and Konami's *Lunar Knights*. He dedicates this manga to his parents for all the love and support they show each day to him. You can see more of his art at http://elsevilla.deviantart.com

## RUBEN DE VELA

**Ruben de Vela** was born and raised in Manila, and graduated from the University of the Philippines. In school, he initially took up Applied Physics, but due to too much doodling, playing too many video games, and reading too many SF/Fantasy books, he shifted his field of study to Fine Arts. He has been trained in animation and worked as a background artist for Toei Animation, as well as dabbled in teaching and creating storyboards for ad agencies. Moving away from his usual role as a colorist, this book is his first major publication as a penciller.

## RAMANDA KAMARGA

Like a superhero, **Ramanda Kamarga** holds a regular job during the day and draws comics at night. An avid gamer, he shares his free time with his wife and his PSP. Ramanda's previous works include *G.I. JOE: Sigma Six*, *Bristol Board Jungle*, TOKYOPOP's *Psy*Comm* volumes 2 & 3, and of course *StarCraft: Frontline*. To see more of his stuff, just visit his website at www.ramandakamarga.com.

## MEL JOY SAN JUAN

**Mel joy San Juan** began working for local Pinoy comics when she was 16 and was published in several manga in her native country of the Philippines. She was discovered by Glass House Graphics' David Campiti while attending his comics creation seminar in Manila, and began working for them a year later. After assisting on assorted jobs, and co-illustrating *Dream Knight,* Mel joy finally landed *StarCraft* as her very first solo pencilling assignment. She gives thanks to her friends and manager for helping her to finish this job.

Thanks for picking up volume 4 of *StarCraft: Frontline!*

Volume after volume, you faithful readers have returned to *Frontline*, seeking stories that explore the *StarCraft* universe, and it has been TOKYOPOP's pleasure to deliver! From the unfolding story of Colin Phash, to the bizarre tale of a fanatic ghost-enslaving cult, to the struggles of the media to shove aside the Dominion's strong arm and expose the truth, to knock-out battles between templar and terran—the *Frontline* series has expanded the world you know and love.

A number of artists and writers in volume 4 deserve thanks for bringing *Frontline* to life. Writers Paul Benjamin, Dave Shramek, Josh Elder and artist Ramanda Kamarga are three-times-over contributors to the series. David Gerrold, Ruben de Vela and Mel Joy San Juan may have just begun their contributions with volume 4, but their work does the series proud! A big thanks goes to Hector Sevilla on his incredible fourth story in as many volumes—and, of course, a giant round of applause for Chris Metzen! It's not every day the Senior Vice-President, Creative Development at Blizzard pens a Jim Raynor story. Our hats off to Chris!

Speaking of creative minds, TOKYOPOP is graciously indebted to the creative team at Blizzard. I'd like to thank our immediate contacts at Blizzard—Jason Bischoff, Micky Neilson, James Waugh, Rob Tokar and Evelyn Fredericksen— for their insightful feedback and excellent suggestions. Without you guys, the *Frontline* series wouldn't be the juggernaut it is today.

And last but never least, thanks to my fellow squad members at TOKYOPOP, editor Troy "Jumper" Lewter and layout artist/*StarCraft* expert Michael "No Problem" Paolilli. We are as one!

Hope Donovan
Editor

TOKYOPOP's Editorial and Design Team get some hands-on ghost training with Nova! Hope Donovan, Troy Lewter and Michael Paolilli

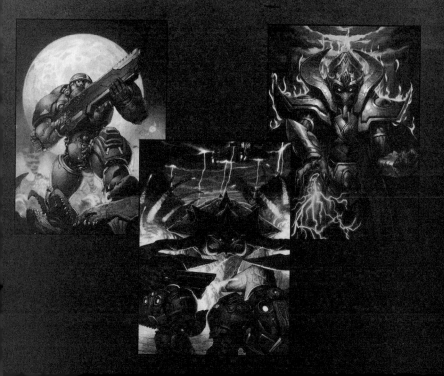

# STARCRAFT

## FRONTLINE
### VOLUME 1

KNAAK | WASHIO | FURMAN | ELLIOTT | BENJAMIN | SHRAMEK
SEVILLA | ELDER | KAMARGA

Each of the three races—terran, protoss and zerg—is closely examined and their motivations revealed...

In a gripping story by Richard Knaak, a thor driver's ego eggs him into attempting an impossible heist...

Psionic boy Colin Phash finds himself at the center of a brutal conflict between terran miners and the zerg...

Talented young Viking pilot Wes Carter must stop his crazed mentor before the man destroys a colony...

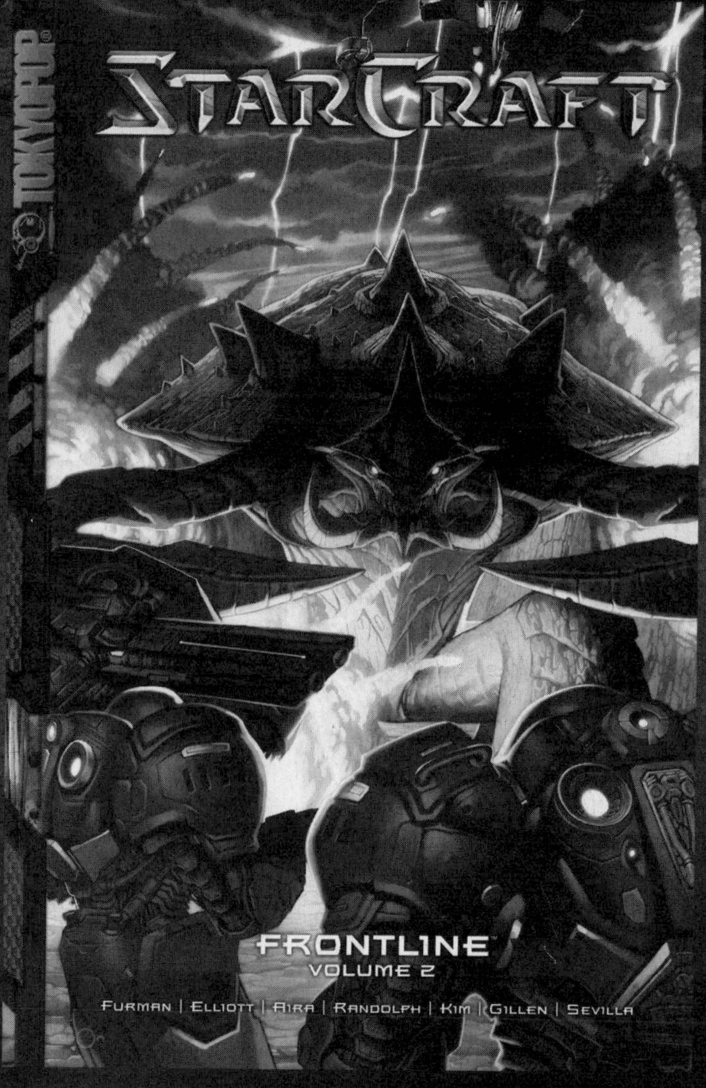

TOKYOPOP
STARCRAFT
FRONTLINE
VOLUME 2
FURMAN | ELLIOTT | AIRA | RANDOLPH | KIM | GILLEN | SEVILLA


The haunting conclusion of Viking pilot Wes Carter's battle against the man who taught him everything about heavy armor...

Feared by all and understood by none, zerg creep comes under the knife in a protoss laboratory...

When a reporter comes face-to-face with atrocity, she must decide whether her loyalty to the truth outweighs her loyalty to the Dominion...

A Kel-Morian crew catches wind of a planet's huge bounty, but comes in contact with its dark secrets instead...

TOKYOPOP

# STARCRAFT

## FRONTLINE
### VOLUME 3

BENJAMIN | SHRAMEK | SEVILLA | ZATOPEK | RODRIGUEZ
RANDOLPH | KYE | ELDER | KAMARGA

His psionic abilities exposed, Colin Phash hides out on a doomed refugee moon, where he's pursued by a fearsome wrangler...

A sadistic scientist captures a protoss high templar in order to perfect his horrifying protoss-terran soldiers...

A lounge singer becomes an unlikely diplomat between the Dominion and the Kel-Morians, but something else may be pulling the strings from behind the scenes...

A high templar loses her connection to the Khala, and is willing to sacrifice even more to become whole again...

# A FRONTLINE VOLUME 4
## STARCRAFT! GHOST ACADEMY
## SNEAK PEEK—CONCEPT ART

They're mysterious, elusive, and deadly. Psionically gifted terrans molded into lethal assassins: these are the highly trained ghosts of the *StarCraft* universe. Ghosts can infiltrate almost anywhere—including your mind. They can move with incredible swiftness, snipe targets from great distances, read thoughts, become invisible, and even call down nuclear strikes. All of these skills and more are learned and refined at the Ghost Academy.

At the Ghost Academy, powerful young students from disparate worlds confront terrifying training exercises, as well as each other, in a highly competitive environment. The following pages showcase several of this exciting new manga series' incredible works in progress, including cover sketches, character concepts, and penciled pages. Prepare to be taken on a journey into the secretive world of...

# STARCRAFT
## GHOST ACADEMY

At this school, failure is not an option.

When the TOKYOPOP editors suggested that we create a sneak peek of the upcoming StarCraft: Ghost Academy manga, we jumped at the chance. We are really thrilled with the way this series is coming together, and we're excited to explore for the first time one of the most closely guarded secrets of the StarCraft universe: ghosts.

Although the academy is mentioned in the novel StarCraft: Nova and the novella Uprising, and StarCraft players can build ghost academies and create ghost operatives in the game, the StarCraft: Ghost Academy manga series is the closest examination ever of this vital (some would say vile) resource of the Terran Dominion.

We hope you enjoy the preview!

The Blizzard Publishing Team

Rob Tokar
Micky Neilson
Evelyn Fredericksen
James Waugh
Justin Parker
Sean Copeland
Cate Gary
Tommy Newcomer
Cameron Dayton
Matt Burns

# CONSTRUCTING A CO

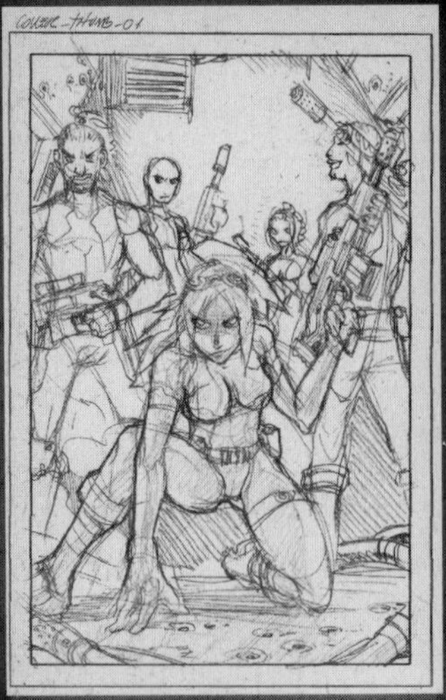

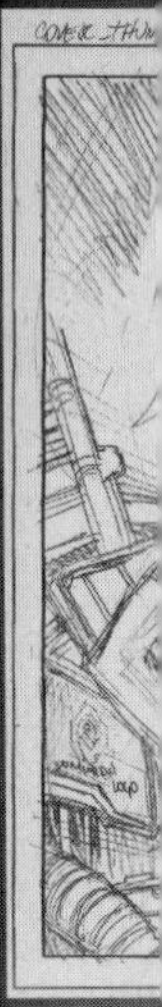

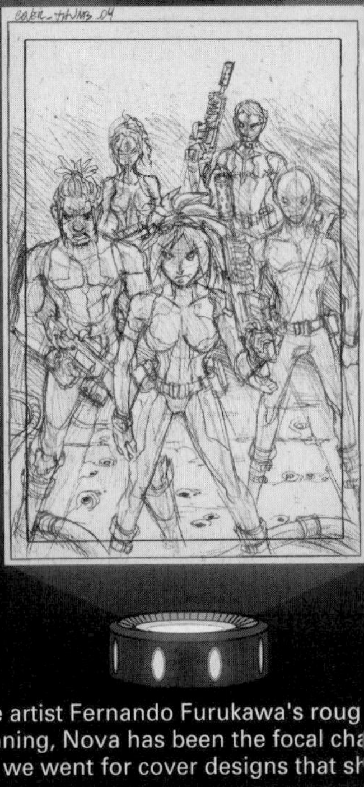

Here you can see artist Fernando Furukawa's roug
From the beginning, Nova has been the focal cha
***Academy,*** so we went for cover designs that sh

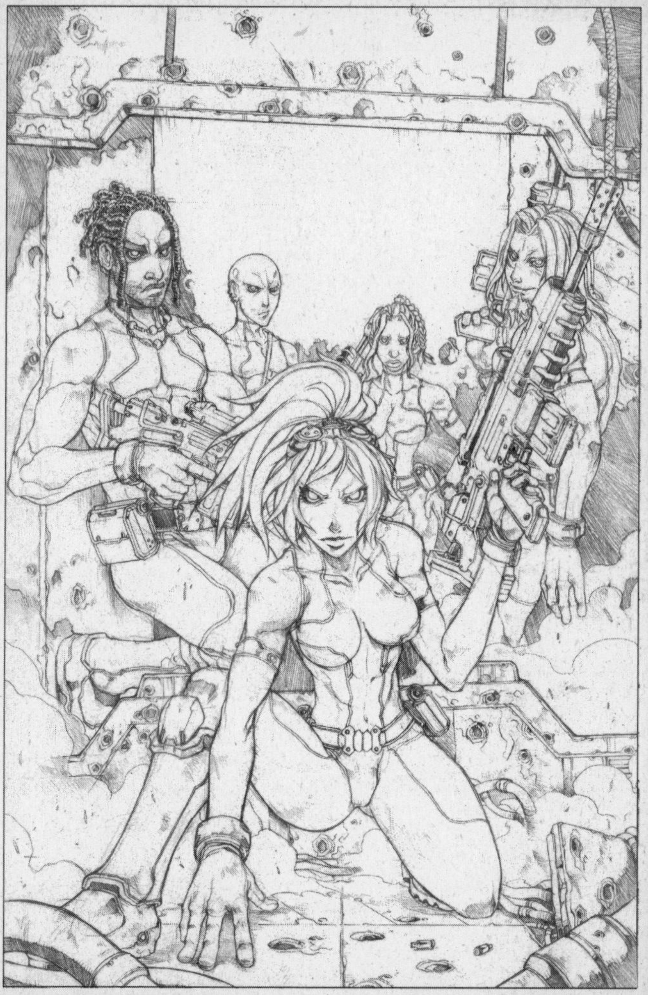

With the basic design picked, Fernando added detail with a pencil drawing...

...and added colors for a fantastic finish! So here we have Nova front and center, surrounded by her peers at the Ghost Academy.

# CONSTRUCTING A CAST:
# NOVA

An iconic ghost in the *StarCraft* universe, Nova was already designed—as many gorgeous, detailed illustrations show. But for *Ghost Academy,* Nova needed to be a little younger. We think "high school" Nova is still pretty badass!

# TOSH

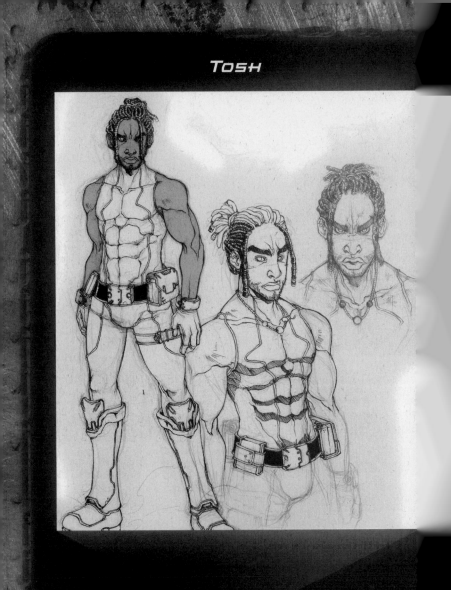

You might say Tosh's time at the Ghost Academy is good preparation for a wild ride...in *StarCraft II!* In the Academy, he's a little bit older than the other students, and has already taken a leadership role as head of Team Blue.

# KATH

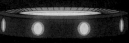

Kath's bright, tough, hot and says it like it is—which is not necessarily
a good thing at the Ghost Academy.

# AAL

Not all the students at the Ghost Academy are exceptional telepaths.
A low-level telepath, Aal's reasons for being at the Ghost Academy
have more to do with his dark past...

Can he use some type of accessories? (earring, necklace, etc?)

Some type of laptop →

Speaking of darkness, Lio is a technopath (which means he can mentally interface with certain machines in addition to organic minds). But, unknown to his teammates, he also has a secret addiction to the drug hab. Definitely not the best vice to have when you're enduring intense ghost training.

# CONSTRUCTING PAGES

**StarCraft: Ghost Academy** is a view into a sinister and infam
institution—but at the same time, that view is through the eye
students. Just like at any school, socializing, learning and grow
all part of the package. And Nova's got a lot of it to do!

The following is a sneak peek of early concept pages for
*Ghost Academy*. Though the art's not final, it's action-pack
and we see Nova in high form!

Hostages have been taken on a grounded planet hopper. Nova and her team must infiltrate the ship and rescue them.

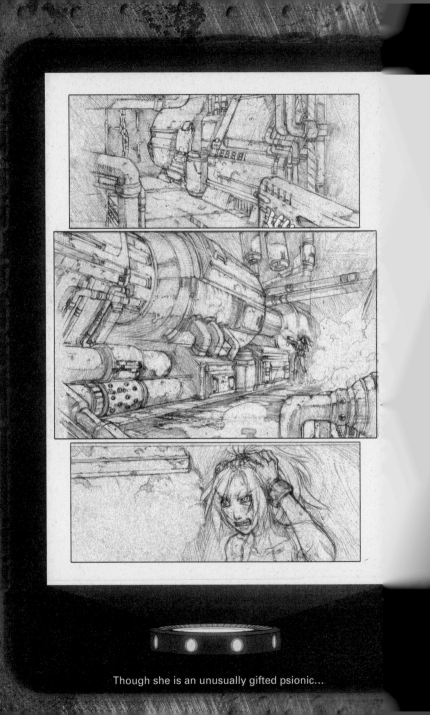

Though she is an unusually gifted psionic...

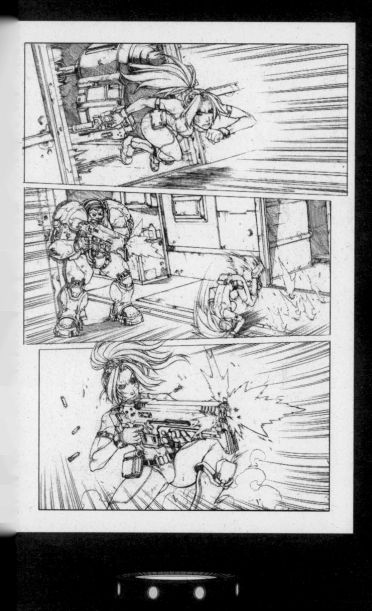

...this sort of mission requires a few of her other skills...mainly enhanced speed, agility and dead-to-rights marksmanship.

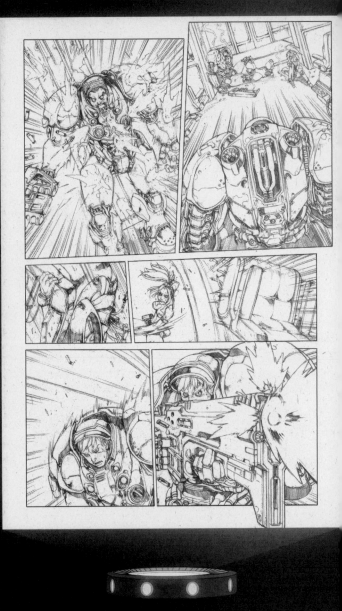

Incredible strength helps too...and maybe a little improvisation.

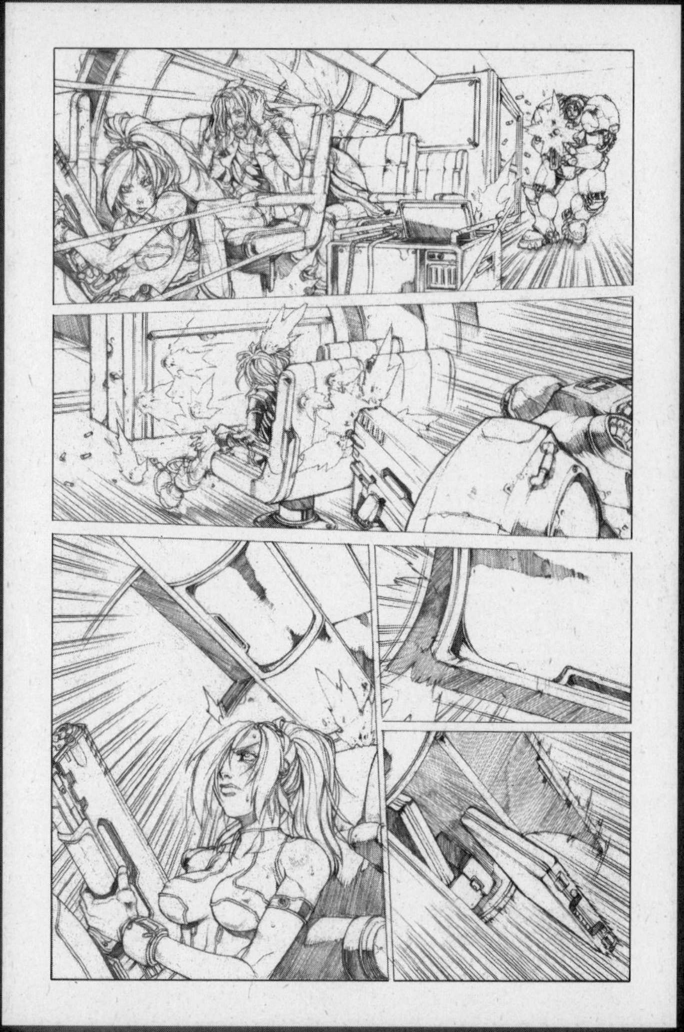

Dominion marines are tough...but no match for telepathy and telekinesis.

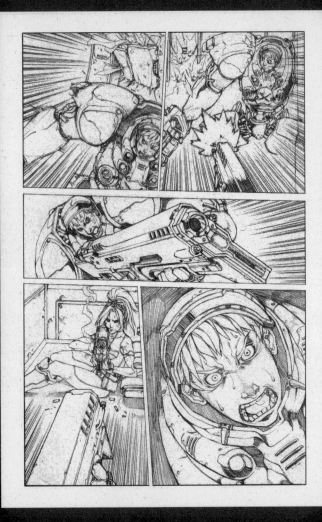

Ghosts are powerful weapons in Emperor Mengsk's arsenal.

And he's training a lot of them.

We hope you enjoyed this glimpse into the Ghost Academy.
Be sure to pick up *StarCraft: Ghost Academy,*
arriving in bookstores **January 2010!**

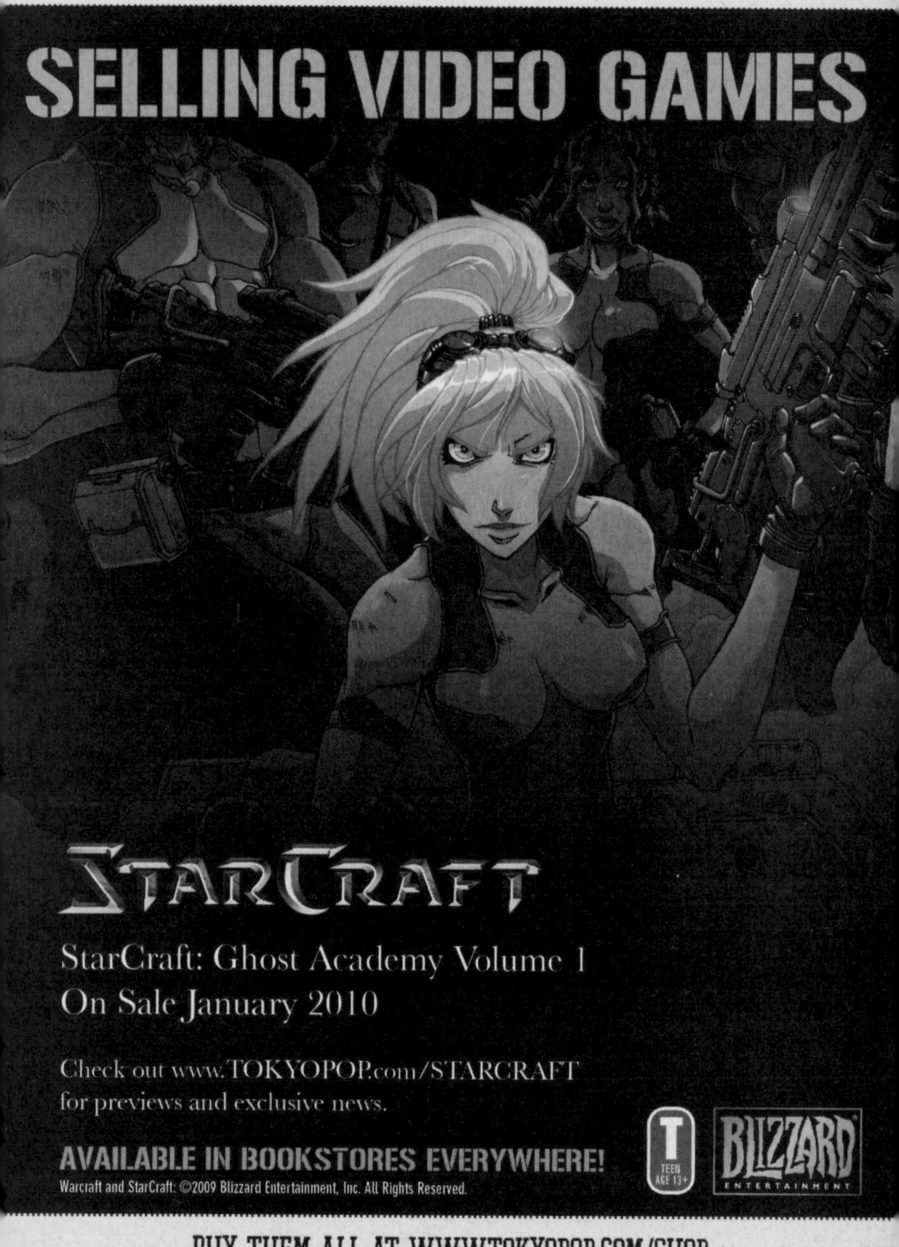
SELLING VIDEO GAMES
STARCRAFT
StarCraft: Ghost Academy Volume 1
On Sale January 2010
Check out www.TOKYOPOP.com/STARCRAFT
for previews and exclusive news.
AVAILABLE IN BOOKSTORES EVERYWHERE!
Warcraft and StarCraft: ©2009 Blizzard Entertainment, Inc. All Rights Reserved.
T
TEEN
AGE 13+
BLIZZARD

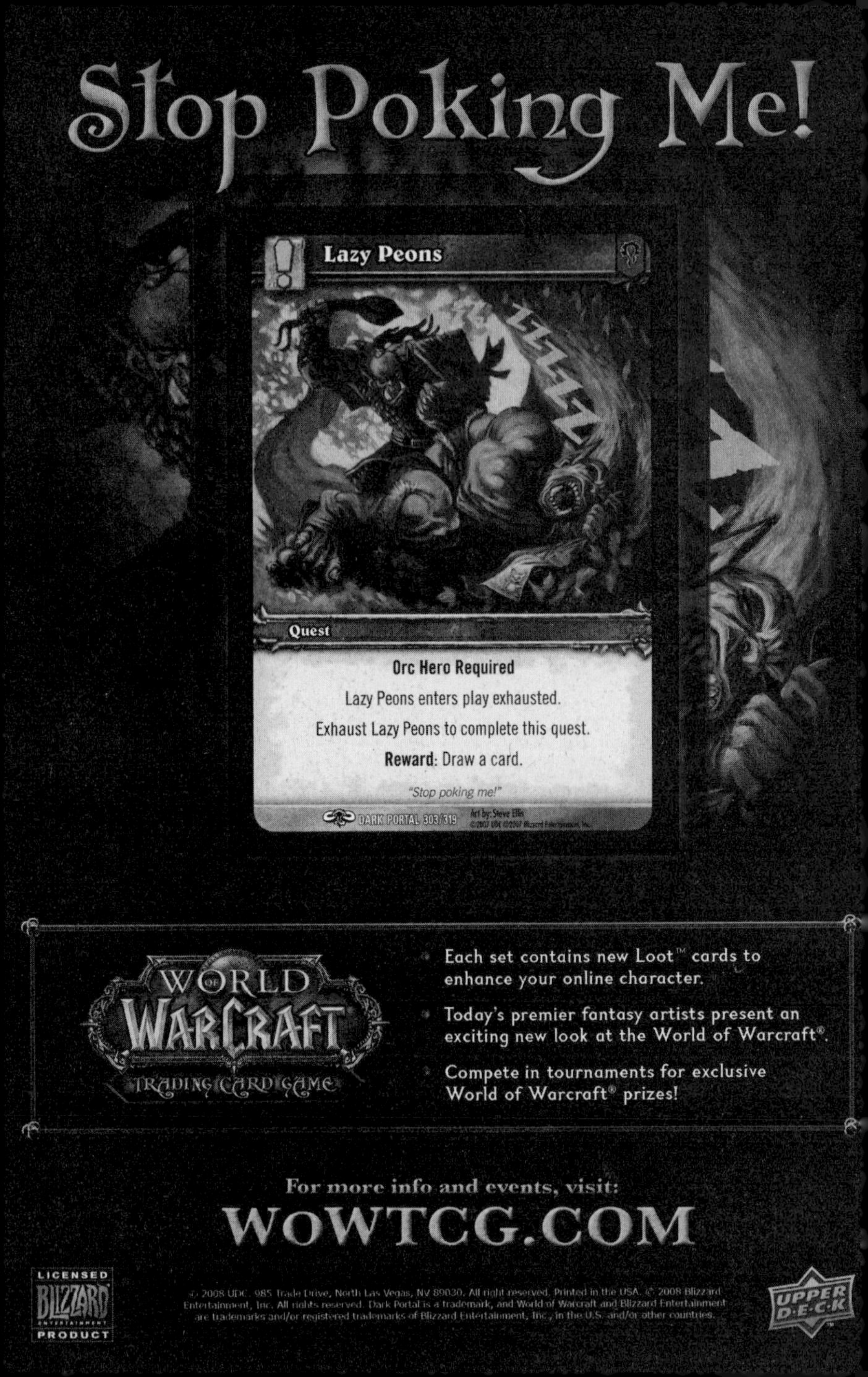
Stop Poking Me!
Lazy Peons
Quest
Orc Hero Required
Lazy Peons enters play exhausted.
Exhaust Lazy Peons to complete this quest.
Reward: Draw a card.
"Stop poking me!"
DARK PORTAL 303/319
Art by: Steve Ellis
WORLD OF WARCRAFT
TRADING CARD GAME
Each set contains new Loot™ cards to enhance your online character.
Today's premier fantasy artists present an exciting new look at the World of Warcraft®.
Compete in tournaments for exclusive World of Warcraft® prizes!
For more info and events, visit:
WOWTCG.COM
LICENSED BLIZZARD ENTERTAINMENT PRODUCT
© 2008 UDC. 985 Trade Drive, North Las Vegas, NV 89030. All right reserved. Printed in the USA. © 2008 Blizzard Entertainment, Inc. All rights reserved. Dark Portal is a trademark, and World of Warcraft and Blizzard Entertainment are trademarks and/or registered trademarks of Blizzard Entertainment, Inc., in the U.S. and/or other countries.
UPPER DECK

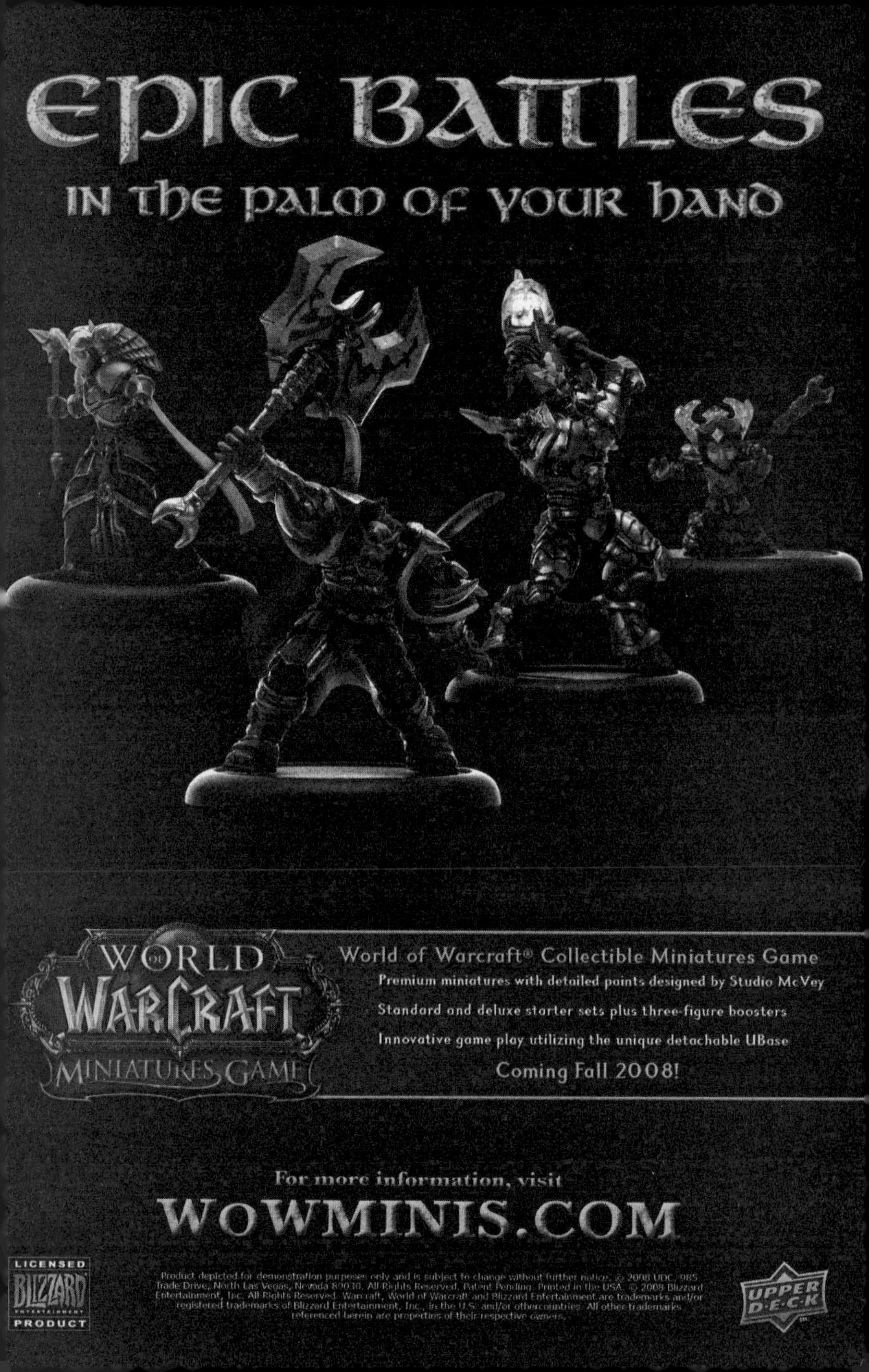
EPIC BATTLES
IN THE PALM OF YOUR HAND
WORLD OF WARCRAFT MINIATURES GAME
World of Warcraft® Collectible Miniatures Game
Premium miniatures with detailed paints designed by Studio McVey
Standard and deluxe starter sets plus three-figure boosters
Innovative game play utilizing the unique detachable UBase
Coming Fall 2008!
For more information, visit
WOWMINIS.COM
LICENSED BLIZZARD ENTERTAINMENT PRODUCT
Product depicted for demonstration purposes only and is subject to change without further notice. © 2008 UDC. 985 Trade Drive, North Las Vegas, Nevada 89030. All Rights Reserved. Patent Pending. Printed in the USA. © 2008 Blizzard Entertainment, Inc. All Rights Reserved. Warcraft, World of Warcraft and Blizzard Entertainment are trademarks and/or registered trademarks of Blizzard Entertainment, Inc., in the U.S. and/or othercountries. All other trademarks referenced herein are properties of their respective owners.
UPPER DECK

Actual Gameplay.

# NO. I'D RATHER KILL RATS.

With millions of players online, World of Warcraft has made gaming
history — and now it's never been easier to join the adventure.
Simply visit **www.warcraft.com**, download the FREE TRIAL and join
thousands of mighty heroes for ten days of bold online adventure.
A World Awaits...